CHATS WITH SOME OF
THOROUGHBRED RACING'S MOST
PROMINENT PERSONALITIES

Best of TALKIN' HORSES

FROM *bloodhorse.com*

EDITED BY RON MITCHELL

EP
ECLIPSE
PRESS

LEXINGTON, KENTUCKY

Library of Congress Control Number: 2008928612

ISBN 978-1-58150-192-6

Printed in the United States
First Edition: 2008

a division of
Blood-Horse Publications
PUBLISHERS SINCE 1916

Best of TALKIN' HORSES
Contents

Continued on next page

RACING OFFICIALS & OTHERS

Best of TALKIN' HORSES
Introduction

By RON MITCHELL

When bloodhorse.com initiated online chats on an irregular basis as an opportunity for readers to have access to the industry's leading owners, breeders, trainers, jockeys, veterinarians, handicappers, and agents, the concept proved popular and quickly became a regular feature titled "Talkin' Horses." The initial chats were truly interactive, with the chat hosts answering questions as they were submitted during a one-hour period. However, the amount of time needed to answer the questions in a thorough and accurate manner resulted in only a small number of the submitted questions being answered. As a solution, the chat format changed so that the questions were solicited several days in advance of the time set aside for the chat. This format resulted in questions and answers that were more complete and had fewer problems commonly found with interactive chats, such as misinformation and typographical errors. While some of the subjects covered in the chats have been topical and timely, much of the content has dealt with philosophies and techniques that have led to the individual host's success in whichever discipline he or she is involved. In an effort to make this information available in a more permanent form that can serve as an invaluable resource for many industry professionals and casual horse and racing enthusiasts, we have assembled the best questions and answers from a broad cross-section of all the hosts of "Talkin' Horses" through the years. It was not easy to select what to include and what, sadly, to leave out, but the result is this book, *Best of Talkin' Horses*. I hope you enjoy it.

Trainers

BOB BAFFERT
RICHARD DUTROW JR.
LARRY JONES
CARL NAFZGER
TODD PLETCHER
TIM RICHEY
JOHN VEITCH
NICK ZITO

TALKIN' HORSES
WITH
BOB BAFFERT

Born in Nogales, Arizona, on January 13, 1953, Bob Baffert is widely recognized as one of the most successful trainers in the history of horse racing. After rising to the top in the Quarter Horse game, Baffert decided to become a full-time Thoroughbred trainer in the early 1970s. Owners Mike Pegram and Hal Earnhardt, who are still with him, were responsible for bringing Baffert into the Thoroughbred game. Besides Pegram and Earnhardt, Baffert also has trained for Robert and Janice McNair (Stonerside Stable); Ahmed Zayat (Zayat Stables); the late Bob Lewis and his wife, Beverly; the late Prince Ahmed bin Salman (The Thoroughbred Corporation); and the late John Mabee and his wife, Betty (Golden Eagle Farm). The Lewises' Silver Charm, whom they purchased for $85,000, gave Baffert his first two classic wins when the colt took the 1997 Kentucky Derby and Preakness. Silver Charm went on to earn $6,944,369, including a victory in the 1998 Dubai World Cup, before being retired to stud. The following year Pegram's Real Quiet won the Kentucky Derby and Preakness before losing the Belmont Stakes by a scant nose. Real Quiet had been purchased for an even smaller sum, $17,000, than Silver Charm. The wins made Baffert the first person in the history of Thoroughbred racing to train Kentucky Derby and Preakness winners in back-to-back years. Captain Steve, third in the 2000 Derby and also owned by Pegram, won the Dubai World Cup in 2001 and earned $6,828,356 during his racing career.

In 2001, Baffert again won two-thirds of the Triple Crown, this time with Point Given, who won the Preakness and Belmont. That year Point Given became the first Thoroughbred in history to win four straight races worth $1 million or more (the Preakness, Belmont, Haskell Invitational Handicap, and Travers). Point Given also was victorious in the San Felipe

TALKIN' HORSES

BOB BAFFERT

Stakes and Santa Anita Derby as a three-year-old. Baffert won his third Derby/Preakness combination with War Emblem in 2002.

Bob Baffert has been voted the Eclipse Award as the sport's outstanding trainer three times (1997, 1998, and 1999) and has trained nine Eclipse Award winners. Baffert also has trained four Quarter Horse champions. At the start of 2008, Thoroughbreds trained by Bob Baffert had earned in excess of $127 million, ranking him fifth all-time. He is the father of five children—Taylor, Canyon, Forest, Savannah, and Bode.

➤ **Of all the champions you've had, who was the hardest to train, who was the easiest, and why?** — Jackson, Tennessee

Honestly, all my champions have presented some sort of challenge. That said, Point Given was probably the toughest because he liked to play around before he went to the track, and he is a very large horse. Keeping his mind focused on the job at hand was tough in the mornings. Fortunately, he was all business in the afternoon. Chilukki was a trainer's dream. She was quiet and kind and did everything effortlessly. One thing all my champions have in common is they were all so thrilling to watch in the mornings and in their races.

➤ **How do you balance family and work when you have to spend so much time at the barn and you have a young child at home?**

— Las Vegas, Nevada

This is the great balancing act of horsemen everywhere. Our job is hard on families. Missed ball games and school events are par for the course. When you get those big wins on the big days, you remember why you sacrifice family vacations and days off. Unfortunately, those wins are hard to come by. I do try to make it to my kids' events even if it means leaving right after training, squeezing in a game, then rushing back for racing. I've missed out on many things in my kids' lives, but I hope they will always have great memories of things like throwing out the first pitch at baseball games, going inside the Yankee clubhouse, and winning the Kentucky Derby. We all sacrifice, but by the same token we all reap the rewards. Training is a 24/7 job. I may not be the first one to the barn in the morning, but I'm there every day. So far it's worked out great. [But] my ex-wife hates me, some days [my wife] Jill hates me, and Bode calls me Bob.

➤ **I have read several quotes attributed to your dislike of the synthetic tracks. Why are other respected trainers touting these surfaces as great for the horses, while you seem to be very unhappy about them, even asking for Santa Anita to return to dirt?** — Shelbyville, Kentucky

I'll start by saying, as with anything, each of us has our own opinions and preferences. I respect my peers and value their ideas and knowledge. In my experience, synthetics haven't lived up to their promise. Horses are still getting hurt. That's the unfortunate part of our business. No matter what surface you're racing on, horse racing can be a dangerous sport. Synthetic supporters have tended to vilify those who don't prefer synthetic surfaces to a well-maintained dirt track.

I, and others, have been maligned for not caring about the welfare of horses. I'm all for safety. My question is, why can't we have a safe and fair racetrack? The two should not be mutually exclusive. To me, horse racing should be a contest where the fastest horse wins when given the opportunity and some racing luck. Synthetics take that away as they tend to play more toward turf-influenced breeding. We already have a turf surface; why are we promoting a second? Our tracks needed reworking, but I'm confounded as to why we jumped headfirst into a situation we know so little about. The only research that's been done has been limited in time, mostly overseas, and only by the people manufacturing it. On a different note, I feel synthetics take a lot of the excitement out of racing. It makes good horses average and average horses good. One thing is for sure,: This year's Breeders' Cup will be interesting.

➤ **How do you handle losing owners, whatever the circumstances, while still at your peak? Would you also speak to the loyalty and patience of Mr. Pegram (Midnight Lute) and Mr. & Mrs. Earnhardt (Indian Blessing)?** — Pasadena, California

Getting fired is always humbling. Usually, the hardest part is losing the horses because we get emotionally attached to them. I've been pretty fortunate throughout my career, when one door closes another seems to open. Mike [Pegram] and the Earnhardts have weathered the good and the bad with me since the beginning. Both have had some great luck and some really bad luck, but they understand the game and have a passion for the horses. In my opinion, if you don't have a passion for this game, you'll never find success in it because

9

BOB BAFFERT

the highs are so high and the lows so low. I consider Mike, Hal, and Patti some of my dearest friends. At this stage of my life and career, I only want to work with people I would be friends with outside of racing.

➤ **It seems you work your horses fast most of the time. Why?**
— Hallandale Beach, Florida

Good horses will work fast. I buy most of my own stock, and I gravitate toward a fast, athletic horse. I like to get a good bottom on my horses before they start because I believe a good horse that's not fit has a greater chance of getting hurt because they tend to give you 110 percent on the track. My horses work fast but gallop more slowly. Some trainers do the opposite. It's worked for me for over thirty years.

➤ **Should there be a lifetime ban from the game if a trainer is caught, even once, doping their horses?** — Austin, Texas

This is a tricky situation as trainers are very vulnerable to outside elements. I personally fought a contamination positive for five years before being exonerated. Even with around-the-clock security, the open nature of the barn can invite trouble if someone wanted to tamper with your horse. As a trainer, this is a very real and scary possibility. On the other hand, if a trainer is caught in the act or has multiple positives, then I believe a long-term or even lifetime ban would be in order. As far as legal medications go, it's the old adage, "Outlaw guns and only the outlaws will have guns." By that I mean, if we get rid of medication, then the cheaters will continue to find ways to take an edge.

➤ **Which was the easiest Quarter Horse you ever trained and the easiest Thoroughbred you ever trained?** — West Union, Iowa

By nature, Quarter Horses are pretty easy to train and keep fit. I can't [say] who was the easiest, but my world champion Gold Coast Express was the toughest. He could not be turned loose from the pony in the morning. Ever. It would be hard to pin down the easiest Thoroughbred. I will say the really good ones are easy to train: Point Given, Chilukki, Vindication, Silver Charm, Indian Blessing, Silverbulletday. It came easily and naturally to them. War Emblem was a bit trickier. I had to call on some of my Quarter Horse background to line him out.

➤ **You have been successful in picking out horses for modest value who later go on to be champions. What are your secrets and what do you look for when you go to a sale, or most important, what do you stay away from?** — Encino, California

I look for athletes first, legs second, and [the] pedigree tells me how much I'm going to have to pay. Most of my good horses were crooked or had some conformation issues. You have to be comfortable with what you can work through.

➤ **Is there a horse that you campaigned against that [you] always had the utmost respect for? Many would guess Free House.**
— Ewa Beach, Hawaii

Definitely, Free House was always a formidable opponent for my old warrior Silver Charm. That rivalry sparked a lot of fan interest in racing. Those two were always exciting to watch when they turned for home, even if my stomach was in knots. The great thing about Silver Charm is that he loved to be headed. He seemed to relish the competition and, more times than not, when a horse looked him in the eye, Silver Charm came out on top.

➤ **What is your view on the current move to limit the use of steroids and other medications in U.S. racing?** — Europe

I believe uniform regulation and testing procedures are in order. I only give medication to my horses as they need it, but I believe if you take away basic medications [then] those who want to take [an] edge will continue to do so with things we've never heard about (cobra venom, and so forth). I believe the less medication allowed, the more cheating you will have.

➤ **I am a Silver Charm fan forever. He is, without a doubt, the greatest that I have personally seen run. Where does he rank in your personal list? Also, why do you think Silver Charm lost the 1998 Breeders' Cup Classic?** — Hudsonville, Michigan

Silver Charm is one of my all-time favorites, too. He took us to great heights, and he did it on every coast and two continents. I feel blessed to have been associated with him and the Lewises. I believe he lost the 1998 Classic by following Swain to the outside. Once he got by Swain, he was out there by

BOB BAFFERT

himself, and I don't believe he ever saw Awesome Again roll up the inside. I'll always believe he lost the Triple Crown the same way as he never saw Touch Gold way to the outside. When he saw him, it looks like he digs back in, but too late. He is as noble a horse as I've ever seen.

➤ **Which horse that you have raced against in your career would you have most liked to train yourself, and why?** — Flint, Michigan

Grindstone. No explanation required.

➤ **From your point of view as a trainer, what would be your ideal working relationship with an owner?** — Saratoga, New York

You have to have a mutual respect. I want an owner to feel confident enough in my ability and experience to allow me to do what I need to do on a daily basis. I've been so fortunate in this business to have had great owners. They've all had great success and they have several things in common. The first [is] they don't try to micromanage the day-to-day operation. They know I'm going to do what's best for their horses. The second thing they all share is a passion for the game. They love horses. That is so important. They enjoy coming to the barn to love on their horses as much [as they] enjoy watching them in the afternoon.

➤ **Do you think there is more pressure on today's trainers to win early with two-year-olds than fifteen to twenty years ago? If yes, does that mean training has to be adjusted in some way?** — Lexington, Kentucky

I just ran across some stats from the 1970s. Back then, they started the two-year-olds earlier in the year and they generally had more starts. I've personally never felt that pressure with Thoroughbreds as much as with Quarter Horses. Horses let you know when they're ready to run, and some naturally come around more quickly than others.

➤ **I saw a photo of you once; you had hopped on [Silver Charm] on the track. How did galloping horses affect your perspective as a trainer, as well as buying horses?** — Washougal, Washington

That was at Churchill Downs after Silver Charm had won the Dubai World Cup. I literally grew up around racehorses. You name it, I've done it. I used to break my own horses. I've groomed, galloped, and even tried my hand as a jockey (wasn't very good). All that experience comes into play with my training. To me, buying and training horses is about gut feeling and instinct. The true art of horsemanship is not something I feel can be taught or quantified. To me, one of the most challenging and rewarding parts of my job is getting inside a horse's mind and uncovering what makes him tick. I've had a lot of temperamental horses where figuring out their quirks was key to unlocking their talent.

➤ **Do you think horses know when they win?** — Wisconsin

Absolutely! I think racehorses have a natural instinct to compete. That's why sometimes when you see a horse with bad form win a race, it can turn his form around. Trainers will look for softer spots to try to get a horse's competitive edge back. I love to see a horse come back to the barn after he or she wins. They have their chest out and their head held high. It's really funny to watch; they're almost childlike.

➤ **What did you see in War Emblem that made you think that he could win the Kentucky Derby?** — Rolling Meadows, Illinois

Well, I loved his race in the Illinois Derby. The way he moved so effortlessly over the ground made me think he was the real deal. When I saw him for the first time, I wasn't as impressed with him conformation-wise as I was with the way he moved. He had a great neck and shoulder, but was a very light horse behind. Frank Springer had done a great job getting a foundation on War Emblem because he was not an easy horse to train. He was very temperamental and a bit of an outlaw. In fact, it took two people to groom him each day. War Emblem is the perfect example of a horse peaking at the right time.

➤ **Do you recall your feelings when it looked like [Real Quiet, 1988 Belmont] was going to win?** — Nicholasville, Kentucky

When he opened up turning for home, I thought I was going to win the Triple Crown. As weird as this may sound, the excitement was nothing compared to what I've felt winning the Kentucky Derby. To me, there is no greater high in horse racing. Real Quiet lost the Triple Crown by an unlucky nose, but, to this day, the toughest beat of my career was when Cavonnier got nosed out in the Derby.

TALKIN' HORSES

Bob Baffert

➤ **How do you cope with the loss when one of the horses in your charge suffers fatal injuries and must be euthanized?** — Sierra Madre, California

It's something you never get used to. Horses are like our kids. The grooms, hotwalkers, exercise riders, we all get attached to them and when they don't come back to their stall it's a lonely, hollow feeling.

➤ **Point Given was such a wonderful racehorse and deserving of being a Triple Crown winner. In your view, what went wrong during the Kentucky Derby that denied him the roses?** — Las Vegas, Nevada

I think it was a combination of things. Speed was golden at Churchill that day. In fact, I had a horse break the track record in an allowance race earlier on the card. Point Given ran into an extremely fast pace in the Derby. At the time, I believe it was the fastest half mile in Derby history. If you watch the race, the horse who ran the best was Congaree. He ran a winning race on the front end of that blistering pace, but wound up third. I believe he could have won the Derby that day. Either way, it's one of those things you chalk up to experience and racing luck.

➤ **What would you love to accomplish before you retire, except for winning the Triple Crown?** — Toronto, Ontario, Canada

I'd like to have a picture with all five of my children—Taylor, Canyon, Forest, Savannah, and Bode—in the winner's circle of the Kentucky Derby.

➤ **When you have a horse that runs up the track (off the board) at odds of 3-5 or 1-2, do you feel, as a trainer, some sort of explanation to the bettors on the poor performance of your horse?** — Wahoo, Nebraska

I'd love to [give] an explanation for the bettors and my owners when my horses lose, but that's not always a realistic expectation. Oftentimes, we don't know for a few days after a race if there's an issue that compromised a horse's chance. Sometimes, there is no explanation as horses, like humans, have the equivalent of a bad day at the office.

TALKIN' HORSES
WITH
RICHARD DUTROW JR.

Richard Dutrow Jr. began as an assistant to his late father at age sixteen and formed his own stable in New York in the late 1990s after his father returned to the Maryland circuit. Dutrow's ascension to the top of the New York trainer ranks began in 2000 when he paired with prominent New York owner and commodities trader Sandy Goldfarb. Dutrow became the leading trainer in New York, taking the title by number of wins in 2001 and 2002. Since spring 2001, he has subsequently tallied eight leading trainer titles at New York Racing Association race meets. In 2005, Dutrow-trained Saint Liam and Silver Train provided him with his first Breeders' Cup World Thoroughbred Championship winners. Winner of the Breeders' Cup Classic Powered by Dodge, Saint Liam was honored as North American Horse of the Year and retired to stud. Dutrow's appearance on "Talkin' Horses" came shortly after he accepted the Eclipse Award on behalf of Saint Liam. [On May 3, 2008, Dutrow won the Kentucky Derby with undefeated Big Brown. This win was followed by Big Brown's win in the Preakness on May 17.]

➤ **Do you train for any horse partnerships (syndicates) and do you think that is a good way to get involved with the game?** — Hollywood, California

We have about seventy-five people who go in on horses with us, but the person who puts most of them [partnerships] together is Sandy Goldfarb. We try to get a lot of people involved in ownership. It's an excellent way to start because you can go in with a small percentage of costs, but you also get to see the bills that come in, like from the blacksmith and the veterinarian. You can learn cheaply as you go and later decide if you want to go stronger or stay at that level.

TALKIN' HORSES

RICHARD DUTROW JR.

➤ **Your father was one of the most astute horsemen I have ever seen. Please tell me the most important things he taught you about training horses.** — Lutherville, Maryland

Taking care of the horses was the most important thing I learned from him. Dad took excellent care of the horses and so do we. He was friends with a lot of his horses, and he enjoyed being around them. He always made sure they had clean towels and saddle cloths and were brushed properly, and so forth. Dad insisted on well-kept horses, and so do I. If I walk by a horse's stall and see something wrong, I am not happy. I have good help [and] am fortunate because the help I have is better these days than it was when he was training.

➤ **Do you have a favorite jockey for all your horses or does it depend on the horse?** — Seattle, Washington

I love Edgar Prado. He is my rider. He fits so many horses in so many different ways. Edgar is just a very, very smart jockey and has the best hands in the game. He is an excellent rider and a very nice person to be around. I like John Velazquez almost as much, but I can never get him [on my horses].

➤ **When Saint Liam first transferred to your barn, did you have any idea what you had on your hands, or did he slowly develop into the champion he is?** — Cold Spring, Kentucky

When I first saw him, I had no idea he would end being the way he ended up. I had high expectations for him when we knew he was coming to me. But we had to take our time with him because he had so many things to overcome. The time I knew he was really good was at the three-eighths pole the second time we ran him. That is when we attacked all the best races we could [find] for him, and he showed up in just about every one of them.

➤ **I understand that bloodstock agent Mark Reid was responsible for getting Saint Liam to you. How much does the work of bloodstock agents affect your work?** — West Grove, Pennsylvania

To us, Mark Reid is not a bloodstock agent. He is a close friend and part of our family. My father gave him his first job as a hotwalker at Bowie. He called one day and said he was going to send me the best horse I have ever had. At first, I took it with a grain of salt. But, he was right. I don't put much stock in what bloodstock agents say because they are out there to sell horses. I like that they give me opportunity to buy horses. Some turn out well and some do not. We are very close with Mark; we don't look at him as a business partner. He knows the horses he puts in our barn are going to be well kept.

➤ **How many horses do you have in your stable and how do you keep up with all of them?** — Lexington, Kentucky

Right now, I have between 110 to 120 horses. It takes up all of my time, but I have very good help in each step. I just can't be everywhere at once. The thing that bothers me about having that many is when a problem comes up and I am not there. If I could be there when problems occur, it would be better. I don't regret it [the large number in training] because I have so many friends who have horses with me, and they want success in this game. I love my horses, but I just can't stop and say I am going to cut down to forty or something like that. It would take away from the fun for them and for me. It just takes up my whole life, but I love it. I think about my horses even when I'm sleeping.

➤ **How do you select your assistant trainers? Would you take an unknown with a good background and strong recommendations?**
— Denver, Colorado

It would be very hard for me to hire an outside person to help us. The assistants I have now all started out with us by rubbing horses, then walking horses, and moving on up to foremen. They know the things I do with horses and how I take care of the horses. They also know what kind of help to hire. It makes my assistants' jobs so much easier if they know the kind of people to hire. I would not take any outsider at this time, mainly because they would have their way of doing things and I have my way of doing things. I am happy with the help I have who have learned through my system.

➤ **When you are looking to claim a horse, do you go strictly by the numbers on the sheets or do you like to eyeball some of their previous races?** — Elmont, New York

I don't go strictly on the sheets in any kind of way. I like watching the horses race on video and studying their past performances. I like to have a plan for a horse before I claim them. For example, I would not want to claim a horse in

RICHARD DUTROW JR.

November that did not like the inner track at Aqueduct, and I would not claim a grass horse because of the condition of the grass courses on the East Coast. I use everything the game has to offer in making decisions on claiming. The more information you have, the better decisions you will be able to make.

➤ **If you could pick one horse from history that you would have liked to train, who would it be? Why?** — Ellinger, Texas

Secretariat, because he was the most exciting horse I have ever seen in my life. I was around the barn at the Preakness Stakes, and I got to meet him at Claiborne Farm after he retired. At Claiborne, they gave us a piece of his tail, which my mom still has framed.

➤ **You have made [progress] in recent years, going from just a few horses [in] the stable [to the] success that you have now attained. What kept you going and focused?** — Saratoga, New York

I have always loved this game and grew up in the racing game. I love the horses and love the competition. That stuff does not leave you. It's what kept me going. The turning point was when I met Sandy Goldfarb. He gave me the opportunity to show those in the racing game that I know what I'm doing.

➤ **What are the important things to you in analyzing your horses' workouts?** — Chicago, Illinois

I don't look at the times that much at all. I don't put much credence in times. I get upset when my horses breeze too fast. The riders know how a horse feels under them, so I like getting a feel for the breezes based on the reports from the riders.

➤ **What enters into your decision to run a horse back in less than seven days?** — Oak Park, Illinois

I could never explain why I started doing it, but it has been very good for us. It's a trial-and-error thing. I like running back within three, four, or five days; after that, it's thirty-five to forty days. I don't like running back in six, seven, or even nine days. I don't get excited about that. Oftentimes, when there is a spot that fits them within four to five days, I run them. I let them tell me if they want to run. [Timing] is very important with these horses—as much as soundness.

➤ **What would you like to see changed about the medication rules and penalties where you race? Do you believe the absolute insurer rule that holds the trainer responsible for everything relating to his horse should be abolished?** — Lexington, Kentucky

I really wish they had the same medication rules throughout the whole country. I would like to see the absolute insurer rule abolished because it does not seem fair. There are a lot of things thrown at me they expect me to be responsible for, and that I should not be responsible for. They should not make a trainer responsible for all that happens [with the horses].

➤ **What treatment did you use for [Saint Liam's] feet?**
— Boston, Massachusetts

He had very brittle feet, with no walls at all. I give all the credit to Alex Leaf, my blacksmith, who is an absolute genius with feet. He started in Maryland, working for my dad, and then went to Dubai, where he worked five years for the sheikhs. He always did what he thought was best for the horse. Nobody else could have come up with the design of the plate he came up with. Alex would fit up some shoes with foam rubber on his heels. We had glue-on shoes we used that were almost bar shoes. Sometimes we used regular shoes, and sometimes I would train him without any shoes at all.

➤ **Because of the toll it takes for a two-year-old to win the Breeders' Cup, do you think we should eliminate the two-year-old race in the Breeders' Cup?** — Columbus, Nebraska

What I really wish is that they would eliminate the two-year-old in training sales. They are out there rushing these horses to try to get the most money out of them. It ruins so many horses. I do not rush my horses into races. I would much rather have a better three-year-old than two-year-old. I am not into the two-year-old picture. I don't know what the rush is. I would rather wait until they have developed more.

➤ **What one change to horse racing would have the biggest positive impact on pari-mutuel handle?** — Bethesda, Maryland

In New York, they should let you split up entries. I wonder why they don't do it. It would help them fill up races and increase handle.

TALKIN' HORSES

RICHARD DUTROW JR.

➤ **Can you give some examples of how you improve your new claims and some of the methods you use?** — Encinitas, California

I do the same for any new horse that comes into my barn. One thing I concentrate on is how they push off and the next thing is how they hit the ground up front. I have a very good hind-end specialist in my vet, and have a blacksmith who makes sure they hit the ground. I try a lot of different things to get them to push off the right way. If they do that and hit the ground, that is half of the battle. A lot of trainers don't have the right people getting on their horses, so they don't know [the horses] are not pushing off the right way. I have very good people getting on my horses. But there are a whole lot of things that go into it. We also give them the best hay, the best straw, and the best grain.

➤ **Saint Liam had so much heart on the track. What was his personality like around the barn?** — Albany, New York

He did not demand any kind of attention. He was a laid-back horse. You could walk by his stall and not know he was in there. He was very quiet, which probably had a lot to do with how he turned out. He just did not demand any attention. He was a pleasure to work with. He did not want you to play with him a whole lot, but I don't think he ever bit anyone. You had to ask him to do things; otherwise, he would just bide his time. It's better for horses to be like him, rather than being more aggressive where they use too much energy on things that don't matter.

➤ **What is most important to you when picking young horses— conformation or bloodlines?** — Boonville, Indiana

I don't usually go to the sale to pick out young ones. I usually have my people do it. I have been starting to look more at young babies. I like looking at the total horse. I don't like picking horses apart. If I like them, I take them.

➤ **How did you feel about Saint Liam winning the Breeders' Cup Classic with Jerry Bailey instead of Edgar Prado, your number one rider?** — Washington, D.C.

I know Edgar could have gotten the job done as well. I would not have cared if my mom rode him that day; it was so much fun.

TALKIN' HORSES
WITH
LARRY JONES

Trainer Larry Jones, a native of Hopkinsville, Kentucky, is known for his strong work ethic and trademark cowboy hat. He rides many of his horses in morning workouts and is also known for personally hauling his horses to race at tracks where he is not stabled. Before becoming a trainer, Jones gained experience working with horses on his farm, where he raised cattle and hogs and grew corn, tobacco, and soybeans. The first horse he owned, a $2,500 claimer named Ala Turf, was a winner. Questioning the way his horses were being trained, Jones took out his trainer's license in 1982 and began his new career. Jones, who is actively assisted in his training by his wife, Cindy, was based at Ellis Park during the summer months until 2006 when a tornado that damaged the Kentucky track led him to Delaware Park. That decision led to greater exposure for Jones on the national scene and led to an association with owner Rick Porter, who operates as Fox Hill Farms. The pair enjoyed immediate success, with Hard Spun finishing second in the Kentucky Derby, then running third in the Preakness Stakes before being retired with earnings in excess of $2.6 million. His other top horses have included grade I winners Island Sand and Wildcat Bettie B. At the time of his online chat, Jones was in the midst of Hard Spun's Triple Crown campaign.

➤ **Do you personally get on all of your horses?** — Denver, Colorado

No. Hopefully, I will have ridden everything in the barn at some time. But there is no way I can get on them all every day. There is no horse I don't ride on occasion. Basically, if the riders come back and have an issue, I will ride that horse the next morning. I make the rotation, get on them when I can. I have seven riders, which includes me.

TALKIN' HORSES

LARRY JONES

➤ **What edge does having a seat on the horses you will be sending to the races give you? Does your agricultural background come in handy?** — Sydney, Australia

I feel like it [riding my own horses] does [help with my success], especially when you have a large stable like I have. It gives me a chance to know more about where my horses are, what they're doing. If my riders are having a problem with a horse, I can get on and tell them what the issue is and what they need to do, so I definitely feel like it gives me an advantage. I don't get to use the agricultural background every day, but it does come in handy, from buying different hays to learning to [analyze] the Weather Channel ... but that's how life is; everything you've learned throughout the years makes you knowledgeable and adds to your experience.

➤ **How early in a horse's beginning training can you tell he will be special?** — Mont Belvieu, Texas

[With] some of them, the first few times you ever lope them you think you've got something nice. But then I've had some very good horses that I didn't know were good until after they started racing; they didn't train well, but, by George, they wanted to win really bad—and that helps. In Hard Spun's case I knew pretty quick. He did everything right from the beginning.

➤ **What was your first job at the track and how did you get started?**
— Aledo, Illinois

Actually, with Thoroughbreds, my first job was being an owner; that's the first license I ever held. Needless to say, with horses I just started riding when I was a kid, like two or three [years old]. My grandfather would put me on mules to ride back to the house from the fields at lunchtime, so I've ridden my whole life. But with Thoroughbreds, my first job was an owner and like a lot of owners, I thought, "I can train as good as my trainer!" So I proceeded to try and show them I could.

➤ **What is Hard Spun's personality like around the barn and on the track? Does he have any unique habits or quirks?** — Aiken, South Carolina

He really is a very nice horse, especially for a horse competing at this level. He rides back and forth to the track like a trail horse. A lot of times, I'll have horses breezing with their exercise riders or jockeys, so I'll sit on him and watch them work and then gallop him. He's a lovely horse to be around, and very seldom do you see him try to bite at anybody. At Churchill Downs we were having a little trouble because he was tired of people being around and he started snapping at people, but as long as he gets his space and time [to himself], he's fine. As far as quirks go, he loves sweet potatoes. He eats them as fast as you can cut them up for him. He could be a pet real easy.

➤ **Just wondered [that] with all the help [received] from the "peanut gallery" in the past few weeks, how did Hard Spun ever lose the Derby and Preakness?** — Philadelphia, Pennsylvania

[Laughing] I guess I just didn't listen well enough. For some strange reason, I tried to do it my way. I had a lot of help, a lot of opinions, and I thank them for being willing to share those opinions with me. But I couldn't apply all the strategies into just the two races.

➤ **I think winning the Triple Crown is probably the most difficult thing to accomplish in the entire sports world. Do you think that we will see a Triple Crown winner ever again?** — Alpena, Michigan

I do. And I agree it is very tough. Being in it this year, I realize more than ever how tough it is. There will be that outstanding horse that will do it. They thought it would never be done when Secretariat came along, and then all of a sudden there were three in the 1970s. It will be done again. It will take a special horse. But that is what it was designed to be. It is not supposed to be easy. That is what makes it so coveted. It is what it was meant to be.

➤ **If you could climb on the back of any of our recent champions, which would you like to ride? Can you explain a little bit how you developed your training philosophy?** — Ione, Oregon

I think it would have been great to have ridden Secretariat. He is my favorite. Seattle Slew, too. As far as philosophy, the biggest thing we try to do is have them well fed, try to keep them in great body flesh, and try to keep them happy. That is where the different training techniques come in. Some need a lot of training, some don't. But try to remember what you are trying to accomplish and read between the lines on what it takes to make it happen.

TALKIN' HORSES

LARRY JONES

➤ **Are sports boots as good as or better than bandages and would you ever race a horse with them on? What do you think of racing horses barefoot? I have also heard that Hard Spun does not like the massages he gets.** — Kenbridge, Virginia

Sports boots are fine; we used to use them with Quarter Horses. Reining horses use them. They are good where you can adjust as you need to, but I would not race in them. I would continue to stay with the bandages. You can't stop and pull up your socks when they start sliding down. You don't get any time-outs in racing. As for barefoot, I don't know if that would be the best thing for them. A lot of horses have feet so bad they would not be able to race without shoes. I do train a lot of horses barefooted; breeze them barefooted. We may only shoe them on race day. And it works. It is a good thing for some horses. I trained Island Sand for six weeks barefoot. [I] had the shoes put on three days before the Fantasy [Stakes]. Over the years, I have trained several [horses] barefooted. The only time Hard Spun seems irritable during the massages is when maybe they have lasted too long, because he gets impatient, or if we get to a spot that is a little tender. But that is what we are doing, locating the tender spot to make sure it is not a problem, to work the old blood out of the spot and work the new blood in. He will not get cranky because of it. He is awfully good for some reason at knowing what is good for him. He goes along with it because he knows it helps.

➤ **What do you like to do for fun when you are not working with the horses? Do you have other hobbies?** — Newark, Delaware

I have two [other] things: I eat and I sleep. But horses are it. If I had an opportunity, I would love to go watch the rodeos, see things, and be around things [like] I used to do, to see how it has changed. But basically, it is all horses all the time. It would be great to spend time with old friends.

➤ **What's the most important thing you learn about your horses from your hands-on (and seat-on) approach to training?** — Florence, Kentucky

Probably that every horse is an individual; that every horse is different. If you train them all the same, you are probably training them all wrong. That is basically it. They are not machinery or automobiles; they are living and breathing creatures and no two are alike. You have to treat them as individuals.

➤ **It is really gratifying to see someone with a strong work ethic doing so well as a trainer. Do you have any pointers or comments you would like to share for those of us in the "blue-collar" [training] crowd?**
— Terra Bella, California

Just that persistence does pay. If at first you get knocked down, get up and do it again. It won't come easy, but anything worth having is worth working for. I'm glad there are others who have the dream, and if you have the dream, go for it.

➤ **What do you look for during the post parade that signals to you that your horse is ready to race? Are there things you don't like to see?**
— Minneapolis, Minnesota

There are things you don't like to see. If they get extremely washy when the horse doesn't normally. But just because a horse is wet with sweat is not a bad sign; if he does it every time, don't be concerned. You look for the things that don't normally happen. You don't like to see things out of the ordinary. I like for the fillies to be calm. They talk about them being on their toes, but my fillies tend to run better when calm and confident.

➤ **Of all the horses you have trained, do you think Hard Spun is the best?** — West Bend, Wisconsin

Yeah, I would have to say that right now. Hard Spun is a unique kind of horse. I don't know how to say enough good things about him. Wherever his feed tub is, that's home. He is great to be around, has natural speed, [and] can play with his opposition early. Normally, with speed they don't have his type of endurance. He is easy to train and ride. He is as close to having a perfect horse as you could have. I never expected to have a horse that can do things like he does. He is awesome; absolutely awesome to have.

TALKIN' HORSES

WITH

CARL NAFZGER

A native of Plainview, Texas, Carl Nafzger was a bull rider on the rodeo circuit before turning his talents to training horses. The trainer met his wife, Wanda, while on the rodeo circuit and they married in 1968, the same year he took out his trainer's license. At the time of his "Talkin' Horses" appearance, Nafzger was preparing the previous year's two-year-old male champion, Street Sense, for a 2007 season that would include victory in the Kentucky Derby. In planning for the season, Nafzger mapped out an unconventional campaign that called for only two prep races before the Derby. All went exactly as planned, with Street Sense winning the Tampa Bay Derby and finishing second in the Blue Grass Stakes before winning the Derby in impressive fashion. The colt went on to win the Jim Dandy and Travers stakes and finished second to Horse of the Year Curlin in the Preakness Stakes before being retired with career earnings of $4,383,200. Nafzger also trained Kentucky Derby winner and champion Unbridled and champion Banshee Breeze. He is also author of Traits of a Winner: The Formula for Developing Thoroughbred Horses.

➤ **When you hugged Mrs. Genter and told her she was going to win the Kentucky Derby with Unbridled, it was one of the most touching moments in this sport. Of the two victories of Unbridled—the Derby and the Breeders' Cup Classic—which one gives you the most satisfaction?** — Bowmanville, Ontario, Canada

They are equal. The historic significance of winning the Derby will never be replaced, and the accomplishment of taking a three-year-old and beating older horses and horses from all over the world in the Breeders' Cup will never go away.

➤ **Does Street Sense have to win both prep races to go to the Derby or is it Derby or bust?** — Edmonton, Kentucky

As long as he runs correct races, he doesn't have to win either of these two races to go the Derby. There are three things we're looking for in the first two races, but really in the first race. We need him to get what I call "deep fitness" that you get out of a race and you can't get out of training him. Second, you have got to get him focused on his game. Then you want him to get his timing, so he's there [at the finish]. And I will be watching for what I watch for in any race, to see if the jockey makes a mistake, to see if the horse makes a mistake, or to see if I have made a mistake. Winning is not that important. These are prep races. This is not the Kentucky Derby.

➤ **I have aspirations of becoming a trainer but am having a hard time getting started. What would you recommend?** — Seattle, Washington

There are a lot of ways to get started, and the way you get started is up to your personality. My wife, my brothers, my dad, and I went to the bank and borrowed $8,000 and went to Keeneland and bought two yearlings. But by that time, I had broken racehorses and sold them in California, worked on a ranch in Cheyenne, Wyoming, and had shod horses and learned shoeing at Cal-Poly. You have to adapt it to your personality. The first thing you want to do to be a successful trainer is to get a good accountant and have a business plan that is no different than if you were going to open a restaurant. The way I look at horse trainers is to draw a circle and divide it into three things—horsemanship, promotion, and management. Some guys have good management skills and have a little horsemanship and a little bit of promotion. I always said a perfect trainer would have a third, a third, and a third. I am not a real good manager. I am not a real good horseman. And I am not a real good promoter. But I am equally good in all three.

➤ **Will the advent of synthetic racing surfaces affect the way you look at sales yearlings?** — Davis, California

As we get more synthetic surfaces, we will be able to utilize our grass horses more. It will be a big benefit to racing. You will have a broader base of yearlings to work out of [at the sales] because you will have more places to utilize a horse with grass breeding.

TALKIN' HORSES

CARL NAFZGER

> **Do you think Street Sense could be the best horse you ever trained?**
> — Saratoga Springs, New York

It is a little early to say, but, yes, he could be. He has to step into some big shoes, and he is doing it. If he keeps going, he could be the best.

> **If you could do one thing to improve the horse racing industry, what would it be?** — Winooski, Vermont

[I would] get us all working on common denominators. I would try to get a common denominator for racing. We have taken some steps that are important. Off-track wagering will gradually bring us together. This has made us start thinking more as a collective group. Coming up with synthetic surfaces has established a common ground. Thirdly, we have to get medications [on the same level] so they are uniform and go from there. We are working on all these things, but there are different approaches being taken to get there.

> **How can I stop my horse from wanting to go wide down the stretch?**
> — Baltimore, Maryland

It could be anything from mental to physical. Like [trainer] Bobby Frankel says, "Don't change equipment before you try to figure out why he is doing it and then work on changing it." You need to figure out why he is doing it. In my experience, 90 percent of the time when a horse is going wide down the stretch, he has a physical problem.

> **Carl, I thought the betting public was crazy to let Unbridled go off at moderately long odds in the 1990 Derby. Six years later, I was thrilled to be close to him, inside his Claiborne stall. What were some of his personality traits?** — Florence, South Carolina

Unbridled was so intelligent I almost expected him to talk to me when I walked into his stall. He had more kids on his back than jockeys [on his back]. He was an unbelievable horse. He controlled the shed row.

> **Is it true you don't believe in hotwalking your horses after galloping? If so, I'm interested to know the benefit.** — Ocala, Florida

We don't hotwalk horses after we breeze them. We give them a bucket of water and then we take our horses into the stall and rub them out. I like the communication between the people when you're rubbing the horse out. It's a quieter atmosphere. It's [the same] with people. After you've run two miles, would you rather get a drink of water and a massage or would you want to walk another five miles?

➤ **Do you [think you'll] ever see the day when the qualifications to get in the Derby will veer away from graded stakes money and to a panel choosing the starters?** — Del Mar, California

You have got to leave it with the horse. That is much better than a judge. The horse has to separate who's going to go in the Derby. If you win a race like the Delta Jackpot, you have qualified because you still had to win that race. The only thing wrong with horse racing is the human. I think we have screwed up the Breeders' Cup because we have a panel decide who is invited to fill out the fields. You have to take humans out of horse racing as much as you can, and that is my opinion of the whole business.

➤ **What were Vicar, Street Sense, Solvig, and Unbridled like at the barn? Banshee Breeze was my favorite, and it was a tragedy when she died. What was her personality like and what was your reaction when the news broke of her passing?** — Rochester, New York

I couldn't believe she died, and I couldn't believe Unbridled died. We went to see Unbridled the day before he died and he was like, "Don't worry. I can handle this." He was just an unbelievable horse. When they get to the breeding shed, you think they will live forever. As for personalities, Solvig had her own territory. Vicar was a very apprehensive colt; he wouldn't relax a lot. Street Sense commands a presence in the barn; he has his space.

➤ **As an owner/breeder/agent I have had the opportunity to purchase a few Unbridled-line offspring. I have found two traits common to all. First, they have incredible natural ability. Second, they seem to have soundness problems due to being a bit upright in the pasterns and straight in the shoulder. Did he have these physical characteristics as well?** — Medfield, Massachusetts

Yes, that was one of his weaknesses and [it's the same] in his offspring, but they showed an extraordinary ability to run.

TALKIN' HORSES

CARL NAFZGER

➤ **Of all the wonderful horses that you have conditioned, which one did you find to be the toughest both physically and mentally; which one got the title of "Iron Horse"?** — Miami, Florida

Banshee Breeze [was the toughest] because all you had to do was get her to the paddock. I think she was one-two-three in seventeen races after finishing sixth in her only start as a two-year-old.

➤ **Do you miss your rodeo days? What do you think your life lessons on the rodeo taught you and has it helped you in the Thoroughbred industry?** — Louisville, Kentucky

Everybody misses their youth. I learned how to be self-sufficient, how to put schedules together; when you're on the road like that, you are totally self-sufficient. You learn discipline and responsibility for your actions. I took all that into racing.

➤ **What is your feeling about bucked shins and does the severity of the [bucked shins] make a difference how you manage the horse?**
— Paris, Kentucky

You definitely want to treat a bucked shin. It's very painful, and you want to take care of it. Horses tolerate very little pain. A bucked shin is something where I back off on them [from training].

➤ **As the trainer of Unbridled, Street Sense, and author of *Traits of a Winner*, what *are* the traits of a winner? [How did you] work with a horse like Street Sense and capitalize on his potential and bring out those traits?** — Seattle, Washington

As I said in my book, the four traits of a winner are "mental, ability, soundness, and the immune system, and class welds it all together." Class is the undefined element in horse racing. How do you bring it all together? You let the horse bring it all together. It is like a coach who does not change a running back's style; you just try to help him perfect his style. There are a thousand ways to train a racehorse, but there is only one result that is acceptable and that is for a horse to relax and respond to his rider's command.

TALKIN' HORSES
WITH

TODD PLETCHER

When he appeared on "Talkin' Horses," trainer Todd Pletcher had just completed a 2005 season in which he had set an earnings record of $20.8 million and was honored with his second consecutive Eclipse Award. While impressive, those achievements seemed to pale in comparison to what he went on to accomplish in subsequent years, with additional Eclipse Awards in 2006 and 2007. Despite not beginning the year until February 10 due to a suspension stemming from a 2004 medication violation in New York, Pletcher established a new earnings mark of $28.1 million in 2007. Utilizing the horsemanship and organizational skills learned from his years as an assistant to D. Wayne Lukas, Pletcher continues to set the bar high. He won his first Triple Crown race in 2007 when champion Rags to Riches defeated males in the Belmont Stakes. Additional champions trained by Pletcher are Ashado (twice), Speightstown, Fleet Indian, Wait a While, Lawyer Ron, and English Channel. He also trained Canadian champion Archers Bay.

➤ **Which single daily training method/technique/routine would you say is the most important in helping you achieve your success?**
— Copenhagen, Denmark

There is no single technique that stands out. I think it is the consistent repetition of a number of techniques that leads to success.

➤ **I have been watching John Velazquez ride for several years, and he has quickly become my favorite jockey. What makes him such a good candidate to work with?** — Elmira, New York

I definitely feel more at ease going into a race with Johnny riding. He is an extremely versatile jockey who rides equally well on dirt and turf, speed horses, and horses that come from off the pace.

TODD PLETCHER

➤ **Do you miss Ashado [sold at Keeneland for a then-record $9 million] being at your barn?** — Batavia, Ohio

Of course, I miss her, but I am happy she has gone to such a good home and think she will make a wonderful broodmare.

➤ **Do you know if you will have an opportunity to train any of Ashado's babies?** — Mt. Gretna, Pennsylvania

I think she will make a very good broodmare who will cross well with Storm Cat. I would love to train any of her babies.

➤ **Since you have over 200 horses under your care, how often do get to put your hands on each one?** — Pleasant Prairie, Wisconsin

I actually have less than 200 horses in my care. I put my hands on every horse that is at the location where I am training on a given day. I am able to supply my owners with the information they need without referring the calls to an assistant.

➤ **I am an aspiring trainer and a big fan. I am an equine animal science major at UC Davis. I worked as a foreman for Marty Jones; I study bloodlines and training techniques; [and] I am working with the farrier at the UC Davis Vet School to learn more about feet. What is the most important thing I could do to become a good trainer?**
— Davis, California

Sounds like you have already made a good start. Try to work for the best trainers you can find, listen well, and then formulate your own opinions.

➤ **Which sires have you had the best luck with in terms of that sire consistently producing nice horses?** — Lexington, Kentucky

Gone West, Saint Ballado, and Distorted Humor.

➤ **How soon can you tell that a racing prospect doesn't fit in with your stable, and what do you do with that type of horse?** — Chicago, Illinois

I think I get the most accurate read on a horse once it starts working five-eighths [of a mile]. Depending on what the owner wants, I might try the horse in a maiden claiming race or at a less-competitive track.

➤ **If you were looking to own and race horses, would you prefer to purchase yearlings or two-year-olds in training?** — Louisville, Kentucky

A combination of both.

➤ **With your vast experience and great success, I would like to know what you look for in a yearling when you are evaluating them as prospective racehorses.** — Boston, Massachusetts

I look for good conformation and balance.

➤ **It seems that the winter talk always gets back to the Triple Crown trail and the time frame between races. Do you feel the schedule needs to be adjusted due to the wear on the runners so early in their careers?** — Berea, Ohio

No. I think it should stay the way it is.

➤ **How do you feel about just turning a horse out after the Breeders' Cup for the winter? If an owner told you they planned to do that, would you consider it beneficial even going into the Triple Crown trail?** — Asheville, North Carolina

I don't think it's a good idea to turn a horse out after the BC that is pointing for the Triple Crown. You never have as much time as you think you do between the Juvenile and the Derby. If you have one hiccup along the way, your schedule gets tighter and tighter.

➤ **Do you feel that young horses are pushed too early to compete in the spring classics? Why do you think so many young, talented horses who run in the classics get career-ending injuries?** — Northhampton, Pennsylvania

I think all races are demanding on horses, and [I] have been fortunate to have a number of horses make it through the spring classics to run again.

➤ **When I look at your barn I can see a lot of excellent horses, but you haven't got any from Argentina. What is your opinion about them?** — Buenos Aires, Argentina

The Argentine horses I have been around are durable and hard-trying.

TALKIN' HORSES

TODD PLETCHER

➤ **Will you ever hire a female assistant trainer?** — Orlando, Florida

My first assistant was female, and I have one female assistant working for me right now.

➤ **What makes a trainer appreciate and respect a Turf writer rather than being annoyed by his or her presence?** — Arlington Heights, Illinois

I appreciate a reporter who comes prepared to an interview and actually asks a question. I especially don't like it when a reporter comes to my barn and says, "So, tell me about Flower Alley ..."

➤ **What was the best thing that Lukas taught you?** — Tiruppur, India

Organization.

➤ **What do you dislike about your profession, other than being away from your family?** — Newark, Delaware

That's the only aspect of it that I don't like.

➤ **At yearling sales, you scour the barns with your father. What is the best horse that you have bought in a father-son combination?**
— London, England

[Millionaire] More Than Ready, with [turf champion] English Channel as runner-up.

➤ **You prefer to have your horses gallop to the starting gate instead of [being helped] by the outrider; is there any advantage?**
— Long Island, New York

I do like to thoroughly warm my horses up before a race. However, I am selective in choosing [the] ones that I think will behave well and not get too aggressive without a pony.

➤ **With you having such a large stable, there must be enormous demands on your time. Is there any thought ever to downsizing or maybe taking a prestigious private position?** — Arcadia, California

I am happy with my current situation.

TALKIN' HORSES
WITH

TIM RITCHEY

Trainer Tim Ritchey, who lives in Maryland and races in Maryland, Delaware, and Pennsylvania while wintering in Arkansas, is known for his unorthodox method of training Afleet Alex, who often went to the track for long gallops twice a day. Ritchey credited much of his training regimen with "Alex" and other horses to his years of riding horses during his youth and as a successful steeplechase rider and trainer. Ritchey was guest host four days after Afleet Alex, who had finished third in the Kentucky Derby, overcame near disaster [after colliding with Scrappy T] in the stretch to win the Preakness Stakes. Afleet Alex went on to win the Belmont Stakes and was honored as the champion three-year-old male of 2005. Following that season, the colt was retired to stud with a record of eight wins from twelve starts and earnings of $2,765,800.

➤ **Afleet Alex's training schedule is heavier than that of most racehorses—and clearly is doing him just fine. [Did] his training [help him] recover so quickly from his stumble or do you think he's just naturally that athletic?** — New York, New York

I think he is naturally athletic, but I would like to think that my training had a part to do with it. I would like to think that because he's had so many miles of training and is so fit mentally and physically, that he [had] the mental and physical ability to recover quickly and pick himself up and go on like that.

➤ **How do you account for the recent Philadelphia Park/Delaware Park success in the Triple Crown series?** — Brookhaven, Pennsylvania

I think some of that is directly attributed to the increase in purses at Delaware Park as a result of slot machines. I don' t know about Smarty Jones and Philadelphia Park, but I know that when the owners of this horse came to me before I bought Afleet Alex it was with the purpose of buying a horse to run at Delaware Park. If you have slots, the bigger the purses are going to be, and the better the horses are going to be.

➤ **What is more difficult for a horse: a step up in distance or a cut back?**
— Saddle Brook, New Jersey

It depends on the horse. If you are taking a sprinter and stretching him out, it can be a difficult thing. If he is a natural speed horse and you are stretching him out, he has to be able to relax in the race, and that depends on the pace. If there is not much speed in the race, he could be able to cruise on the front end. If you have a distance horse lacking speed and is going short, if the pace is fast he will be able to pick them up late as they fall back, even if he is not a sprinter. Pedigree has an effect as well.

➤ **Do you think that your background [as an eventer and steeplechase rider] contributed to the unique training regimen and success for Afleet Alex? What do horses in training for a race and horses in training for a three-day event have in common?** — Lexington, Kentucky

I think it [my background] definitely affected the way I trained this horse. I have done it with other horses in the past and it has been very successful. In both, you have to be mentally and physically fit. With a three-day event or steeplechase horse you do more with them, getting them out a lot more and for longer periods of time. It makes them a lot tougher, a lot fitter, and it sharpens their agility, which you have to have in a three-day event. Timewise, you can't do it with every horse in your stable. I wish I could do it with a lot of my other horses, but that is not possible with the limited training hours at the track. My long-range plan with this horse was to build him up physically and get enough of a base under him that he could get through the Triple Crown preps and the three races and be able to rebound quickly after each race.

➤ **What instructions were given to jockey Jeremy Rose for the Preakness and how did they differ from the Derby?** — Seattle, Washington

Basically, they were same instructions. It was more circumstances in the Derby, where Jeremy had to go through holes and move right and left to find the holes when they opened and those spurts take little bit out [of] every horse. I wanted him to make one sustained run, and he was not able to do that in the Derby because he had to move so much. I think he could have made up a length somewhere in the Derby, but in the end [it] was not meant to be and in the Preakness it was meant to be. I believe a lot in faith and destiny.

➤ **You say that Afleet Alex is a very laid-back horse who never gets upset or lets anything spook him. Do you think [it's] because Alex learned to accept and trust humans to care for him so early in his life that might have contributed to his wonderful temperament?**
— Stow, Massachusetts

Yes. Since he was basically raised by humans, I think he has developed a great trust in people that I have never seen in any other animal, including dogs, or even in people-to-people relationships. He really has a special thing for children—he loves them. He has never been abused and has complete trust in humans. It has helped his disposition and the whole procedure I took with him. Robert Scanlon did a tremendous job in breaking and preparing him.

➤ **What training procedures will you use up to the Belmont to "ensure" Alex gets the 1½ miles?** — Midlothian, Texas

Early in his career and even early in his three-year-old season, many questioned whether he could go around two turns, and he proved them wrong. I purchased this horse to have a horse that could go a route of ground. There is a tremendous amount of stamina in his pedigree. The key to getting any horse to go a distance of ground is to get them to relax, and this horse relaxes so well that he can just lope along until Jeremy asks him to pick it up and make his run. He certainly trains like he will run a mile and half, or even two miles.

➤ **In addition to a rigorous exercise program for Alex, what other ingredients help him maintain his fitness? Do you use special feed, or any dietary or vitamin supplements?** — Grass Valley, California

I feed a complete feed that has a lot of beet pulp. Basically, that is all he eats. He gets fed three to four times a day. He gets fed the same as everybody. He is not that big of a horse, I would say he weighs just under 1,000 pounds and stands 15.3 hands, but he gets fed as much as a bigger horse because he does so much. He has maintained his weight very well.

TALKIN' HORSES

TIM RITCHEY

➤ **What caused Afleet Alex to come in third in the Derby?**

— Englewood, Colorado

I think it was the fact Jeremy had to use him two or three times to get through tight holes, and with a horse like this you look for one run. He also got bumped around two or three times and when he did make his run he had to steady [himself] at the head of the lane behind three or four other horses.

➤ **What made you so confident that your horse would win the Preakness?**

— Lutherville, Maryland

After really watching the Derby, I thought he was the best horse in the race but due to circumstances and fate, he wasn't meant to win. He came out of the Derby very well, and he had trained very well between the Derby and the Preakness. He had to overcome a lot of adversity to win the Preakness, but good horses do that.

➤ **Has being on the road with Alex through the preps and Triple Crown races taken away from your responsibilities with the rest of your stable and how have you handled that?** — Marrakech, Morocco

I do a lot more training on the phone [and] I have a great crew of people. I try to get back to Delaware as much as I can. The last time I looked we had a 30 percent win rate.

➤ **How much of Alex's success can be attributed to him, to you as the trainer, and to Jeremy Rose?** — Hoboken, New Jersey

I would think it would be 80 percent horse, 10 percent me, and 10 percent Jeremy. Good horses make trainers and riders look much better than they are, and bad horses make them look worse than they are. It is not rocket science. You just have to keep them healthy and fit.

➤ **Has Afleet Alex's success and publicity had an effect on your career?**

— Hammond, Indiana

I have had quite a few inquiries from people wanting me to train for them. But I tell them I have to be very loyal to the people who have supported me over the last ten to fifteen years and if stall space becomes available, I will take on new clients at that time. But so far, I have not taken any new owners.

➤ **Should Afleet Alex win the Belmont, will it forever be a nagging thought in the back of your mind regarding his third-place finish in the Kentucky Derby?** — Lexington, Kentucky

I am sure everybody who has won two legs of the Triple Crown thinks about it. But you can't dwell in the past and have to look forward to the future. I am very happy he came out of the Derby OK and won the Preakness and would be very happy if he wins the Belmont.

➤ **Is it fair to say the Belmont favors a fresh horse, rather than a horse that has been put through the grueling test of the first two legs of the Triple Crown?** — Warminster, Pennsylvania

I would think it is fair to say [history] does favor horses who have not gone through all three races. But that was my thought in December when I came up with a plan and schedule that would have him ready and fit to go through the Belmont. I think my horse is going to be prepared for the race and he will run his race, and hopefully no fresh horse will come out the woodwork.

➤ **Why is Alex the type of horse from whom you want a "sustained run?" I'm not sure what it means.** — New York, New York

When you have horse who must take a stalking position, just off the pace, especially going a distance of ground, you need one good run where the horse and rider can get into a rhythm. As in the Derby, Jeremy had to make little bursts three or four times to put him in the position he was in at the end, and I think those little bursts that he had to make cost him more than a length.

➤ **When you bought this horse as a two-year-old, what made him stand out from all the other, better-bred horses?** — Syracuse, New York

He just was a very athletic horse in his workout, even though he worked in :22⅖, which was in the lower 50 percent of those that breezed that distance. But it was the way he did it that I liked. It was very fluid. When I inspected him, he was a very, very straight and correct horse and had an athletic walk. And he had a very good mind. When I looked at him, there were other horses bucking and acting up and he just stood there.

TALKIN' HORSES
WITH
JOHN VEITCH

When he was inducted into the Hall of Fame at the National Museum of Racing in Saratoga Springs, New York, in August 2007, trainer John Veitch joined his late father, Sylvester Veitch, in the elite club. Veitch, the chief steward for the Kentucky Horse Racing Authority, trained champions Davona Dale, Our Mims, Before Dawn, and Sunshine Forever during his career, but his best-known horse may be Alydar, who was part of the great rivalry with Affirmed in 1977 and 1978. Davona Dale and Alydar are members of the Hall of Fame. Veitch trained for Admiral and Mrs. Gene Markey's legendary Calumet Farm from 1976 to 1983 and surfaced on the 1978 Triple Crown trail with Alydar, who finished second to Affirmed in all three races. In 1984, Veitch became private trainer for Darby Dan Farm, for which he trained 1985 Breeders' Cup Classic winner Proud Truth and 1988 champion grass horse Sunshine Forever. He retired from training in 2003.

➤ **Are horses more fragile now than when you started training or is it just a matter of how we view things?** — Lexington, Kentucky

I think they are more fragile. It goes back to the very fundamentals of what mare is bred to what stallion. We have had probably twenty years of intense, pervasive use of medication in this country that has allowed some horses with basic unsoundness to race and to pass along that unsoundness to their offspring. The pervasive use of Lasix to prevent bleeding has weakened the system. When I was a boy and my father was training for C.V. Whitney, we had a group of mares that were just pensioned off because their offspring were unsuitable for racing. Instead of continuing to breed them and weaken the breed, they were just retired. [Of] the colts that had not been productive at the racetrack, [most of them were gelded to keep people from breeding to them].

That was the philosophy of the day. Of course, most of the better pedigreed horses in America were being bred by a small group of major stables. It was a sport to them and all of the emphasis was not on making money. They had more money than they could spend and had all gone to the same schools. One of the places where they could show they were better was on the racetrack, by breeding a better racehorse and hiring a smarter trainer. With a breeding concept that has gone commercial, and the pervasive use of medication, which disguises some horses' weaknesses so you really don't know if you're breeding to a sound horse, things have changed. In the course of two or three decades, we have gone from producing the soundest racehorses in the world to one that is not as sound. You are going to find some people who have foresight in the betterment of the game and the horse itself as an ideal way of doing it. But once you've turned that corner, it is difficult to go back. When you have money that is involved rather than what is right for the game, it sure is a blocking agent.

➤ **How did you get the Calumet job and what was it like working for them?** — Encino, California

[Farm manager] Melvin Cinnamon called me in December of 1975 and said that Admiral and Mrs. Markey wanted to make a change. Every year they had a brilliant two-year-old that never seemed to make it to its three-year-old year. They wanted somebody who was young who would take the job. Most people don't realize that by then Calumet had fallen on some hard times. In April of 1976, Melvin Cinnamon called me again and asked if I could meet him again on the fourteenth in Miami where Admiral and Mrs. Markey had a home. I went over to have lunch with them, and I thought it was just an interview. The first thing the Admiral said was "Melvin, have you told Mr. Veitch what his salary is going to be?" I was shocked.

The next morning Melvin and I went over to the stable at the Hialeah racetrack and Melvin gave the news to the former trainer that I was going to replace him. We had twenty-four horses there and a few at the farm that were recovering, and by the end of the year I had nine left. They were in pretty rough shape. It was a bad year for Calumet. I went to their home in Florida in December to resign at the end of that year after having the job for only about nine months. Mrs. Markey would not accept my resignation and explained to me that she had given me a lot of bad horses to train and I would have better material to work with and that is how it turned out. They were wonderful people to work for—knowledgeable, understanding, supportive. There was never a time they told me what to do. I was hired as their trainer and they had confidence in me. They were wonderful—the word for it is "class." They loved the sport—win, lose, or draw. They were wonderful to work for, as was the whole Calumet family —the people who had worked on the farm all their life. They were so supportive and pleased when the stable came back to life again.

➤ **I recently re-read *Wild Ride* [about the rise and fall of Calumet]. [Have] your opinions changed regarding the events of Alydar's death and the reasons behind Calumet's demise?** — Pompano Beach, Florida

My feelings have always been that something nefarious happened to the horse. I can't apply blame to anybody, but the incident happened under some very suspicious circumstances that were unexplainable to me.

➤ **It has been well-documented how much Alydar's victory in the Blue Grass Stakes meant to Mrs. Markey. Was that your most gratifying win because of that?** — Bowling Green, Kentucky

I was not totally convinced that the Blue Grass was the best stepping stone to the Derby. In those days, there were only nine days between the Blue Grass and the Kentucky Derby and I thought maybe two weeks would be little bit better. Somebody will say "five days is not a whole lot of difference." But there is a considerable amount of difference. It would have given me time to do a little more with Alydar before Churchill Downs. But Mrs. Markey was old and somewhat infirm and Admiral Gene Markey was also in poor health. Working through Ted Bassett and Bill Greely at Keeneland, they made a special effort for her to come and see the horse run. It really meant a lot to her to come and see her horse participate in the Blue Grass. And it worked out beautifully. It was the last race that she and the Admiral ever saw in person. The horse came through for her. His effort in the Blue Grass was sensational.

From the point of overall gratification, it didn't happen with Alydar or a Calumet horse. It happened with a horse owned by John Galbreath and Darby Dan Farm. It was with Proud Truth winning the Breeders' Cup Classic. Proud Truth had sustained a saucer fracture in his cannon bone about a week before the Belmont Stakes, which made us miss almost all of the summer. When we got him back in training, I didn't have a day to spare, from the standpoint of preparing him for the Classic. I sat down with a calendar, and worked backwards, beginning on the day of the Classic, looking at what I was going to do, when I was going to do it, how I was going to do it, what races I was going to run him in, and what I needed to accomplish from a standpoint of getting him up to the race. And it worked perfectly. He was the ideal horse to do that with because he would give you anything you asked him for in the morning. It was a wonderful day for Darby Dan Farm, for Proud Truth, and for me.

➤ **In hindsight, was there anything you might have done with Alydar that might have helped him beat Affirmed; e.g. change of equipment, jockeys, learn to change leads, run up the rail?** — Chantilly, Virginia

I really don't. I have gone over it a thousand times in my head. One thing the public probably doesn't know is that Alydar almost never changed leads in the afternoon, but in the mornings he changed leads perfectly. When I would work him in the morning, he would change leads like a ballerina. But in the afternoon he would not. I think more than anything else it was concentration. When you are running at that speed and he was running with so much heart and dedication, you really don't want to mess with it. In the heat of battle he's giving you everything he's got and it was just something we couldn't control. It would be one thing if he wouldn't do it in the morning, which would give us something to work on. It did put him at a little bit of a disadvantage. I took blinkers off after the Preakness before going into the Belmont. And a number of riders rode him. Jorge Velasquez rode him the most and was a perfect fit for him, although Alydar had so much natural ability almost any rider could have ridden him and done well. I would like to have another shot.

➤ **After Alydar's injury at age three, he didn't seem to come back as great as he was before. Can you briefly explain his injury and how, with the advancement of vet medicine, a horse may have an easier recovery today?** — Floral Park, New York

Alydar broke his coffin bone —the outside wing on his right front. That is one injury that veterinary science really has not advanced on because that bone is so porous and it does not heal very well. Because it is inside the hoof there is very little that can be done without invading the hoof and possibly

43

weakening it forever. In hindsight, we probably should have retired Alydar, but my thinking and that of the farm manager was that Mrs. Markey was very old and frail and not in good health and she might not have the opportunity again to see a horse of that caliber for Calumet. We wanted to take a shot to see if we could bring the horse back. Unfortunately, he did not come back as well as he had been as a three-year-old. Fortunately for Calumet, we had quite a few good horses after that. Margaret Glass, the farm office manager, felt that added years to Mrs. Markey's life.

➤ **What things have changed the most from your days as an active trainer with regards to training methods and concepts?**
— Lexington, Kentucky

The [biggest] change I have seen in the last thirty years has been the shift to the major horses in America being sold at auction. In my early years at Calumet and during my boyhood, most of the better horses in America were raised on most of the major racing stables' breeding farms and they were raised to be warriors. The breeding trends were to produce a very solid racehorse, where [raising horses] commercially it is more of a fad. You kind of have to raise them like hothouse tomatoes and protect them from blemishes or from getting any bumps or bruises. Also, a lot of training methods have altered considerably. You used to see horses trained harder and raced more often. Now, we have mega stables that would never have existed in the old days because most of the traditional owners realized a trainer could not possibly supervise and do a good job with a huge number of horses. They wanted their horses to have some personal attention.

➤ **[Is] the current trend toward mega stables bad for the industry or is it good because of the publicity generated by those stables with so many big stars?** — Lexington, Kentucky

I think it is damaging to the industry. When you concentrate a large number of the quality horses in such few hands, it hurts the racing secretary's ability to fill races and it hurts the diversity of the field. Basically, you have a situation where some excellent horsemen are leaving the game because they just can't make a living at it anymore. I don't think that the concentration of the quality horses benefits anybody, particularly the fans. I am certainly not criticizing the mega trainers because they work very hard and most of them are extremely talented horse trainers. It's just that I don't think the owners get a fair shake either. Most of the modern owners are using statistics to pick their trainers and the trainers are not going to run a horse that is not going to do well. And they have the opportunity to pick and choose who they run and where they run. I think that a lot of quality horses that don't fit into a system and who need really special handling, especially when they are young, fall through the cracks.

> **I loved Davona Dale and just wondered if you could tell me how she was to train? How was she away from the track?** — Cedar Rapids, Iowa

She was just fantastic. From a standpoint of pure athletic ability, she was probably the best horse I ever trained. Up to a mile and a half, she was absolutely sensational. Of all the great horses Calumet had in its history, there was only one horse that had more consecutive stakes wins than she did and that was Citation. She ranked right up there with the very best. She was an ideal horse to train and an ideal horse to manage. She was almost a pet in the stable. You could do anything with her. She would be lying down in the stall and you could go into the stall and put your hand on her neck, she would not bat an eye.

> **How has your perspective of the regulatory side of the industry changed now versus [when you were] a trainer?** — Lexington, Kentucky

Not a great deal. As a trainer you had to train by rules and respect them and now as a regulator I enforce them. Everybody should play on a level playing field. But now that I am on the side of enforcing rather than obeying those rules, my viewpoint has not changed a bit. What is fair for one should be fair for all.

> **Please describe some of the behaviors of your most difficult horses and also your kindest. Who was the most generous?** — Portland, Oregon

Our Mims could be difficult and she was particularly difficult after she was retired from racing and became a broodmare. She wanted to be the queen of the paddock. But she was really not that difficult in training. I had a horse named Tim the Tiger, who was a graded stakes winner for Calumet Farm and was almost dangerous to be around. When I was serving my apprenticeship and working for Elliott Burch, Arts and Letters was a horse you really had to respect. He was dangerous to be around if you didn't know what you were doing. Those were the most difficult horses I had. From the standpoint of generosity, almost all the good ones—Davona Dale, Our Mims, Alydar, Before Dawn, Proud Truth, Sunshine Forever—were just super-generous horses with their ability. I was amazed just to look at them, at what was inside them that made them so special.

➤ **Has any thought been given to having all equine drugs monitored by the authorities, full disclosure to the public, and severe sanctions to those who choose to violate the policy?** — East Saticoy, California

Dealing with medication is something that Thoroughbred racing and all competitive sports have been dealing with for a long, long time. We have developed a system, just like the Olympics, NBA, and NFL, in which we screen and monitor all the substances out there and spend a tremendous amount of money every year at laboratories all across the United States for testing, monitoring, creating new tests. There is some abuse, there is no doubt about that. Whenever you have a lot of money to be made, there are people who are going to try to do it nefariously. But we try to police our sport to make sure that everybody plays on a level playing field. I believe everything that can possibly be done is being done. With people trying to beat the system, they sometimes think they are one step ahead of us and sometimes they are, but we have got some very dedicated people that are in the pharmacological and chemical business of trying to detect those things and develop new approaches. We do have severe sanctions for people when someone is caught using a class I drug, which is a drug that will enhance the performance—those are the stimulants.

➤ **What was your biggest challenge as a trainer after Alydar retired? Have you ever forgiven Laffit Pincay for the incident in the 1978 Travers or spoken to him since? Will you ever consider returning to train?** — North Providence, Rhode Island

The biggest challenge to any trainer when a star retires from your stable is to replace him. Shortly after Alydar, Davona Dale came into the stable and then, Before Dawn. But the biggest challenge is to find a replacement for your star.

From the standpoint of Laffit Pincay and the Travers, I was upset with Laffit because I thought he saw it coming and dropped in on Alydar. I thought it could have been a great tragedy if one or both of those horses were seriously injured.

It is in the past. Oftentimes, and I have done it myself, in the heat of battle you do things you regret and I certainly hold no malice toward the great rider that Laffit Pincay is. Our paths crossed many times when he was still an active rider and we were very cordial to each other. There were never any acrimonious words exchanged between him and me. I did not get the opportunity to use him as a jockey because he was on the West Coast and I was on the East Coast, but I would have because he is one of the great ones.

> **Which is worse: dealing with the jockeys [in your role] as a trainer or a steward?** — Lexington, Kentucky

Dealing with jockeys as a trainer [is worse] because a trainer has very little power over a jockey. As a steward, I have a great deal of power over a jockey.

> **What is your favorite track and what race did you not win that you would like to besides one of the Triple Crown races?**
> — Lexington, Kentucky

I have two favorite tracks—Keeneland and Saratoga. Both are unique and both are vested in the tremendous tradition of Thoroughbred racing. They are different, but they are the same. There is just an atmosphere about them that is unmistakable and cannot be duplicated any other place in the world. I cannot say there is a race I wanted to win but did not, but I would have liked to have a Horse of the Year one time. I was very disappointed when Proud Truth was not three-year-old of the year after winning the Breeders' Cup Classic, beating older horses. I felt that he was somewhat slighted. I thought Proud Truth's effort—not only considering his injury and missing almost all of summer and early fall races—in the Breeders' Cup and the stake before that was a tremendous display of ability, I thought he should have been three-year-old of the year.

> **You've trained many great horses, but of those, which horse did you feel had the most heart?** — Albany, New York

There is no doubt that Alydar had the most heart. Alydar never came back and acted like he was discouraged (after losing a race). He came back and gave his all, regardless of who he ran against. Mrs. Markey didn't want to back down and wanted to run in the races we felt were appropriate for a horse of his ability. From a standpoint of heart, no other horse I ever [trained] had as much.

TALKIN' HORSES
WITH
NICK ZITO

Trainer Nick Zito was the guest host one week after being inducted into racing's Hall of Fame. The trainer of two Kentucky Derby winners—Strike the Gold (1991) and Go for Gin (1994)—as well as winners of each of the other Triple Crown classics—Louis Quatorze (1996 Preakness Stakes) and Birdstone (2004 Belmont Stakes), Zito reminisced about the best horses he has trained, including Eclipse Award champions Storm Song (1996) and Bird Town (2003), and the rigors of the Triple Crown trail. Birdstone's Belmont was one of the all-time biggest upsets in racing history as it spoiled the Triple Crown for Smarty Jones.

➤ **Who is the best horse you ever trained?** — Toronto, Ontario, Canada

That's a very good question. The horse that had the most talent was Unbridled's Song. I think Bellamy Road could be his equal. Strike the Gold, no question, was the most determined. He never ran a bad race. I've had so many great horses, it's hard. Talent-wise, I could give you fifteen, but I think [overall] it's Unbridled's Song and Bellamy Road.

➤ **What are your thoughts on the use of the whip in horse racing?**
— Grand Rapids, Michigan

One of the things is that the whip is overused. If you look at the great jockeys, you'll see that they don't overuse the whip. If you look at Pat Day, he's a great example, because he didn't use the whip that much. He was more of a "hands" jockey.

➤ **I was wondering if there was one special horse that you fell in love with as a child that drew you to the sport?** — Cedar Rapids, Iowa

Of all of my favorite horses, one that kept attracting me to the sport was Kelso.

He won the Jockey Club Gold Cup five times. That definitely attracted me. We used to say "Kelso" this and "Kelso" that. He was like Michael Jordan.

➤ **Do you think the horse makes the trainer or does the trainer make the horse?** — Lexington, Kentucky

Mostly, [it's] the horse, but it's still a combination. It's nice to know what you're doing, so you don't mess [the horse] up. Good horses make good trainers. It's not often that good trainers make good horses. If you're excelling at what you do, it's a combination. You can have a great plane, but you need a pilot; know what I mean?

➤ **I was wondering if you have any thoughts or ideas about what could be done to make racing more appealing or open to young fans?**
— Merrick, New York

The racing bodies have to get involved. It needs to be mandatory. State agencies should be mandatory. It's not affirmative action, because it's not. They should give kids a job for the summer. You have to do more. We're talking about people's lives here. We should have some kind of programs going to give some kids some jobs. They [kids] don't have to be from a farm; they could be from the projects. It doesn't matter.

➤ **Of all the horses you have trained, who would you consider to be your personal top five?** — Eureka, California

The most talented were Unbridled's Song and Bellamy Road. The best— that's a very tough question—[probably] were Albert the Great, Louis Quatorze, Strike the Gold, and Birdstone. The Cliff's Edge might have been one. He was a very unlucky horse. A.P. Valentine got hurt. Stephen Got Even was a very good horse. Thirty Six Red got it all started for us. There have been some very good horses.

➤ **What advice would you give for an aspiring racehorse trainer?**
— Medford, New Jersey

The logical answer is put the work ethic first [along with] the love of the horses. It's two things. They go hand in hand. And you have to sacrifice. That would be it.

TALKIN' HORSES

NICK ZITO

➤ **Up to now, what has been your most memorable race victory?**

— Cinnaminson, New Jersey

We've had a bunch. Strike the Gold in the Kentucky Derby. Of course, Birdstone. Commentator, because I was going into the Hall of Fame on Monday after his Whitney. The Whitney has to be way up there. There's been so many.

➤ **How did you come to be a horse trainer?** — Tallahassee, Florida

I started from the bottom. I became a hotwalker, and it got in my blood. I worked my way up to a groom, to an assistant trainer, to a trainer with one horse—then four horses, eight horses, and twenty-four horses. That's how I did it. A lot of luck and a lot of hard work.

➤ **How do you rate Birdstone's Belmont [over favored Smarty Jones] among your classic victories?** — Caracas, Venezuela

I think that's one of the all-time best. It was a part of history—thirty-three million people watching [on television]. For all the ramifications it had—all the people looking at Smarty Jones—it had to be one of the best, if not the best.

➤ **Was there a particular time that you consider the "low point" in your career?** — Buffalo, New York

One was right before Thirty Six Red came. I wondered if I'd reach the pinnacle. Of course, then he came along. I was probably a little low there, because I was looking for "the" horse. But racing has its highs and lows every day.

➤ **You have a great talent for picking out winners. What are the two most important things to you when selecting a yearling?**

— Dumas, Texas

Walt Robertson (of Fasig-Tipton) told a friend of mine, "I never know what Nick looks for." I basically go by feel. There's a lot of luck. I can't explain it. We already know the conformation, right?

JERRY BAILEY

RUSSELL BAZE

PAT DAY

GARRETT GOMEZ

CHRIS McCARRON

MIKE SMITH

GARY STEVENS

TALKIN' HORSES
WITH
JERRY BAILEY

Hall of Fame jockey Jerry Bailey participated in an online chat one month after announcing his retirement in January 2006. One of the most successful riders in history, Bailey rode 5,893 career winners with purses of more than $300 million. He won 216 grade I races highlighted by two wins in each of the three Triple Crown events—Kentucky Derby, Preakness Stakes, and the Belmont Stakes—three Kentucky Oaks wins, fifteen Breeders' Cup victories (including five Classic wins), and four winning rides in the Dubai World Cup. Bailey is also the author of Against the Odds: Riding for My Life, *a moving account of his personal struggle to deal with the pressures and demands of such tremendous success. Upon retirement, Bailey joined the racing broadcast teams at ABC and ESPN.*

➤ **Why do you think it is so hard to win the [Derby]? Do you think the Derby should be limited to smaller fields?** — Louisville, Kentucky

One of the hardest things for a jockey [who is] in demand to do is to pick the right mount. Most top riders have their choice of several horses. But owners and trainers usually need a commitment at least two races prior to the Derby, and since these three-year-olds progress and regress rapidly at that time of year, a good choice in March might not be the right one in May. Even if you do pick the right one [Empire Maker, as an example] your mount has to remain healthy. No, I do not think the field size should be smaller; it would be an injustice to prior winners to change the rules now.

➤ **What did you eat for your first big meal when you knew your riding was completed?** — Cincinnati, Ohio

My first lunch, I ordered a Reuben sandwich, something I had been wanting to do for at least ten years. I could only finish half of it.

➤ **You did a significant amount of riding for Paul Mellon and Ogden Phipps. Can you share your thoughts?** — Saratoga Springs, New York

I didn't get to know Ogden Phipps very well, so it is impossible for me to compare him to Mr. Mellon. Mr. Mellon was a very kind and philanthropic individual. He always took the time to speak not only to me, but to my wife and son whenever we met.

➤ **What races stand out to you as especially sweet memories [and] what races would you most like a second chance to ride?** — Springfield, Missouri

My best race memory is the [inaugural] 1996 Dubai World Cup [won by Cigar]. I really wouldn't say that I would ride any races in my career differently, but I certainly would have chosen a different post position [number eleven] in the 2003 Kentucky Derby [with runner-up Empire Maker] if I had it to do over.

➤ **If you had the power to change one thing in horse racing, what would it be?** — Miami, Florida

If I could change anything in horse racing, it would be to market the human stars more [the jockeys and trainers] because, even though the horses are our product, the great ones aren't around long enough to market and create a public following.

➤ **Is there any truth to the rumor that you were very close to getting the Smarty Jones mount? I can't help but wonder what would have happened if you were riding him in the Belmont.** — New York, New York

No, there is no truth at all to the rumor that I was close to getting the mount on Smarty Jones. Their connections never even intimated that they wanted to change, at least not to me.

➤ **How much of your success do you attribute to outworking [other jockeys] and preparation?** — New York, New York

Until the last few years, I would be at the track at least five mornings a week. Even recently, with traveling back and forth to Florida from New York, I was out in the mornings four days a week. Even if I did not actually get on a horse, the public relations with the trainers went a long way. If they were out there working, why shouldn't the jock be out there as well?

TALKIN' HORSES

JERRY BAILEY

➤ **What has been the most dangerous spill or accident you had at the track?** — Caracas, Venezuela

My most dangerous spill occurred in the Fall Highweight Handicap at Belmont Park in the fall of 1985. I broke my back in three places, [broke] three ribs, and [broke] my foot in three places.

➤ **You come across as too competitive to sit around doing commentary. Are you 99.9 percent retired or 100 percent retired?** — Orlando, Florida

I am 100 percent retired. My competitive spirit will be addressed not only by golf, but trying to succeed in bringing racing to fans in a way that you've never had it before. I will call them like I see them; I will relate to the public exactly what we think and do out there as jockeys.

➤ **Mr. Bailey, as a handicapper my grandfather told me once that when betting horses racing in the slop, one should always look for horses with the shortest legs. Any truth to that theory?** — Essington, Pennsylvania

No, I have never heard that one. However, I do believe that a slighter-built horse has a bit of an advantage over a big, heavy horse on an off track.

➤ **Jerry, could you comment on your relationship with other jockeys?**
— Chicago, Illinois

I have had a couple of true friendships with other jockeys, [but] it is extremely difficult. To be a successful jockey, you certainly cannot give "friendly breaks" to your friends out on the track, and you or your agent are constantly trying to get on the best mounts, even at the expense of another jockey's feelings.

➤ **How much difference does the trainer make when you are talking about a great horse?** — Jersey City, New Jersey

A great horse will be great in the care of an average trainer, or being ridden by an average jockey, but a truly good trainer can extend the length of a great horse's career.

➤ **Jerry, which do you consider the best overall horse you rode, and was there one that you let get away?** — Olive Hill, Kentucky

The best horse I rode was Cigar, and the best horse that I almost rode was Ghostzapper. I had worked him out and Bobby Frankel was under the impression that I didn't like him. Oh, well.

➤ **Generally speaking, how [does] Saint Liam stack up? He's a deserving Horse of the Year and I will miss seeing him run.** — Cold Spring, Kentucky

How good was [2005 Horse of the Year] Saint Liam? It is impossible to compare horses from different years, but he was among the best I have ridden.

➤ **Pat Day said you were one of the jockeys with a good sense of humor. Who were some that could make you laugh?** — Alpharetta, Georgia

Bill Shoemaker had a great sense of humor, but the funniest jockey I have ever come across has to be Bryan Fann. He rode through the Midwest and was the leading jockey at Monmouth Park in New Jersey in the late 1970s.

➤ **Where does Empire Maker rank among the horses you've ridden?**
— Gainesville, Florida

[Belmont Stakes and Florida Derby winner] Empire Maker had more raw talent than any other three-year-old I had ever ridden. If he had stayed sound, he would have done some incredible things.

➤ **Why didn't you just hang around and ride only on the weekends —rather than retire—or is that just not possible?** — Ocala, Florida

Riding just the weekends and expecting to remain at a high level is impossible. A jockey needs to compete on a regular basis to keep his or her skills at a peak level, even if it is just two or three mounts a day during the week.

➤ **Last year I saw Cigar at the [Kentucky Horse Park] and he still looks like he could run today. What do you think was the number one reason that made him so great?** — Dallas, Texas

I think that God was the number one reason that Cigar was great. He was blessed with immense talent and speed, but the reason he was so great for an extended period of time was [due to] his trainer, Bill Mott.

TALKIN' HORSES
WITH
RUSSELL BAZE

Legendary Northern California rider Russell Baze was a guest on "Talkin' Horses" during his quest to become the all-time leading North American rider. [He accomplished that feat December 1, 2006, when he rode his 9,531st winner. Later, in 2007 he became the first rider to reach the elusive 10,000-win plateau.] A native of Vancouver and a member of the Racing Hall of Fame since 1999, Baze is a ten-time winner of the National Turf Writers Association's Isaac Murphy Award, which recognizes the rider with the highest percentage of winners from mounts in a year. He also won the 2002 George Woolf Memorial Jockey Award and received a special 1995 Eclipse Award as the first jockey ever to win 400-plus races four years in a row. Baze is a third-generation rider, coming from a family long involved in horse racing.

➤ **Please share with us something of the personality of the late [2005 champion sprinter] Lost in the Fog [who died in September 2006 due to complications from cancer]. Do you have a favorite horse you have ridden?** — Tustin, California

"Fog" was a champion, but he wasn't a pet and could get quite aggressive with those who worked with him. He's the best horse I've ridden. Down through the years I've ridden many good horses. The ones that find a place in my heart are the hard-trying veterans who overcome problems and still keep on trying.

➤ **What do you consider your strongest assets as a rider?**
— Bigfork, Montana

My ability to read a race—how it is setting up and how to position my horses to take advantage of developments throughout the race—and a strong desire to succeed or win.

➤ **In all your career, what are the main points that you can say were crucial or significant?** — Newmarket, England

The two main decisions of my career are probably: 1) Deciding to hire Ray Harris as my agent and remain in California year-round and 2) Moving to Southern Cal for three years to try my luck at getting some good horses to ride in the classic races.

➤ **Do you have any big plans for the day you break the record?** — Richmond, Virginia

Not really. I'll probably have to ride the next day, so I won't be able to go too crazy.

➤ **How has the Lord influenced your life as a jockey?** — Salem, Oregon

There is no doubt that I have been blessed throughout my career. Simply being preserved each day to return the next day and race is a great blessing in itself.

➤ **What criteria do you use to determine the mounts you choose to ride? In your opinion, what is the difference between riding a quality horse and a $5,000 claimer?** — St. Marys, Georgia

My agent chooses mounts for me based on which horse stands the best chance to win in a given race based upon the conditions for that race. Good horses are easier to ride, generally, than cheap horses.

➤ **Can you tell us all the Bazes who are or were riders, and [describe] how you are related?** — Kent, Washington

First came my grandmother, Mable Baze. Then, her oldest son, Earl, my uncle. Then, my dad, Joe. Then, my cousin, Gary. Cousin Earl. My brother, Jeff. Myself. Cousin Mike. Little brother, Dale. Second cousin ,Tyler (cousin Earl's son). Second cousin, M.C. (cousin Mike's son).

➤ **What is generally the most difficult thing to do when navigating a horse race?** — Marco Island, Florida

Judging the moves of the other riders and their responses to the situations that occur during a race is the most challenging aspect for me.

TALKIN' HORSES

RUSSELL BAZE

➤ **What was the closest you have ever been to disaster that suddenly turned to triumph?** — Tuscaloosa, Alabama

I had a horse my Uncle Rex was handling in the gate leap at the start, nearly knocking my head into the overhead bars. We got a mile behind the field, but [I] was able to get up in time.

➤ **How did you feel when Lost in the Fog passed away?**

— Hot Springs, Arkansas

My first thought was that this explained why he had performed as poorly as he had in his last start. Of course, I was very sad when he passed away, but by the time that day arrived I had had a chance to get my mind around the idea that he wouldn't be around anymore.

➤ **Had you not become a jockey, what would you have likely pursued as a profession? Also, did you feel family peer pressure to work in horse racing?** — Lexington, Kentucky

I was not pressured to enter the world of horse racing, but when I showed an interest and an aptitude for riding, my father did everything he could to help me be the best that I could be.

➤ **In general, can a jock have a strong influence on how well the horse breaks? Do you feel you can help a horse break sharply from the gate, especially if the horse has a history of not breaking well?**

— Waukegan, Illinois

Yes, the jockey definitely has influence on how the horse breaks. It takes a lot of concentration and focus to make sure your horse is standing with his feet underneath him in the starting gate and is alert but not anxious. If a horse doesn't want to break, I am not going to be able to make him. But I can help a horse leave the gate as well as he's willing to leave.

➤ **What is your opinion of California fair racing compared with racing at the other tracks in northern California?** — Modesto, California

The fair racing serves a purpose for the horses of lesser quality to have their time in the limelight. It's also a good place for younger horses to develop towards greater things in the future. Definitely, it's a lot different mindset when you're riding on the fair circuit. You have to ride at different tracks, with different configurations and surfaces, every two weeks, but it is very good at keeping your mind flexible by having to adjust to different track variables.

➤ **How many times have you been injured and what was the most serious? Other than exercising in the mornings and riding in the afternoon, do you have any workout regimens?** — New York, New York

I have been injured numerous times, but the most serious was when I broke the vertebrae in my back. I missed six weeks. On Tuesdays [when there is no racing], I have a regimen that includes pull-ups, push-ups, crunches, and running the stairs, and upper body work with a sports band. Normally, it takes me about forty-five minutes to go through the whole workout.

➤ **While it is a certainty that you would have set the record regardless of where you rode, do you think it would have taken longer if you competed regularly on the Southern California circuit?**
— Midway, Kentucky

It definitely would have taken longer if I had remained in Southern California. The competition for mounts in Southern California is extremely fierce, especially when I was down there.

TALKIN' HORSES
WITH
PAT DAY

Hall of Fame jockey Pat Day—winner of one Kentucky Derby, five Preakness Stakes, and three Belmont Stakes—was guest host the week after announcing his retirement as racing's all-time money-winning rider (nearly $298 million in purses) with 8,803 career victories to devote himself to a life of service with the Racetrack Chaplaincy of America, a national organization that serves the spiritual, physical, emotional, and social/educational needs of the workforce at tracks throughout the United States. Day won four Eclipse Awards as outstanding jockey and was inducted into the Racing Hall of Fame in 1991.

➤ **I read once that you considered Lil E. Tee one of your worst Derby mounts. What was it like winning the Derby and is it a bigger thrill to win on a favorite or on a longshot?** — New York, New York

That's a mistake. I never have considered him to be a bad Derby mount. He is my only winning mount so I don't know what it's like to win on a favorite. Thank you and God bless.

➤ **Lady's Secret was a special horse. Can you share any memories of this great mare?** — Orange, California

[She was] one of a kind. Great racehorse. Very headstrong but a fun ride. [I have] fond memories [of her].

➤ **Who are the best female and male horses you have ever been on?**
— DeRidder, Louisiana

[The] best females were Dance Smartly and Lady's Secret. [The] best male [was] Easy Goer.

➤ **What other jockeys do you most admire now and/or were inspired by? What made you decide to become a jockey?** — Waldoboro, Maine

I have great admiration, appreciation, and respect for all riders. It's a very competitive, close-knit group of individuals. I became a jockey because the Los Angeles Lakers didn't come with the right amount of money. Just kidding. I know now that I was being directed by God and thank Him for this.

➤ **What horse do you think was the most talented that you rode during your career?** — Cincinnati, Ohio

Easy Goer was the most talented. He had a big engine, a lot of heart and desire, and was very well trained by Shug McGaughey. He did what he did with continuing ailments.

➤ **What career advice would you give to a young jockey today, not necessarily about riding skills but how to conduct himself and what to be concerned with?** — Richmond, Virginia

Work hard and be a person of integrity. Take advantage of and show appreciation for any and all opportunities.

➤ **Did you ever [work with] a trainer that you felt [did] not want to win a race by giving you instructions like, "Don't do too much with her (or him)" or "This is not his (or her) best distance so don't go all out"?**
— Kalamazoo, Michigan

No, but I always had the horses' best interest at heart and never purposely did anything to hurt them.

➤ **When you ride a horse that you really like and that you feel also likes you, how do you make yourself known to this horse upon mounting for a race? Is it more to it than just communicating through touch and voice when you are in the saddle?** — Djursholm, Sweden

It is the whole aura, and I have been blessed with an innate ability to communicate with the horses and they oftentimes respond readily for me, whether it is to settle in the early stages or give me their very best in the drive.

TALKIN' HORSES

PAT DAY

➤ **If you could choose how you and your career are remembered, what would you want your legend to be?** — Kansas City, Missouri

[I would like to be remembered as] a rider that tried hard, gave his best, and truly enjoyed the great sport of horse racing and the people involved.

➤ **Frequently, I thought you were cut off by interviewers when the subject of your faith came up. How did you handle this? Did you have trouble reconciling your faith and your participation in a sport so dependent on gambling? Also, I wonder what horse would you most like to have ridden, but didn't get to?** — Kentwood, Michigan

God has promised that His word would not return void. I trust that whether or not it made the paper, it would accomplish what God would have it to. I had no trouble after receiving the revelation from God that I was to stay in racing but have never used my position to promote the gambling aspect of our business but rather to share the love of Jesus. As for which horse—all the champions!

➤ **When you decided to leave racing, why was the departure so abrupt?**
— Los Angeles, California

It was a decision that was difficult to come to, but upon receiving direction from God, I knew it was time to retire. I knew also it was not a time to procrastinate but to move forward.

➤ **If you were to address the hierarchy of Thoroughbred racing in America, what would you suggest be done to make racing stronger and better for all concerned?** — Saratoga Springs, New York

There are some incredibly knowledgeable and caring people who are looking at that very issue even as we speak, and I trust that they will come up with the proper answers. Racing has been around, and will continue to be around, for a long time.

➤ **We know you have a terrific sense of humor. Who were some of the jockeys or trainers that could make you laugh?** — Alpharetta, Georgia

Ray Sibille, my brother-in-law, has the world's greatest attitude and was always pulling jokes on everybody. It was a joy to ride with him. Jerry Bailey was quite a prankster also, especially if jockey Bryan Fann was around.

➤ **Of your 8,803 victories, which one meant the most to you, and why?**
— Olivebridge, New York

Five victories stand out. The one that meant the most to me was Lil E. Tee in the 1992 Kentucky Derby for obvious reasons: It's the cornerstone of American racing and known around the world. The next was Foreblunged, my first winner. [Then comes] Danas Woof Woof, who secured the national races-won title. Wild Again in the inaugural Breeders' Cup Classic. And I took my career to the next level with With Anticipation in the Sword Dancer at Saratoga in 2002, who, when it appeared that I had left him with too much to do and not enough time to do it, got up and won and put me in the lead in the all-time earnings list.

➤ **Could you talk about what it takes for a rider to be able to get on a horse and know that he or she is either sitting on a potential star or sitting on a horse that has something wrong physically?**
— Charles Town, West Virginia

We generally have eight to ten minutes in the post parade to warm-up our mount and get a feel for them. It's fairly easy to tell if the horse is not traveling smoothly. Certainly, [it is easy] after riding for several years and garnering the experience.

➤ **I was wondering who you think was the greatest horse you ever rode against?** — Warminster, Pennsylvania

Most likely [it was] Cigar. His record speaks for itself, but I have been beaten by some of the best. But I have beaten the best on occasion.

TALKIN' HORSES
WITH
GARRETT GOMEZ

Jockey Garrett Gomez was North America's leading money-winning rider in 2006 at the time of his online chat in early 2007. Not only did he repeat his earnings' title in 2007, but he had a record seventy-five stakes wins during the year and won an Eclipse Award for outstanding rider that season. In consecutive years—2006 and 2007—Gomez rode two winners on the Breeders' Cup World Championships cards. A native of Tucson, Arizona, whose father, Louie, was also a jockey, Gomez won his first race at Santa Fe Downs in New Mexico on August 19, 1988. Gomez had a twenty-one-month absence from racing, beginning in 2002, during which time he sought help for substance abuse. Since his return, he has been more successful than at any other point in his career. In late 2006, he donated $10,000 to the Winners Foundation, which assists racetrackers with substance and alcohol abuse problems.

➤ **If you could have ridden any horse in the history of Thoroughbred racing, who would it have been and why?** — Whitefish, Ontario, Canada

Probably Secretariat. He was an amazing horse and was the best of his era. He is one of the horses that sticks in everybody's minds when they think of horse racing. He might not have been the best horse ever, but as far as the general public goes, they know Secretariat. Some of the races he ran, he didn't break very well, and you wondered what he was doing and then he ran right by them. That had to be an amazing feeling.

➤ **Have you ever wanted to quit riding? If so, what made you stick with it?** — Kennett Square, Pennsylvania

Yes [I wanted to quit riding]. My passion for riding [made me stick with it]. I need to stay physically and mentally fit.

➤ **I have long considered you an extremely talented jockey. Can you tell me which jockey [jockeys] had the greatest influence on your career?** — Atlantic Beach, Florida

My father [Louie], Chris McCarron, and Eddie Delahoussaye. But there were very many [other] jockeys that influenced me.

➤ **Who was the best horse you have ridden?** — Bratislava, Slovakia

There have been so many good ones, all of whom had different styles and abilities, that it would be hard for me to pinpoint any one that was better than the others. Also, I am on some really good horses right now and one of them could fall into that category at some point.

➤ **Would you want your son to become a jockey?** — Louisville, Kentucky

If he wished to be although there are a lot better and safer job opportunities I would be happier with him doing. But if he wanted to be a jockey, I would give him 110 percent support, just like my father did for me. He never pushed me into the game but has supported me from the beginning.

➤ **What do you consider your biggest strength as a jockey?**
— Menomonee Falls, Wisconsin

I think one of my biggest strengths is getting a horse to relax early on in a race, no matter where he is positioned. The horses can feel at ease under me. There are certain riders who are known as speed riders, and you can see their horses are cranked up when they get to the gate and at the break. I think I get along well with horses that are little more uptight, and I can get them to relax during the race and show what their true abilities are.

➤ **Trainers are always looking for a weight advantage. Do you believe a few pounds make a difference to a thousand-pound horse?**
— Saddle Brook, New Jersey

No; not a few pounds.

➤ **What is the most important characteristic of an elite racehorse? What do the good ones have in common?** — Reston, Virginia

Heart. They want to win.

TALKIN' HORSES

GARRETT GOMEZ

➤ **How did it feel to cross the finish line first in 2005 with Stevie Wonderboy at the Breeders' Cup [Juvenile]? Was it one of your best riding moments?** — Honolulu, Hawaii

[It was] like a feeling you can't describe. Yes, it was the best moment of my career. You only win your first Breeders' Cup once.

➤ **Can you comment on the effect [agent] Ron Anderson has had on your career?** — San Diego, California

Ron is the best in the business. I'm able to relax and do my job.

➤ **A lot of riders always say they ride the favorite the same as a longshot, but is there truly something different you might do on a longshot to try to help the horse win?** — Lake Forest, Illinois

Yes, [you] cut corners and [have to] be even more patient.

➤ **What does your diet and exercise regimen consist of?**

— Pikesville, Maryland

Airplane food, lots of work, golf, and lots of water.

➤ **If you were to win the Kentucky Derby, is there a special trainer you would want to win it with?** — Arcadia, California

No, I just want to win it.

➤ **Do you believe the trend towards synthetic surfaces is an advantage to a strong finisher such as yourself?** — Del Mar, California

You need to finish strong no matter what [the] surface [is].

➤ **While you have achieved fame as a rider and look better on a horse than your dad, who could get more run out of a horse?**

— Raton, New Mexico

My dad was a great rider. And, a great teacher, and I hope that it shows.

➤ **Do you believe you can win every race if you can run the right race?**

— Green Bay, Wisconsin

Even the perfect ride won't always get me the win.

➤ **Do you remember when you were first trying to make a name for yourself? Was that harder than reestablishing yourself as a "go to" rider for major stakes races as you have done in the last three years?**
— French Camp, California

It's all hard work. It's an everyday grind. I'm just thankful to be in the position that I'm in now.

➤ **All great jockeys seem to have a clock in their head telling them precisely where they want to be at every given second, respective to their horse's running style. How hard is it to develop this internal clock?** — Gaithersburg, Maryland

I work on it every day. It has a lot to do with "feel" also.

➤ **[Can you] describe the difference between riding a pacesetter/presser versus riding a closer? How do you know that it's "go time" on a closer?** — Tustin, California

There are many scenarios that tell me when to push the button. Fractions of the race, the way the horse is traveling, and traffic.

➤ **Is it easier to ride a front-running horse or one who likes to lay back in the field?** — Louisville, Kentucky

They are both the same. However you can get along with the horse, you ride them that way. It doesn't matter if it is a front-runner or a closer. It is all according to the trip you get. There is not too much difference, really.

➤ **I remember seeing your dad, Louie, ride at the Downs at Santa Fe. I remember your mom pushing you along in a stroller. How are your mom and dad doing?** — Poway, California

My mom and dad are doing very well. They live here in California with me, and it is great to have their support. They come to the track, and they watch me everywhere I go. They got the opportunity to go to Saratoga with me. If it weren't for them, I wouldn't be doing any of this.

TALKIN' HORSES

WITH

CHRIS McCARRON

In a riding career that spanned twenty-eight years, Hall of Fame jockey Chris McCarron won two Eclipse Awards, rode the winners of six Triple Crown classics and nine Breeders' Cup World Championship races, and numbered among his achievements being the first jockey to pass the $200 million mark in earnings. Among the top horses he rode were Alysheba, Sunday Silence, John Henry, Paseana, Precisionist, Lady's Secret, Flawlessly, Glorious Song, Turkoman, Bayakoa, Northern Spur, Storm Cat, and Tiznow. After retiring with more than 7,000 winners and just over $260 million in purses won, McCarron served as general manager of Santa Anita Park and vice president of industry relations for Magna Entertainment Corp. McCarron has relocated to Central Kentucky and has established the North American Racing Academy, a school for jockeys and riders.

➤ **I've always admired you ever since that incredible Derby in 1987 when Alysheba stumbled and picked himself up. What do you think happened in the Belmont [fourth-place finish]?** — Springfield, Missouri

Alysheba was a tremendously gifted athlete. His agility saved us from falling in the Derby, and with sixteen horses behind us, what a wreck that would have been if we did go down. As far as the Belmont is concerned, I'm not really sure why Bet Twice was so much better on that day. I know it was not the distance or lack of Lasix. It could have been that Alysheba was finally tailing off a little considering he ran in the Blue Grass just after coming off throat surgery, then won the Derby just nine days later, then two weeks later ran in [the Preakness Stakes in] Baltimore. I do know this: My ride cost him second money. I used poor judgment when I decided to take him back off the pace, got into trouble, and left him with too much to overcome. However, I don't think it was fourteen lengths worth of trouble. Bet Twice was the better horse on that day.

➤ **I have always loved Lady's Secret. Please tell us what it was like to ride her. Was she very different from the colts?** — Richmond, Virginia

Lady's Secret was awesome! She brought a very tough attitude with her into every race.

➤ **During your career, you rode a lot of outstanding horses, but which was the greatest of them all?** — Hackensack, New Jersey

Alysheba. I don't think we saw how good he was. He liked to play around when he was in a race. He was becoming more mature during his four-year-old season and then went to stud. He would have been an unbelievable five-year-old.

➤ **Tiznow's back-to-back Breeders' Cup Classic wins are my greatest "in person" Cup moments. Also, I was at the 1987 Preakness Stakes when you and Alysheba powered past Bet Twice.** — Florence, South Carolina

Tiznow's victory over Giant's Causeway [2000 Breeders' Cup Classic] was deceptively handy. He had such tremendous stamina. His victory over Sahkee [2001 Classic] was much more hard-fought. The way he trained up to the Classic in 2001, I was not sure which Tiz was going to show up that day. Fortunately, the right one did. I could not believe how easily Alysheba handled Bet Twice in the [1987] Preakness. I did not need to ask him for his best until inside the eighth pole. I began my career in Maryland, so to go to my "second" home and win was a tremendous feeling.

➤ **Is there going to be an age limit for admission to the riding academy? I am thirty-eight years old and interested.** — Montreal, Quebec, Canada

We don't have an official age limit, but to be starting out as a jockey at thirty-eight, you may be a little "long-in-the-tooth" as they say. However, the North American Racing Academy [plans to] be offering courses for those individuals looking to pursue other careers in racing, such as training.

➤ **After having so much success in Maryland back in the 1970s, what influenced you to go to California rather than New York for the next stage of your career?** — Lutherville, Maryland

Simple. The weather!

TALKIN' HORSES

CHRIS McCARRON

➤ **I will never forget your ride on Tiznow to repeat his Breeders' Cup Classic victory. Where does that moment rank in your top riding memories?** — Karachi, Pakistan

It ranks with Alysheba's Derby and [with] Precisionist winning a grade I at a mile and a quarter and [then] later winning the Breeders' Cup Sprint.

➤ **Who would you rate as your toughest ride? Your kindest horse?**
— Portland, Oregon

Well, I'd say I got more nervous prior to riding Precisionist than any other horse because he was so fast and so aggressive that if I moved a muscle on him he would be gone. I always thought, "I just hope I don't get in his way." He was an incredibly kind and generous horse. But I'd have to say that the kindest would have been Flawlessly. She was simply a sweetheart. A child could have ridden her. I feel blessed to be the one who rode her most often.

➤ **You rode an unwanted horse to a Breeders' Cup win in Sunday Silence [1989 Breeders' Cup Classic]. What were your feelings going up against Easy Goer?** — Ione, Oregon

I am convinced that Sunday was a horse that could negotiate the turns more effectively than Easy Goer could. Two instances bear this out. In the Preakness, Pat Day got the jump on Pat Valenzuela going into the far turn and opened up about a length and a half. Then, coming out of the turn, Sunday was head and head again. In the Classic, going into the far turn we had about a half-length advantage on Easy Goer, but coming out of the turn, we were four lengths ahead of him. That was the victory right there. [But] Belmont, with its big sweeping turns, suited Easy Goer's big, long, beautiful stride. That was a terrific rivalry between two great horses.

➤ **Back in the 1940s, Hollywood Park had races for apprentice riders only. Do you have any plans to enter into arrangements with tracks in Kentucky for such races?** — Washington, Utah

That would be great. In Panama and Puerto Rico, they stage all-apprentice races as part of the students' graduating from the schools there. They conduct these races on Mother's Day, and it is quite festive. Hopefully, we can do something similar.

➤ **[My] eleven-year-old daughter is interested in working (eventually) as a jockey or exercise rider. What advice would you give a person to prepare for attending your academy later?** — Dry Ridge, Kentucky

Most important [is for her to] complete her high school education. Get as much experience working around horses as possible. Then, she should enroll in the North American Racing Academy. We have received application requests already from high school freshmen and sophomores. Wish her luck for me.

➤ **I have read so much about John Henry, and it seems he has so many sides to his personality. What would you say is the key to understanding his winning ways?** — Kenwood, California

Well, first of all, by the time I acquired the mount on John, he was push-button, very professional. He was always the most difficult around the barn. But on the track he was all business. Since he had, I think, seventeen different riders during his illustrious career, I don't think I know anything about him that at least some of the other riders did not learn. The most important thing I learned was that he was a "momentum builder." It took him a little while to get going, but once he did, it was all over. The late, great Charlie Whittingham spent the better part of five years trying to figure out a way to beat John. Then one day a reporter asked Charlie if he ever would, and Charlie responded by saying, "Beat him? I'm just trying to outlive him." Charlie was the greatest.

➤ **Will you be very involved in the actual training of the students at NARA?** — Roswell, Georgia

I will be very involved. I will be the head instructor as far as the riding is involved. I will be very involved with the communications courses, in which we will focus on how to deal with the public, media, trainers, and owners. I have three good friends that are on our board—Laffit Pincay Jr., Eddie Delahoussaye, and Steve Cauthen—and they are very interested in what we're doing; otherwise, they would not be on the board. I will extend invitations to all three so they can come in to lecture. In addition, I will be asking local trainers to come over and share their views of what they expect of riders. I will be inviting breeders over because the jockeys need to understand how much is at stake and what it means to bloodlines when a horse hangs on by a nose for a third in a grade I race.

TALKIN' HORSES

CHRIS McCARRON

➤ **Do you get to visit John Henry very often? Does he treat people he's familiar with much better than relative strangers or is he the same tough customer to everybody?** — Memphis, Tennessee

He is the same tough customer to everybody, but I think he has a modicum of respect to those who are around him all the time, that they won't back down when he is aggressive or mean to them. It takes a courageous and experienced person to show the horse who's boss without getting hurt or hurting the horse. He is an incredibly intelligent being and recognizes those who take care of him more than strangers and, therefore, there is an automatic respect. [John Henry died at the Kentucky Horse Park in 2007 at age thirty-two.]

➤ **Given what happened to Barbaro in the Preakness and looking back to what happened in the Breeders' Cup to Go for Wand, what is it like for the winning jockey of the race knowing some horrible circumstance mars an otherwise wonderful moment?** — Atlanta, Georgia

You heart just sinks and goes out to the [other] riders and horses. It dampens the victory immensely. Unfortunately, it is part of any sporting event. There are human athletes getting hurt all the time, but it becomes more difficult to handle when it happens to an animal. One that stands out in my mind was in 1983, when I won the Jockey Club Gold Cup on Lemhi Gold. Timely Writer was on the lead on the far turn when he broke down and took some other horses with him. I remember a distinct lack of celebration in the winner's circle because everyone was so concerned for the horses and riders.

➤ **A retired jockey I asked about raising the weight standards said that he never raced at a track where there was a shortage of jockeys. What's your opinion?** — Saddle Brook, New Jersey

I believe that Thoroughbreds could carry a little more weight without it being a burden and causing any problems.

➤ **Who has gained the most weight since retiring: you, Pat Day, Gary Stevens, or Jerry Bailey? Come on Chris, 'fess up.** — Alpharetta, Georgia

Well, I don't know how much weight the others have gained, but I have increased my waist by two holes in my belt. Actually, I've put on ten pounds. I weigh 122, disrobed.

➤ **Which of the horses you rode had the "quirkiest" personality that made them really stand out not just on the track but on a one-to-one basis around the shed row?** — Daytona Beach, Florida

John Henry was a very domineering horse. He was probably the most competitive and alpha male of all the horses I was around. Sunday Silence would also fit that profile. He used to have to go to the starting gate with a halter on and a shank under his lip. Alysheba was quirky in the sense he went through his whole three-year-old season almost like a kid. He would stop and go and stop and go, not the horse he was as a four-year-old.

➤ **What was Tiznow like to ride? I know he was known for his antics during workouts sometimes, but what was his personality like?**
— Philadelphia, Pennsylvania

Tiznow was the opposite of John Henry and Sunday Silence. He was incredibly kind around the barn and was difficult on the track because he had a strong mindset and wanted to do it his way. I had to coax him into doing things.

➤ **[Sometimes when] well-meaning but misinformed friends ask if I think it's cruel to "force" horses to run races, I tell them the story of your ride on Touch Gold in the Belmont, making sure Silver Charm didn't see him coming. [Which] horses you rode were particularly game or competitive?** — New York, New York

It's actually a very good question, especially the first part. I believe horses are much more intelligent than people give them credit for. Since they are bred to run, the majority of horses thrive on the competition. I could go on forever on which horses I rode who were really competitive because I rode so many good ones. When I think about the ones who were incredibly competitive, Precisionist jumps out at me. The most famous ones [also] come to mind, such as Flawlessly, Fappiano, and Alysheba.

TALKIN' HORSES
WITH
MIKE SMITH (WITH STEVE HASKIN)

Four days after Giacomo's stunning victory in the 2005 Kentucky Derby, winning jockey Mike Smith participated in a special online chat with Steve Haskin, the senior correspondent for The Blood-Horse *and an award-winning Turf writer renowned for his Kentucky Derby commentary. Sent off at 50-1 odds, Giacomo became the first Derby winner for Smith, a Hall of Fame member and a two-time Eclipse Award winner who rode Holy Bull, Giacomo's sire, to a twelfth-place finish in the 1994 Derby. Giacomo went on to finish second behind champion Afleet Alex in the Preakness Stakes and was a multiple grade II winner at age four before being retired to stud.*

➤ **Mike, how did you originally plan to ride the race, and did it unfold the way you expected it to?** — Union Bridge, Maryland

It happened almost the way I planned it, other than getting hung outside on the first turn. I'd planned on sitting back and making one big run. And I knew I'd have to go through a lot of traffic. But it all worked out.

➤ **Mike, what was the key to your ride and Giacomo's success on Saturday?** — Richmond, Virginia

Being patient and picking the spots I picked. I picked some great spots to weave in and out in the whole race. Every spot I picked worked out for us. I don't think I'd have won if we didn't get through every single time. It doesn't always work that way.

➤ **Mike, you said Giacomo was your Derby horse from the first time you got on him. What made you so sure so early on?** — Poplar Grove, Illinois

His balance. The way he carried himself. He felt like a good horse, and he looked a lot like his father. He reminded me of Holy Bull in a lot of ways, and I just fell in love with him.

➤ **Steve, how do you feel Bellamy Road and the other Derby favorites fit into the picture compared to Giacomo now? Do you still think they are better horses?** — Waldoboro, Maine

Yes, they are better horses, but the better horses don't always win the Derby. And the ones who are better don't show it until they win the Derby.

➤ **Steve, horses that don't have the typical "stayer" pedigrees through their sires that handicappers have sought in the past have had recent success in the Derby. Are we overrating the traditional "stayer" sire lines for potential Kentucky Derby winners? Or will the staying lines like Princequillo roll back around?** — Cedarville, Ohio

Stayers are a dying breed, and the Princequillo line is rapidly fading into the past. I can count on one hand the number of true staying influences in a horse's four-generation pedigree. And that's not where the Derby winners come from any longer.

➤ **Mike, how is riding Giacomo different from Holy Bull? Any differences in their personalities?** — Hollywood, Florida

Holy Bull was more aggressive all the way around. He was aggressive to be around and also aggressive when he ran. He was quicker than Giacomo. He was a very, very fast horse.

➤ **Steve, when will the graded stakes earnings for limiting the Derby field to twenty horses be updated? Why not make the rule "graded stakes earnings at a mile or more?"** — Reno, Nevada

Excellent point. I feel a point system based on grade I, II, and III races would work. But yours could work as well. It sure would eliminate a lot of non-Derby horses [from running in the Derby].

➤ **Steve, why are horses that are basically milers, based on their breeding, now winning the Derby regularly?** — New York, New York

The sire is having less and less of an impact on Derby-winning horses. Any

TALKIN' HORSES

MIKE SMITH (WITH STEVE HASKIN)

sire, and I mean any, can sire a Derby winner. But you also have to have a strong, classy female family, which these recent winners have had.

➤ **Steve, how in the world could you have missed [selecting] Giacomo?**
— Versailles, Kentucky

My job is to make a final analysis based on works, gallops, and observations. When a horse ships in three days before the race [like Giacomo] and has only two gallops, I can't justify picking him when I've been watching all the others closely for two weeks. But I can honestly say no one has ever asked me how I could have missed picking a horse that pays more than $100 to win the Derby. Normally, $100 horses are not what you'd consider "'obvious."

➤ **Mike, did knowing you were on a longshot make you ride your horse any different than you would when on a favorite?** — Kenosha, Wisconsin

No. I had my game plan and it didn't matter what his odds were. I felt like I was on the favorite. I wasn't saying [before the Derby] that he'd win, but I knew he would run big. I had confidence.

➤ **Steve, I can't wait to read your explanation as to how the "racing gods" allowed Giacomo to win the Derby** — Miami, Florida

My editor frowns on the "Derby gods" angle, so I've been trying to minimize its use as much as possible. But since you asked, the Derby gods do not smile down on the horses, but [on] the people. And I can certainly see Mike Smith as a worthy recipient of the Derby gods' generosity.

➤ **Steve, the time for the final quarter mile and final time of the Derby were atrocious, given the track conditions. Is this the American breeding program coming home to roost? Isn't this how milers run at one and a quarter miles?** — Chicago, Illinois

This is exactly how milers run one and a quarter miles, and we better get used to it. Stamina is a thing of the past, and the ones who do have stamina are simply too slow. Those horses were slowing down quite a bit in the end, and it's hard to believe only one horse was able to close and get it done.

TALKIN' HORSES
WITH
GARY STEVENS

You might say Gary Stevens simply went into the family business. The son of a successful trainer and his rodeo queen wife, the native of Caldwell, Idaho, groomed horses during his youth and at age fourteen was riding on the Quarter Horse circuit. Stevens, whose brother also is a jockey, won the first Thoroughbred race of his career at age sixteen at Idaho's Les Bois Park. Stevens led all jockeys in earnings in 1990 and 1998 and ranked among the top ten money winners sixteen times between 1985 and 2001. He was inducted into the Racing Hall of Fame in 1997 and received the Eclipse Award as North America's Outstanding Jockey in 1998.

Before his retirement in 2005 to become a racing analyst for television, Stevens had ridden eight Breeders' Cup winners and had eight victories in Triple Crown races. Included among the best horses ridden by Stevens were Kentucky Derby winners Winning Colors (1998), Thunder Gulch (1995), and Silver Charm (1997); Preakness winners Silver Charm (1997) and Point Given (2001); Belmont winners Thunder Gulch (1995), Victory Gallop (1998), and Point Given (2001); and Breeders' Cup winners War Chant (2000 Mile), Anees (1999 Juvenile), Escena (1998 Distaff), and Silverbulletday (1998 Juvenile Fillies).

Stevens hit an exacta in 2003 when he portrayed jockey George Woolf in the blockbuster Seabiscuit, *during the filming of which he met his future wife, production assistant Angie Athayde-Stevens. He is also the author of* The Perfect Ride, *a book recounting his experiences.*

➤ **What do you like most about what you're doing now? Do you miss riding?** — Cedar Rapids, Iowa

Commentating gives me the same adrenaline rush as riding so that helps me not miss riding. I miss being in the jocks' room, but I still get to see my friends and be involved in the sport I love. I like being able to eat and not having to

GARY STEVENS

maintain a low weight. The thing I like most is the live shows! You never know what is going to happen, and I get to be involved and tell everyone my opinions and observations of the race.

➤ **Since most trainers' and jockeys' racing careers are longer than those of horses, wouldn't it be a good idea for the industry to focus on its people instead of its horses when marketing the sport?**
— Bethesda, Maryland

We have all been saying this for a long time. The horses have a shorter career span, so I think it would be great for them to focus on the personalities in the sport and help build up the personalities to bring attention to the sport.

➤ **Who do you think is the best horse you ever rode?**
— Phillipsburg, New Jersey

The best horses are Point Given and Rock Hard Ten. I can't pick between the two, but my favorite horse is Silver Charm.

➤ **I am still smarting over Silver Charm's defeats in the [1997] Belmont and [1998] Breeders' Cup Classic. If he [had] won those two races instead of finishing a hard-trying second, he would be a legend.**
— Hudsonville, Michigan

Silver Charm was the real thing. He had heart, which is what made him my favorite. If he saw a horse coming, he would not let them pass. I always wonder if I had done something different, could he have won? I was depressed for about six months after the Belmont. But the Triple Crown will be very hard to accomplish ever again. He is a legend regardless of his [second-place finishes].

➤ **I have always wondered if the jockeys, during the race, can hear the announcer's call. Or does the crowd noise and track noise make it impossible to hear?** — Roswell, Georgia

It depends how focused you are. If you are very focused, you don't hear it. You know what the other riders are doing without hearing the call. If you are winning easy, you hear the call while coming down the stretch. Otherwise, you are focused on what is going on in the race and with your fellow jockeys and horses. On Derby Day, you really hear the crowd noise.

➤ **You've said Rock Hard Ten was the best horse you ever rode. How did it feel to sit on him and know that he was so push-button?**
— Union City, California

There was no better feeling. I never got to the bottom of [Rock Hard Ten or Point Given]. They were just freaks. To know all you had to do was ask, and they would accelerate was an awesome feeling. That, I miss.

➤ **How did you feel when you played George Woolf [in the movie** *Seabiscuit*]**? Was it just like racing horses? If a young rider came up to you asking for advice, what would you tell them?**
— Diamond Bar, California

Playing George Woolf was an awesome experience. It was like racing horses except I had a stunt double who rode! It was different because if we messed up, we could do another take, but when we race you have one shot to do it right. I would tell a rider to never give up and work hard. Hard work and dedication pay off. You can never rest on your laurels.

➤ **What impact did Rock Hard Ten's retirement [in November 2005] have on [your decision to retire]? Also, how good of a horse was he or could [he] have been had he not been retired?** — Grand Rapids, Michigan

I was considering retirement, and my wife and I had been discussing it. I didn't know if I was going to retire when I did or if I was going to wait and ride the Rock through the Dubai World Cup, as I thought he would be the favorite. When [trainer] Richard Mandella and [owner] Ernie Moody called me and told me he was [being retired], I decided to retire the following week. Horses like that come along once in a blue moon and after I had ridden him and Point Given, I thought it would be a while until I had another one like [them], if ever. I never got to the bottom of him, but it is very hard to keep a horse sound forever and luckily the Rock had great owners and trainers who cared about the horse.

➤ **Gary, how are your knees now that they have had a good rest?**
— Seattle, Washington

My knees are not good. If I have a good day, I think, "Oh, maybe I could still be riding," and then I try to go up stairs and I remember why I'm not riding.

TALKIN' HORSES

GARY STEVENS

➤ **Of all the outstanding horses you have ridden, which one would you consider to be the most difficult to figure out?** — Miami, Florida

There are so many that have strange quirks. Some are bad. Some are good. Some you get along with, and some you don't. I would [sometimes] tell a trainer, "I don't match this horse. He/she can really run but not with me on them." The most difficult [horse] to figure out would be Gentlemen.

➤ **Since retirement, what do you miss most about riding in races? Also, how is the Hollywood thing going?** — Weston, Connecticut

I miss hanging out in the jocks' room with my friends. I am lucky because I get to see them at the races. I miss hanging out in the jockeys' room, and I miss the competitiveness. I have some scripts I am looking at and would love to do more [movies], but I am loving the broadcasting.

➤ **During your long career as a jockey, you experienced a special bond with gray equines, or was it just coincidence?** — San Juan, Puerto Rico

Thank you! I won three Derbys and two of those were on grays. I always had a bond with fillies for some reason. I had a lot of great gray horses, so maybe I did have a special bond. You may be on to something here.

➤ **If you were "Czar of Racing," what would you do to hook the kids of today on this great sport?** — Louisville, Kentucky

To hook kids and fans today, I would not charge to enter a racetrack. I would not charge for parking. Get the fans in the gate. Our industry hasn't been marketed right, and we really need to market the personalities.

➤ **What do you think the future holds for racing in California?**
— Lexington, Kentucky

The synthetic surface will help for sure. There are other issues, such as year-round racing, not having a national jurisdiction that makes laws/rules consistent throughout, and incentive programs (or lack thereof) and workman's comp [regulations] that make jockeys/trainers/owners leave California. We have a chance to save it, but a lot has to be done. Track surfaces need to be fixed, racing days limited, and incentives and purses upped while workers' comp comes down or is paid by other ways.

➤ **Do you believe that horse racing would be a healthier sport (healthier for business, healthier for jockeys, and healthier for the horses) if year-round racing was eliminated?** — Del Mar, California

If racing were not year-round, it would be better for everyone. The horses are worn out and, therefore, have more injuries and breakdowns. The jockeys are mentally exhausted and need a break. I would always take a break after the Breeders' Cup World Championships because, mentally, you can't go year-round. The owners and trainers could have a semibreak over the holidays and tracks could fix the surfaces, and so forth. The fans would like it, too. When you limit the racing, they want to be there during the season, but how it is now, they know they can go year-round. There is a reason Saratoga, Keeneland, and Del Mar are so successful.

➤ **What do you think is the biggest mistake owners make with two-year-olds?** — Matawan, New Jersey

The biggest mistake is rushing them to be developed for the Triple Crown. Develop them slowly, and let them tell you when they are ready instead of letting the racing schedule tell you when they are ready. I'm not saying the next Secretariat should skip the Triple Crown, I'm just saying don't force your horse to be ready if [it's] not.

➤ **Thanks for all the great rides and memories. Of your Triple Crown wins, which is the most memorable, and why?** — Islandia, New York

They are all memorable. My first Derby win on Winning Colors because it started it all, or Victory Gallop when I ruined the Triple Crown for Real Quiet. My good friend owned Real Quiet and my good friend Kent Desormeaux was on him. It was the closest spoil in Triple Crown history. It was as perfect to a perfect ride as I've ever had. But they were all special—including [riding] Thunder Gulch for Michael Tabor, after I had just lost a good friend, and [riding] Silver Charm for the Lewises.

➤ **What's been the most fun since retiring: broadcasting, getting to eat anything you want, or growing your hair?** — Burbank, California

All of it. The hair just happened after I stopped wearing the helmet every day. Eating has been great, as has golf. And the broadcasting is truly wonderful.

TALKIN' HORSES

GARY STEVENS

➤ **[Will] Barbaro's injury and the immense public support influence safety standards for the animal athletes?** — St. Louis, Missouri

I loved Barbaro before the race, but it is horse racing and anything is possible. I don't think he was injured before, and I spoke with [jockey] Edgar [Prado] and that is what he thought as well. I think safety standards for horses are pretty good. We are on the right track by putting in synthetic surfaces. There should be national jurisdiction that dictates medications and such. I think his injury brought attention to the sport. It has brought a huge donation to the center that cared for him. So, unfortunately, it has helped our sport, but you hate to see it at the cost of a great athlete's health. If he could have won the Triple Crown, I think we all would have preferred attention that way!

➤ **When you rode Winning Colors and Serena's Song, did you use a different strategy when they were running against colts than in their races against other fillies and mares?** — Nicholasville, Kentucky

Fillies are like women; you have to have them think it is their idea. You can't fight or nudge them as much to do something. For some reason, I was able to do this with the fillies; now the women, that's another story! If anyone could tell me how to do that, I would love to know.

➤ **In the 1998 Belmont, you got Victory Gallop up by the narrowest of noses to swipe the Triple Crown from Real Quiet. Was that a moment of joy or were you disappointed for the sport and Bob Baffert as you two came close the year before with Silver Charm?** — Davie, Florida

It was both. I felt what Desormeaux must have been feeling when I lost the year before. I think a Triple Crown would be great for our sport, but I got paid to win races and that day I accomplished that goal.

➤ **Which "near miss" horse most deserved the Triple Crown?**
— Salt Lake City, Utah

Silver Charm.

Owners/Breeders

COT CAMPBELL
ALICE CHANDLER
PENNY CHENERY
TERRY FINLEY
BARRY IRWIN
MAGGI MOSS
JOSH PONS
J. PAUL REDDAM

TALKIN' HORSES
WITH
COT CAMPBELL

*Dogwood Stable president Cot Campbell is known as the "father of Thoroughbred racing partnerships" and as one of the most successful practitioners of ownership through partnership. South Carolina-based Dogwood Stable has formed and managed partnerships since 1969 that have campaigned a stable of runners that includes champion Storm Song, Preakness Stakes winner and Kentucky Derby runner-up Summer Squall, and steeplechase champion Inlander. Campbell is the recipient of many honors, including the John W. Galbreath Award and the Clay Puett Award. Campbell was feted as the 2004 Honor Guest of the Thoroughbred Club of America and served as chairman of the Sales Integrity Task Force that produced the Thoroughbred Owners and Breeders Association's Code of Ethics for Thoroughbred Auctions. He is the author of two books published by Eclipse Press (*Lightning in a Jar *and *Rascals and Racehorses).* Dogwood also sponsors the Dominion Award that is presented annually to deserving backstretch workers and unsung heroes of racing.*

➤ **I know it's hard for an owner to pick a favorite horse, but could you tell me who your favorite horse is and why?** — Cedar Rapids, Iowa

I have had a wonderful life thanks, in part, to racehorses. I have to like the horses that contributed so much to Dogwood's success. They are first, Mrs. Cornwallis, who really put me in the horse business when, through her great victories, she publicized the concept of group ownership, which was unheard of in 1971. Next was Dominion, who struck a mighty blow for Dogwood in 1978 when he came charging down the stretch at Saratoga and won the Bernard Baruch. He indicated that Dogwood was "here to stay." Obviously, Summer Squall—the best horse we ever had—was a major factor in my life. He was a big-time horse for three years and then went on to a distinguished stallion career, with us buying many of his babies, including the champion Storm Song.

➤ **My fiancée and I share a love for horses and the racetrack. We are talking about joining a syndicate. What would you recommend as a way to get our feet wet?** — Bellefountaine, Ohio

Buy what you can afford, of course, and don't spend money that you're going to have to be frantic about. Do your homework, get some references from the syndicate manager, and feel good about the chemistry between you and that manager and you and the horse or horses. Don't go too cheap—better to forget the whole thing. But again, don't be desperately dependent on success. It is hard to come by.

➤ **What do you think is a reasonable price markup of a partnership horse?** — Teaneck, New Jersey

We try to buy a horse at public auction that has fallen between the cracks. We seek a bargain, and we hope [that] when marked up and presented to our prospects, we can justify the cost of the horse based on the average yearling price for that sire's progeny. In other words, does the conformation of the horse and the pedigree make the price tag inflated after being marked up? Based on that, there may have been a 20 percent markup or there may have been a 60 or 70 percent mark up. Hypothetically, a $500,000 yearling (a higher price than we ever pay) would be presented [to investors] for $575,000 or $600,000.

➤ **Many of your horses are trained by Todd Pletcher. To what do you attribute Mr. Pletcher's unprecedented success?** — New York, New York

Todd Pletcher is first a gifted horseman. Second, he trained with the best. Third, he has remarkable organization abilities, and fourth, and certainly not least, he has the most remarkable memory I have ever seen in a human being. This he would need to handle all of the details, and I have yet to see it falter.

➤ **What was the inspiration for your green silks with the yellow polka dots? They are among the most recognizable in the sport.**
— Fargo, North Dakota

Our colors of green and yellow have no great scientific basis. Since we are Dogwood Stable, the color green was perhaps indicated as a major theme of our colors, and we liked the way that yellow went with it. They have been around for a while now, and they are recognizable.

TALKIN' HORSES

COT CAMPBELL

➤ **I would love to participate in a syndicate but cannot afford the price. Will you ever consider having an occasional offering with more than the four shares to spread the cost somewhat?** — Alpharetta, Georgia

I used to do partnerships with as many as forty shares, but it was like belonging to the public library. Too many people. There needs to be a feeling of closeness with the horse, and we need to be able to provide the proper amenities. With four shares we can [do that]. Occasionally we sell half-shares in more than one horse, and this can on occasion leave a half-share "dangling." That is about as good as we can do.

➤ **At the 2006 University of Kentucky Equine Law Symposium, a great deal of time was spent discussing integrity in the public and private sale of horses. One prominent local attorney posed the following hypothetical: Suppose a [buyer] makes a deal with a seller; let's assume he guarantees the seller $300,000 for hip #123, but if there is anything over $300,000 the overage will be split 50/50 between the two, regardless of the eventual purchaser. What is your take on this scenario? Is it a legitimate business practice?** — Lexington, Kentucky

I think your hypothesis and the legitimacy of it depends entirely on whether the buyer is indeed going to be the buyer, or is he buying it for someone else. If the latter exists, then it is an illegitimate business practice and would seem to be fraudulent. If he is going to be the end user of the horse, if he gets it, then I don't see anything wrong with it. However, it is highly desirable for all commerce at horse sales to be entirely transparent and the perception that would go with his guaranteeing $300,000 and splitting the overage is undesirable. Tricky question.

➤ **What is the significance of going four generations back when looking at pedigree? Are there certain characteristics being carried when going back four steps?** — Los Angeles, California

I don't pay much attention to the fourth generation in a pedigree. The truth is, if you look back far enough you can always find a name that would justify high expectations in a racehorse. I do feel strongly about pedigree. When the going gets tough in the middle of the stretch, I want a horse to be able to reach back and call on his mama and daddy.

➤ **I took a picture of Summer Squall running in the 1989 Aiken trials [and] I knew he was special. Your special memories, please, of this determined runner.** — Florence, South Carolina

Summer Squall was special. He acted like a good horse from the moment I bought him as a yearling. He understood racing, and he liked to mix it up. The worst thing a horse could do in a race with Summer Squall was to bump him. It made him mad as hell, and if he wasn't going to beat you to begin with, he would after he was bumped. I see him often in Kentucky where he is pensioned. He always comes running over to get a peppermint, and I get a big kick out of it.

➤ **I have noticed that the general public who are not horse racing fans don't consider jockeys to be great athletes. Of course, the horse is the primary factor, but what is your opinion of jockeys as athletes?**
— Roswell, Georgia

Jockeys are incredibly marvelous athletes. In addition to riding huge animals in heavy traffic in the afternoons, they have to appear at dawn each day to work horses, and then spend the afternoon chatting up owners in the paddock and responding to tired old jokes. Then throw in the fact that most of them have to starve themselves to make the weight. Notwithstanding all of that, the physical exertion of riding a horse in a race is incredibly demanding. I salute jockeys.

➤ **I recommend your books to anyone involved in or remotely interested in Thoroughbred ownership. Given recent headlines and publicized experiences about auction dual agency and other auction-related controversies (such as conformational corrective surgery), as well as the issues around medication controversies, would you take a harder stand on these issues today than you did in your book?**
— Albany, New York

I agree with Dr. Larry Bramlage [that] any corrective surgery that is designed to permanently improve the conformation of a horse is good. I suppose I would take a harder stand on steroids. However, this is a tricky subject because steroids are most beneficial in some cases. Still, there is an international furor about the use of steroids in humans, and from a perception standpoint, racing would be better without it.

TALKIN' HORSES

COT CAMPBELL

➤ **I was wondering what was your most memorable moment in your career with racehorses?** — Mt. Pleasant, South Carolina

My most memorable moment was—strangely—winning the Bernard Baruch with a horse called Dominion. It happened in 1978, and it came at a time when Dogwood needed it, and that win with that grand, game racehorse seemed to establish us firmly in the upper echelon of racing. I'll always be grateful to Dominion.

➤ **Aiken and South Carolina have a rich and storied history as a place for training Thoroughbreds. What are the attributes that set Aiken apart from other areas as a training center?** — Aiken, South Carolina

There is no magic about Aiken as a training center. The climate is ideal, with a change of seasons, but no severe winter weather. Our racetrack is a fine one, and horses flourish on it. I think the atmosphere and personality of Aiken make good people want to come and live here. Therefore, there follows a concentration of high-class talent in the area and that makes it flourish. The training center has always been underpromoted, and I think that will change.

➤ **Who has been the best horse you have been associated with, both in terms of success on the track and/or in terms of overall enjoyment?**
— Louisville, Kentucky

The best horse we've ever had would have to be Summer Squall. He raced for three years, won a classic, and I think should have been two-year-old champion in 1989. He was undefeated that year. He made about $1,800,000 and was syndicated for a value of $8 million.

➤ **How do you think that we can shift [the current mentality of] "race to breed" back to an "earn your way" [mentality in the breeding shed]?**
— Toronto, Ontario, Canada

I don't think there is much likelihood that the breeders will back off their current approach, which is to breed for speed. Sadly, there are not enough horses on the racetrack that are owner-bred. Breeders [do not necessarily try to] produce a racehorse, but one that will look pretty in the sales ring. Breeding is a tough business. It has its own set of headaches, and I'm glad I'm not in that endeavor.

➤ **Could you name some three- to four-year-olds from the past you think would have beaten [2006 champion three-year-old] Bernardini?**
— Belmont, New York

I think Bernardini is wonderful, but I think Kelso—on his day—could beat any horse that ever drew breath. I think there will never be another one like him.

➤ **I notice at the sales you buy early and often and then you're done. Is this by design in your buying strategies?** — Cranston, Rhode Island

I do buy early at horse sales. I think the first thirty hips that sell at a sale sell before the rhythm of the sale has been established, and I think buyers are tentative about jumping in early. I am not, and if I like a horse, I'll move aggressively to buy him early.

➤ **Having entered and won Breeders' Cup races, please tell me if you think a horse from Europe who has never run on dirt before can win the BC Classic.** — Sunset, Florida

I think it's very difficult for a European horse to come across the Atlantic Ocean and run on our dirt tracks in environments that are unfamiliar to them. Giant's Causeway almost got the job done, [finishing second] in the [2000] Classic. But, he was one of the most gifted racehorses I ever saw. Swain came close, had he not gone to the outside rail. I'm glad they keep trying. It's good for racing.

➤ **I'm encouraged to see that [synthetic] surfaces help the racehorse to get around the track with less risk of injury, but I bemoan the fact that we are breeding more unsound horses. With the breeding emphasis leaning toward speed, do you think we will return to breeding for stamina to help keep the breed sound?** — Lexington, Kentucky

I feel that as long as there is big money available at the auctions for yearlings that are bred to be precocious, there will be little incentive to breed for stamina. I used to buy a lot of horses in England, France, and Argentina, where the bloodlines offer more stamina. However, too many American horsemen began doing the same thing and the prices soared out of reach. It is sad that the breed is becoming ridiculously unsound.

TALKIN' HORSES

COT CAMPBELL

➤ **Do you think the sale companies are doing all they can to police their auctions for fraud or illegal kickbacks? [Do you have] any suggestions for them?** — Houston, Texas

I think the sales companies are doing what they have to do to police the auctions for fraud and illegal kickbacks, and no more. Some of them have clearly dragged their feet. They don't want to be policemen, and I don't blame them. At the same time, they would be happy not to have any larcenous activities [associated with] their auctions (behind the scenes, of course). They have a fine line to walk.

➤ **As someone who is in a smaller-scale partnership with some success, I would like to know what is the trick to success? How do you get the racing luck?** — East Brunswick, New Jersey

We buy horses in the $100,000 to $250,000 range. I like horses with strong families, good conformation, of course, and I am willing to accept a small fault. I have had great luck doing this. My feeling is that if you went into the paddock before the running of a major stakes race and examined every horse, 75 percent of them would have faults that would have been knocked by a veterinarian at a yearling sale. There are some faults, of course, that I cannot live with.

➤ **What is the significance of going four generations back when looking at pedigree? Are there certain characteristics being carried when going back four steps?** — Los Angeles, California

I don't pay much attention to the fourth generation in a pedigree. The truth is, if you look back far enough you can always find a name that would justify high expectations in a racehorse. I do feel strongly about pedigree. When the going gets tough in the middle of the stretch, I want a horse to be able to reach back and call on his mama and daddy.

TALKIN' HORSES

WITH

ALICE CHANDLER

Alice Chandler is the owner of Mill Ridge Farm, which she started in 1962. The farm comprises 1,050 acres in Fayette County, Kentucky. Mill Ridge is a major consignor to the Keeneland sales, races a few horses for itself, and boards horses for many successful breeders both in the United States and abroad.

Mrs. Chandler has been a racehorse owner for sixty years. She is the daughter of Keeneland founder and Kentucky horseman Hal Price Headley. Headley's influence as a breeder remains strong through the descendants of several broodmares, notably his champion Alcibiades, whose descendant Sir Ivor went on to win the 1968 Epsom Derby, only the third American-bred to do so in nearly two hundred runnings.

In addition to standing stallions at the farm, Mill Ridge has bred many stakes winners: Sir Ivor, Keeper Hill, Nicosia, Ciao, Hadif, Honor in War, Secret Hello, Flemensfirth, Golden Gear, Rash Statement, Pillow Talk, and Rose Park. Mill Ridge has raised on the farm the following top horses: Ramruma, Cetewayo, Kumari Continent, Bienamado, Point Given, Scorpion, Spain, Symboli Kris S, Giacomo, Tiago, Sweet Catomine, Artie Schiller, Dessert, Dr. Arbatach, and Johar. The dam of 2006 Kentucky Derby winner Barbaro, La Ville Rouge, also resides at the farm with her 2007 foal, a full brother to the Derby champ. Another full brother, Nicanor, was also raised at Mill Ridge.

➤ **Can you give us an update on Barbaro's full brother, who [is a yearling of] 2008?** — Clearwater, Florida

He is growing and has plenty of bone. He is quite a lengthy colt, a medium bay with a double cowlick in his forehead, and a large white snip on his left nostril.

TALKIN' HORSES

ALICE CHANDLER

➤ **Who are some of the other women currently in racing that you have respect for and think do a great job?** — Nashville, Tennessee

Helen Alexander, Kristin Mulhall, Charlsie Cantey, Dell Hancock, Janine Sahadi, Linda Rice, Christine Janks, Charlotte Weber, and the late Trudy McCaffery.

➤ **I've had the pleasure of touring your farm twice ... the employees are so courteous and friendly. Who is the coolest stallion to be around?**
— Cleveland, Ohio

My people are a great part of the farm. My dad threw me up on Man o' War when I was eight years old! Pretty cool, he was!

➤ **Would you discuss the issues and difficulties you encounter in finding and standing new stallions in Kentucky's highly competitive market?**
— Wynnewood, Pennsylvania

Finding a new stallion is as competitive as winning the Kentucky Derby. It mainly concerns timing and money.

➤ **What effect do you see artificial surfaces having on the breeding of racehorses?** — Ocala, Florida

They will take a lot of the emphasis off of the American speed sires.

➤ **What is your view on steeplechase races? Will they gain greater attention?** — Raleigh, North Carolina

I am not a big fan because of the obvious danger of falling. I do not know why they should gain greater attention.

➤ **Do you think that performing corrective surgery on a crooked weanling would be considered fraud when you went to sell him as yearling?** — Arcadia, California

No. At Mill Ridge we treat every horse the same [whether] it is destined for the sale or the racetrack. We have raised several superior runners that never went through a sale but did have corrective limb procedures. We make it a practice to provide any information on a corrective limb procedure to any prospective client who requests it.

➤ **What can you share about [stallion] Menow's personality and conformation?** — Pittsburgh, Pennsylvania

Menow, Pharamond II, and Tom Fool all had incredibly kind dispositions and kind, happy personalities. Menow died with his head in my lap … sad day.

➤ **The Thoroughbred racing industry seems to ignore a tremendous pool of future owners and breeders. As a [female] pioneer of the sport, how would you attract more women?** — Fort Washington, Maryland

Any segment of the Thoroughbred industry has its ups and downs and may not lend itself to every female.

➤ **I'm nineteen [and] a huge Thoroughbred horse racing fan. Could you suggest any sources of information on starting out in owning shares in racehorses?** — Canterbury, Connecticut

I would like to refer you to the Thoroughbred Owners and Breeders Association's New Owners Program, which can then recommend you to many successful racing partnerships.

➤ **Did you ever imagine the effect [the former top stallion] Diesis would have on the present day list of top-class runners worldwide as a broodmare sire? It is also very interesting to note the patronage by Sheik Hamdan [al Maktoum] to Diesis and the results those mares have obtained; did he know something way back then?**
— Lexington, Kentucky

It is interesting that you should say that. Sheikh Hamdan was the first one to buy a share and breed a mare to Diesis, and he supported him his entire career. I am sure that he was aware of Kris, his [successful] brother.

➤ **It seems to me that all many owners want is more money, so they take three-year-olds and send them to the breeding shed when they could race a lot longer. [Is this] one reason attendance [at tracks] is down?** — Syracuse, Indiana

When a horse is a serious racehorse and has proven him or herself, it is sometimes difficult for the owner to risk running it. Things do happen no matter how hard we try to keep racing safe.

93

TALKIN' HORSES

ALICE CHANDLER

➤ **I can see the images in my mind of your ascent to the helm of Mill Ridge, you father's advice not to sell Attica rattling in your brain. How did you decide to breed her to Sir Gaylord? How did you find out about Sir Ivor winning the Epsom?** — Portland, Oregon

I loved Sir Gaylord from the get-go—his pedigree, looks, and ability. It seemed the thing to do. My mother, my son, Mike Bell, and I went to Epsom. I looked up the stretch and Tattenham Corner looked miles away, and the finish was uphill! [Sir Ivor] had only run a mile before. We had a festive dinner and flew to Ireland the next day! I'll never forget it!

➤ **Is there a particular horse on the farm that stood out most to you in terms of personality?** — Portland, Oregon

[Kentucky Oaks winner] Keeper Hill would be one. She was fun to watch race and is a very people-oriented mare. Diesis was always a favorite. I watched him run as a two-year-old in England and asked Lord Howard de Walden early to let us stand him at Mill Ridge. He is buried behind the office and I miss him. [Stallion] Gone West loves treats over the fence and is fun to play with. [Stallion] Johar has traveled a lot but has settled in well. He is a nice horse.

➤ **I would love to own a racehorse and get involved with the racing industry. Can give me any suggestions?** — Elkton, Maryland

Before you invest your money in any horse venture, be absolutely certain that this money is disposable income.

➤ **What would be a good avenue for a young person to take if I would want to eventually be a consignor in the future? Work experience? Education?** — Lexington, Kentucky

Come to work for a farm that sells and works with the sales yearlings and hopefully, take them to the sales. Many farms in the Lexington area use young people who have only had a few months' experience.

➤ **During your career in the Thoroughbred industry, what has been horse racing's greatest innovation?** — Lemont, Illinois

Airplanes. The fact that we can move horses anywhere that we need to, to race or breed, has changed the game enormously.

➤ **Nicanor [recently] left to begin training; it will be awhile before he can be assessed as to racehorse potential. However, what was his personality like at Mill Ridge?** — Nashua, New Hampshire

He is a nice colt, a light bay with a star in his face. He was tough and competitive. He should end up being the size of Barbaro. He has more white in his face than Barbaro.

➤ **You've bred and raised more yearlings than anyone could count. From foaling to yearling sales time, what do you think is the most important part of raising those babies?** — Philadelphia, Pennsylvania

We try to leave all of our broodmares out[side] until foaling time comes. The weaned foals and the yearlings are put up for a few hours in the morning to be fed, and then turned back out again. I believe the closer to nature a horse can be, the better it grows. I like to see clean X-rays, straight legs, size, [and a] good head and eye.

➤ **As a major sale consignor, are you ever approached to sell a horse privately on [the] sale grounds before it enters the ring? If so, what are the ways you handle a situation like that?** — Paso Robles, California

Generally, we would say no, but if it was the owner's wish to sell the horse privately before going into the ring, the horse would 1) be withdrawn from the sale or 2) an announcement would be made by the auctioneer that ownership had changed since the printing of the catalog [in keeping] with the sales company's condition of sales.

➤ **What ranks the highest and the lowest [moments of the sport] in your eyes?** — Scottsburg, Indiana

Winning a big race (Sir Ivor's English Derby) and selling a big horse are big highs. Losing a horse through an accident, age, or on the racetrack is the toughest.

TALKIN' HORSES
WITH
PENNY CHENERY

Secretariat was the first Triple Crown winner of the television age and his stunning thirty-one-length victory in the 1973 Belmont Stakes remains one of the most incredible feats in all of sports history. His owner, Penny Chenery, considered by many the unofficial "First Lady of Racing," was honored in 2006 with the Eclipse Award of Merit for her lifelong contributions to racing. Ms. Chenery, who took over the reins of her ailing father's Meadow Racing stable during the development and campaign of Secretariat, has served as president of the Thoroughbred Owners and Breeders Association and the Grayson-Jockey Club Research Foundation for equine research. She has also been a key player in the effort to provide a dignified life for retired racehorses as a strong supporter of the Thoroughbred Retirement Foundation.

➤ **I'm curious to know who made the decision to breed Somethingroyal to the great Bold Ruler, which resulted in Secretariat?**
— Montreal, Quebec, Canada

In the early 1960s, one of my father's good friends in racing was Ogden Phipps, whose mother owned the great Bold Ruler. He was so popular that you couldn't buy a season. Bull Hancock, the owner of Claiborne Farm where Bold Ruler stood, conceived of the idea that a mare be bred in two consecutive years to Bold Ruler with the proviso that the owner of the mare and Mr. Phipps flip a coin to see who got first choice of the resulting foal. This was offered to select farms and only to their choice mares. There was no dollar stud fee. You had to give up one of your foals as the stud fee. My dad and Mr. Phipps had done this at least two times before I began managing Meadow Stable. I believe we had Bold Ruler's very first stakes winner, a filly called Syrian Sea, who was a full sister to Secretariat. So I was simply following my dad's established pattern in sending Somethingroyal to Bold Ruler. It was a no-brainer.

➤ **In today's racing climate, the vast majority of breeders are in the market to sell, which is why more and more Kentucky Derby winners are auction purchases not homebreds. Given this atmosphere, how remarkable was Meadow Stable's accomplishment of winning consecutive Kentucky Derbys with homebreds Riva Ridge and Secretariat?** — Los Angeles, California

Statistically I can't respond, but my father bred horses for thirty years and raced or rode the majority of them, so we had no tradition of selling the horses that Meadow Stable raised. I think we were just a product of the times. That's what people did in the 1960s and 1970s—breed to race. It is still more satisfying to me, and I hope some day I can come close to my father's achievement in breeding horses.

➤ **Riva Ridge "hooked me" on racing as a seventeen-year-old the spring of 1972. Your comments, please, on his place in racing and in your heart.** — Florence, South Carolina

Riva Ridge's success as a racehorse was crucial to the continuation of my father's Meadow Stable during my father's long illness. As a racehorse, I suspect he is just one more talented classic winner. He is still first in my heart because he came through when I was faced with pressure to sell all of the horses as my father was no longer able to see and enjoy them.

➤ **With Riva Ridge running at the same time as Secretariat, was it hard for you not to favor one over the other?** — Cedar Rapids, Iowa

Secretariat was so handsome and charismatic that he stole all of the attention from Riva Ridge. Sentimentally, I always favored the underdog, Riva, because his earnings and achievements enabled me to keep my father's racing stable in operation longer despite Dad's growing incapacity. I loved them both, but I had a special fondness for the timid Riva, who needed my affection more than the big star Secretariat.

➤ **When Secretariat died, how much of an interest in him did you still actually own?** — Lexington, Kentucky

None. He was entirely owned by the syndicate; I had sold my share. I owned no fractional share, but he owned my heart.

TALKIN' HORSES

PENNY CHENERY

➤ **Were you contacted when Secretariat became ill with laminitis?**

— Orange, California

Secretariat's last illness was quite swift. I was not kept in daily update since I was no longer a syndicate member. But Seth Hancock did call me on the Sunday and tell me that he was very concerned over the progress of the laminitis. I learned of Secretariat's death when a reporter called me early on Tuesday morning to ask for my reaction to his death. I was, of course, shocked and could hardly believe it. All I could do was go in to the office of the Thoroughbred Racing Communications and be on the phone with racing fans who mourned him. Author Bill Nack joined us, and we did an overnight television call-in show, live television. I couldn't be alone with this terrible news.

➤ **I believe some people advised you early in Secretariat's career to change trainer and jockey. What made you decide to stick with them and did you ever wonder if you made the right choice?**

— Surrey, British Columbia, Canada

Well, I don't recall anyone urging me to change trainers once Lucien [Laurin] had raced Secretariat. Initially, I had not wanted to use him as I had enjoyed training with a young man, his son Roger. Although he was not my first choice, after I watched Lucien for a month I would not have entertained any suggestion to replace him. The night of Secretariat's defeat in the Wood Memorial was a bleak affair. I did blame Ronnie [Turcotte] for having ridden what I considered a complacent race, expecting stablemate Angle Light to tire and come back to him. But instead Angle Light galloped home unchallenged and we were all in confused disappointment. Much later I learned of an abscess that bothered Secretariat during the race. Actually, that defeat took some of the pressure off our camp from the press because [Secretariat] was no longer invincible. It made his subsequent victories all the sweeter.

➤ **[Do] you think racing needs to radically change its product to succeed long-term?** — Lexington, Kentucky

I have long felt that racing needed to market its product, i.e. competitive racehorses, in a more dramatic way that people can connect to. It's not just about the stats and more about the stories of the horses and the owners and jockeys. It's the human-to-horse connection.

➤ **There is little doubt that Secretariat is the greatest racehorse in American history. Do you think his world record time of 2:24 flat in the Belmont Stakes will ever be broken?** — Webster, New York

Not unless they have wings ... There are two records that Secretariat achieved that I hope and expect will never be broken: his Belmont record and his Derby record. There are brilliant horses being bred today but few of them have the bone and soundness that Secretariat possessed. That, plus his unusually large heart, enabled him to run freely to establish his speed records. He was not hampered by physical shortcomings, which allowed him to run for the joy of it in the Belmont. He also won the Man o' War Stakes on turf as he pleased and established a grass record on the turf at Belmont that I think still stands.

➤ **Many people have speculated about the negative effects of increasing inbreeding, which they claim has led to the diminishing quality of Thoroughbreds. Do you think there is a significant difference between today's top Thoroughbreds and those of Secretariat's and Riva Ridge's generation?** — Palo Alto, California

I definitely feel that today's Thoroughbred is more fragile than those of thirty years ago. This is partly due to the market's needs for early performance, fast two-year-old workouts at sales, for instance. In reading history from seventy-five years ago, purists bemoaned the inbreeding they saw in pedigrees. With such a limited genetic pool we may some day breed ourselves into futility, but I hope not to see it.

➤ **When did you get the first hint that Secretariat was someone special? What do you have to say about his performance as a stallion?**
— Tiruppur, India

Secretariat emerged as someone special in his first stakes victory. He always broke slowly. Ronnie told me he needed time to get his big rear-end in gear. So he had an added challenge of making up that lost ground. I notice that he chose different points in a race to make his move. And I always felt it was his decision, not Ronnie's, as I don't think you can urge a horse to make those explosive moves. As a stallion, Secretariat could only pass his large heart to his daughters; it's on the X chromosome. And so their performance in the stud exceeded that of his colts. His daughters were terrific broodmares.

TALKIN' HORSES

PENNY CHENERY

➤ **I was just a little girl glued to the television set for every race Secretariat ran. It was always thrilling to watch him loop the field and romp home. Can you please tell me what your favorite moment was with Big Red?** — Kelowna, British Columbia, Canada

I think the outstanding memory I have of Secretariat as a racehorse was when he made a great leap in the first turn of the Preakness Stakes and circled the field. This was especially important to me as Riva Ridge had been beaten in the Preakness the year before and denied a Triple Crown. After seeing how Secretariat inhaled his field, I was confident going into the Belmont, but nothing could have foreshadowed the way he did that—*that* being winning the Belmont.

➤ **In my early twenties I journeyed to Claiborne to see Secretariat; [it was] one of the highlights of my life. His beauty and talent were obvious to anyone who saw him, but please tell us about his personality.**
— Lubbock, Texas

Secretariat was pretty much what you saw. He was a cheerful, mischievous horse as a youngster. During his days at Claiborne, he emerged as a classic showoff. He loved all of the attention he received from the fans. He knew he was the star and sometimes would be put out when other stallions would be led out to be viewed, tossing his head and saying, "Hey, what about me?" His ears went up at the click of a camera. If he heard a camera, he would stop and put his ears up. His grooms tell me that he was feisty in a playful way, but never mean. You had to be on your toes to groom him, but it was all a game. He truly loved [groom] Eddie Sweat.

TALKIN' HORSES
WITH
TERRY FINLEY

Terry Finley is the founder and president of West Point Thoroughbreds Inc., one of the oldest and most successful partnership companies in the industry. A graduate of the U.S. Military Academy at West Point, Finley is a former Army captain and Airborne Ranger who holds an MBA from Boston University. Since beginning in 1991 at Philadelphia Park with a $5,000 claimer named Sunbelt, West Point Thoroughbreds has raced grade I winners Dream Rush and Flashy Bull as well as graded stakes winners Awesome Gem, Ethan Man, High Finance, and Seattle Fitz. Since its inception, West Point Thoroughbreds has campaigned more than 400 horses and has introduced more than 2,000 individuals to Thoroughbred ownership. Specializing in the syndication of two-year-old racing prospects, West Point Thoroughbreds currently has approximately sixty horses in training. Finley is involved in all facets of the industry and serves on numerous industry boards.

➤ **Do you help select all your prospects or do you use agents ? What are some of the most important qualities you look for in a prospect?**
— Chicago, Illinois

Well, it's a team effort. Our primary bloodstock agent is Buzz Chace, but I attend all the sales and inspect all the horses myself, as well. We come up with our short list, and we decide on who to go after and who to eliminate. In the end, I make the final decision, so I am very involved in the selection process. I've been doing it for over fifteen years now, and I've gained a lot of institutional knowledge. One thing that is very important is that you have to keep your number of distractions down [while] at the sale and be as focused as possible. As for what I look for in a horse, I like to look at the whole package—their overall makeup, how they carry themselves, their attitude, and their overall demeanor. I

TALKIN' HORSES

TERRY FINLEY

want to buy a horse that moves well and looks like an athlete doing it. They have to vet well or we will skip them. We also pay attention to pedigree. We have a lot of partners who are savvy about a horse's breeding and the influences of their bloodlines. So we want to cater to their wants and needs, too.

➤ **Does West Point ever transition racing partnerships into breeding partnerships, [such as] when a filly/mare's career is over? Or do you just sell the horse?** — New York, New York

Well, most of the time we sell our fillies when their racing career is over because that financial model makes the most sense. When people get into a racing partnership, their main objective is to campaign racehorses and then get out. However, with the kind of high-quality fillies we currently have, we would not rule out any options.

➤ **I was told [West Point charges a fee] so much above the purchase price because of the service that a partner receives. What do you provide that the other syndicates do not?** — Kaufer, New York

We do provide the best customer service in the industry, but it's not the only factor that goes into our syndication prices. We include the horse's training and maintenance for their two-year-old year, mortality insurance, and maintaining the staff at West Point Thoroughbreds. West Point is the only partnership in the country that's fully compliant with SEC regulations and registration, and we believe these kinds of business practices set us apart. We realize that we are not for everyone, but our entire staff is experienced in both the racing industry as well as in corporate America. To me, it's like the difference between staying at a Holiday Inn Express and staying at a Ritz Carlton. Both places have a bed, a bathroom, pillows, and blankets, but they offer two very different versions of the same product. It's the same with the partnership industry—there are different companies that offer different business models. We understand that our model isn't right for some people, but it's worked out very well for others.

➤ **What is your biggest challenge in trying to relay [the thrill of racing] to the general public?** — Baton Rouge, Louisiana

This is a challenge the entire industry faces as we all try to attract new people to racing. And, to me, there is nothing more exciting than a good horse race. We try to incorporate the thrilling benefits of owning a racehorse in our marketing materials and communications with new prospects, but for the most part, they're already pretty much interested in the sport. After all, why would they talk to us unless they were open to owning a racehorse? Our toughest hurdle in selling horses is getting people to look past the finances alone. We all realize that the financial model is not great, so you have to convince people to look at the overall experience, the competition, and the excitement of the game.

➤ **After several years of "mediocre" results, to what do you attribute your breakthrough season?** — Lexington, Kentucky

We are certainly enjoying things this year. I might not call our past years' results mediocre, but I think we've been doing all right. We are very forthcoming with these statistics as we post all historical data on our Web site. You can see that our win percentage has always been good. Competing at the top level of racing (New York, Kentucky, Southern California, Florida, and so forth) certainly presents a lot of challenges, but I think we've held our own these past several years. I think our sustained success is attributable to the fact that we learn more each year about how to select our horses, where to place them, and to whom we can sell them. We just keep getting better.

➤ **What equity stake does West Point take in horses that it acquires (aside from equity in horses that don't syndicate 100 percent)? Does the corporation shoulder any of the risk, aside from the initial outlay of capital, or is that burden relieved in concert with the realization of profit drivers factored into the syndication price?** — Edison, New Jersey

Coefficient of risk is a big factor in our pricing model. We don't raise money before we make our purchases, and we incur a significant capital outlay each spring when we pay for roughly twenty-five new horses. We do not take a position in the horses ourselves if we can help it. It's our goal to sell each horse out completely. If we don't, we keep the unsold interest.

➤ **[Have] there been any discussions for West Point to eliminate the monthly management fee it charges?** — Scottsdale, Arizona

I get that question a lot, and while we have made changes to our business model over the years, we have maintained our management fee. It covers more than just the decision-making process for our horses. West Point Thoroughbreds has an incredible infrastructure that is set up to meet our clients' needs. I have assembled a team of professionals who do their jobs better than anyone I've seen, from our financial reporting to our compliance with the SEC to our communications. It is because of this approach to the management of the stable that our partners keep coming back. They appreciate the level of sophistication and professionalism of the company. Regarding the management of our horses, I am a macromanager, but the decision-making process with the trainers is very much a collaborative one. Neither party is the sole decision maker. This has worked very well for us over the years.

➤ **Terry, what steps do you take to ensure the horses' well-being after the track?** — Saratoga, New York

Our horses are very important to us, and it's our job to make sure they're cared for properly. When a horse isn't cutting it on the racetrack, we retire them and find them a good home on a farm or a facility. We'd much rather do this than run a horse at the bottom of the claiming ranks and risk them getting into the wrong hands. My trainers, partners, and I have a lot of connections and resources. We are also big supporters of organizations like the Thoroughbred Retirement Foundation. They do an amazing job along with many other organizations of helping to place retired horses. All that said, there's no doubt that retired racehorses will continue to be an issue in racing. We produce too many racehorses right now. If 40,000 horses are born each year, where are they all going? We try to do our part, and I would urge others to continue to work hard to make sure that we give back to these great animals.

➤ **In your experience, what's the greatest misconception people have about the Thoroughbred industry before investing?** — Cincinnati, Ohio

That's tough to say, but most people don't realize just how much goes into getting a horse to the races. They tend to think these animals are machines and can race every three weeks. Anyone who has owned a racehorse knows how much goes into holding these guys together. You're lucky to get to the starting gate, let alone win a race. Then to go on and win big races is quite a feat. Most fans only see the races, and they don't get the opportunity to fully appreciate all the hard work everyone puts in to get the horses ready to run.

➤ **For a [fairly] young person with a nonhorse background but with aspirations of one day being involved in managing a racing/breeding operation, what skills are most valuable?** — New York, New York

Well, my background was certainly varied. I worked on the backstretch at Philadelphia Park as a teenager then went into the military after attending West Point. I got a master's degree in business and did some sales work before starting West Point Thoroughbreds. You need to read everything you can about racing. Read some of the biographies of people you admire. Try to pick the brain of a person you look up to as a mentor and throw yourself into it headlong. There's no substitute for experience. It's been over fifteen years for me, and I am still learning. Always be willing to keep learning, because that's what will get you ahead.

➤ **How is your client retention rate?** — Paramus, New Jersey

Our client retention is good. We have about 350 partners currently. A few of them have been with me since the very beginning, but the company in 1991 was very different than it is now. We focused a lot on claiming partnerships then, and now we've gotten away from them. As a result, the demographics of our partners have changed over the past five to ten years. All partnerships will have turnover every year, and we're no different. We realize it's a tough game, but we do our best to keep clients as long as possible.

➤ **Could you walk us through the experience of winning your first grade I race [with Flashy Bull]?** — Irvine, California

The experience itself was unbelievable. As a person who respects the game of racing as much as anyone, I know how difficult it is to hit the wire first in a grade I race. After Flashy Bull crossed the wire, I was speechless. I'll admit that the emotion poured over me when I met him on the track to lead him into the winner's circle. Things especially started to sink in a couple weeks after the race. It's been great. You start to remember the other horses you had such high hopes for, the calls you got from trainers saying a horse got injured or isn't as good as you hoped, and it also made me think of the 1978 Kentucky Derby with Affirmed and Alydar. That was the first big race I went to, and to win a grade I at Churchill Downs with a horse that took us to our first Kentucky Derby really put a punctuation mark to the moment.

TALKIN' HORSES

TERRY FINLEY

➤ **What should be done to ensure transparency at auctions and do you feel some of the same measures should also be taken with regard to racing partnerships?** — Saratoga Springs, New York

Transparency is very important to me. Our clients are very much informed about everything that is going on with their horses, their finances, and the company. Regarding my advice with the auction market, it really comes down to the people you deal with. My suggestion is to ask a lot of direct questions, get references, and do your homework. As in any business transaction, let your gut be a big factor in your decision-making process. There's a reason why some companies have been around for years and have great reputations. And there's a reason why other companies change names, business practices, and fall apart quickly. Sure, there have been some stories reported about wrongdoing in this business, but I can assure you that the overwhelming majority of people that I encounter are good, honest, hardworking people. I hope that going forward this point will continue to be brought to the public's attention.

➤ **Was Dogwood Stable your inspiration to go with syndicating? What methods do you use, and how much do you usually spend on one horse [on average]?** — Mt. Pleasant, South Carolina

Dogwood is the pioneer of the partnership model. We all owe Cot Campbell a debt of gratitude for what he's done for racing. He's a distinguished man and an excellent ambassador for the racing community. He should definitely be inducted into the Hall of Fame for his consistent contributions to the sport of racing. We all probably took some inspiration from Cot, but our business model is slightly different. My background was very business-oriented, so when I first formed the company I decided to approach it the same way. West Point Thoroughbreds has a board of advisers and a very disciplined approach to how we do business. It's why I keep mentioning practices like our compliance with SEC regulations. We want everyone associated with us to know exactly what we are doing. That includes how we buy horses. We buy just about all our horses at public auction. Most are bought as two-year-olds, but others are bought as yearlings or weanlings. When you buy at public auctions, people know exactly what we pay—transparency is very important to us. Anyone can look at the auction results and see what we buy and how much we bought them for. That way, when we start selling the horses, you don't have to guess what we really paid for a horse. It's all there in black and white. This year, our two-year-olds ranged from $45,000 to $575,000. It's a huge spread, but the majority of the horses we purchase are in the $100,000 to $200,000 range.

➤ **Given that you are a syndicate, do you get a volume discount with certain trainers?** — Bridgeport, Connecticut

We do not receive or want volume discounts. We send our horses to top trainers who do everything they can to provide our horses with the best care possible and oftentimes the day rate doesn't even cover their costs. So, we don't want to cut any corners when it comes to the care of our horses. We've heard of volume discounts being provided [by trainers] to some owners, but that's just not our style.

➤ **Are there specific sire lines you look for at the two-year-old sales?** — Little Rock, Arkansas

Sales companies do such a good job in the selection process that they really take care of the initial filtering process. Naturally, there are some sire lines we have not had success with where it makes sense that we might shy away from them. Although 95 percent or more of horses won't win a stakes race, so you can't be too biased. Each horse is an individual, so we won't discount a horse solely because we haven't had success in the past with a sire or a particular consigner. One interesting thing we are now taking to account is the synthetic factor. It appears that pure sprint stallions are not having as much success with runners on synthetics. Take, for example, our [stakes-winning] filly Lear's Princess. Four or five years ago, we probably would have not bought a filly by Lear Fan. Commercially, her pedigree was not the sexiest thing out there, but we believed that she had the potential to excel not just on the dirt or turf but also the synthetic surfaces. We look for those types of opportunities at the sale.

➤ **How do I convince my wife that investing in racehorses is a good idea?** — Miami, Florida

We actually get this question a lot, and the partnership realm is a good place to start when your spouse is reluctant about racing. At WPT, we have a great community of men and women who enjoy sharing the ownership experience and the excitement with a group of friends. It's not like having a husband that goes out to the golf course with his buddies—this is something a husband and a wife can share together. Before you know it, your wife will be tracking the horses as closely as you are and (with luck) handicapping better too!

> **[Did any] of your partnerships decline a sizeable offer to turn a horse over to the breeding shed and instead continued his or her career on the track?** — Paris, Kentucky

It's good for the sport to keep good horses racing, but sometimes the financial reality makes that difficult. In a partnership, even a significant purchase price will not be a lifestyle-changing event for partners who own a small portion of a horse. As a result, we don't get the same interest from agents that sole owners might. There aren't that many sizeable offers out there. We hear more about the superstar deals because they are the exception, not the rule.

> **Knowing of your commitment to your own integrity, the well-being of the horse, and your investors, how do you manage the pressures of each without sacrificing one or more of them?**
> — Nottingham, New Hampshire

It's not as hard as you might think. Doing the right thing may not always be the popular decision or the easiest decision, but it never pays to sacrifice your integrity. I know that I have to wake up each morning and look at myself in the mirror. I try to do the right thing at every turn in managing the company, servicing our clients, and taking care of our horses. I'd like to think I'll be rewarded for that in the end.

> **How do you recruit new partners?** — Indianapolis, Indiana

The vast majority of our business comes from referrals, which I think is a testament to how we do business. Other than that, we work very hard in our marketing and communications. We advertise, direct market, attend events, and make cold calls. Our Web site [also] is a very effective tool. People search the Internet, and when they come to our site I think they realize that we're a top-class organization. Of course, when you win big races like we have, people also tend to notice you more.

TALKIN' HORSES
WITH

BARRY IRWIN

Former journalist Barry Irwin and partner Jeff Seigel formed Team Valor, which puts together racing partnerships, in 1992 after previously operating under the nom de plume Clover Racing Stable. Among the top horses raced by Team Valor/Team Clover solely or with other partners were Prized, My Memoirs, Captain Bodgit, Star of Cozzene, The Deputy, Golden Ballet, Cashier's Dream, Ipi Tombe, Irridescence, Becrux, and Sweet Stream. In 2006, Irwin was honored by the Race for Education with its inaugural Valedictorian Award for his efforts on behalf of the organization, which provides scholarships to children of those employed in the horse industry. He is also an outspoken advocate of enhancing the integrity and ethics of the racing industry. In a column published in The Blood-Horse *magazine in December [2006], Irwin wrote: "In America, not one state racing jurisdiction or racing association or owners or horsemen's group is fully dedicated to firmly establishing the integrity of racing. Only lip service, to a greater or lesser degree, is practiced, because ensuring the integrity of racing is costly and not considered a priority, even though without it, survival of the sport is fragile. The message has been intellectualized but not internalized. Our leaders must come to the realization that unless integrity is made the number one priority, the sport is doomed."*

➤ **[How many] horses [do] you attempt to purchase at auction each year, and what percentage [do] you get?** — Lexington, Kentucky

In the United States, we rarely are successful in getting what we want at public auction because the prices are so high. We buy just a few each year at home. Abroad, however, it is a different story. In South Africa, we get everything we want. We bought ten yearlings there last year. In other countries, such as Germany, we pretty much get what we want, too.

TALKIN' HORSES

BARRY IRWIN

➤ **Captain Bodgit was my favorite horse. How much return on investment did the partners get on that deal?** — Baltimore, Maryland

There are two types of returns on investment in my business. One is financial; the other is satisfaction. In financial terms, the partners had an investment of $500,000 in the horse. His net earnings after winning the Wood Memorial and the Florida Derby, as well as placing in the Kentucky Derby and Preakness Stakes, more than covered his original cost, and half of him was sold for stud duty for another $1.25 million. You can do the math. I will tell you, however, that I would wager that each and every partner in the horse would have considered the partnership a tremendous success even if they had never received a dime back in earnings. People by and large do not buy horses just for return on investment. There is a certain amount of excitement in winning a grade I race. You cannot quantify this in terms of dollars and cents. Shocking, huh?

➤ **Why do owners who are already multimillionaires syndicate their Triple Crown-winning horses to stud soon after the Belmont?**
— Winooski, Vermont

To many people, and I happen to be one of them, the point of racing is to prove which one is best so that he can go to stud and attempt to better the breed. Once they have proven who is best, there is no further point in racing a horse. It is more important to the breed to get them to stud. As for the first part of your question, I never met a wealthy owner that did not want to know what his horse was worth, and they all want to cash in to justify the millions they have already invested in this enterprise.

➤ **There are many partnership programs in the marketplace, but you seem to have taken the concept to the next level. How do you select your prospects?** — Mebane, North Carolina

There are basically three types of horses we buy, but they all have one thing in common, which is "blue sky," or room to improve enough to allow one to dream of racing glory. We buy unproven stock (yearlings, two-year-olds), horses that are lightly raced, and thoroughly proven stock. Most of what we buy falls into the middle category. We have bought more unproven stock lately because the cost of horses that have raced has skyrocketed in the past few years. And we buy the occasional totally proven horse. In order of importance, these are the criteria for us in selecting our stock: athleticism, temperament, conformation, and pedigree.

➤ **What is the secret to picking out a good racehorse?** — Arlington, Virginia

There is no secret. I have spent a lot of time studying movement of athletes, both human and equine. I think this is helpful in selecting horses.

➤ **What race would you like to win above all [others], and why?**
— Chicago, Illinois

I think the most difficult race in the world to win is the Prix de l'Arc de Triomphe. There are no gimmes in the Arc. It is a thorough test of a champion because the field is large and full of top-class animals. The intensity generated in the final 400 meters is intoxicating. There is no other race in the world like it.

➤ **What is your opinion of the current effort to eliminate the use of anabolic steroids in racing?** — Saratoga Springs, New York

The impact of steroids on horses has not been the subject of many studies, other than how it affects female racehorses when they are retired to the breeding shed. I cannot get very worked up about the administration of steroids when there are other more important battles to be waged and won, such as policing performance-enhancing drugs. I think the only reason to rein them in is to be on a level playing field with horses from abroad, who are not allowed to use them. The perception abroad of American horses is that they are pumped up on steroids and hopped to the gills. Anything we can do to change this perception is a good thing.

➤ **I see you occasionally buy horses in Europe and bring them back here and run them on the dirt whereas most [people] buy them and run them on turf. What criteria do you look for in them, besides the obvious [one] of breeding, that makes you believe they will be successful on dirt here?** — Quarryville, Pennsylvania

Horses that run well on the turf skip over the top of the grass. Horses that run well on dirt run through it. It takes a stronger horse to make a dirt runner. Conformation can be a key. Stride rhythm and length are important, as well. But the most important thing we look for is style. In Britain and Europe, class is more

BARRY IRWIN

important than style. In America, class is secondary to style. If the horse has the right style, it will do well in this country. Martial Law [Santa Anita Handicap] and The Deputy [Santa Anita Derby] were modest at best in England, but they both had the right type of style to make their mark in California, where the ability to lay close [to the pace] and accelerate at the right time is crucial.

➤ **You paved the way for horse owners to get into the game at a reduced cost by joining or forming a partnership. [What] key factors [must] a prospective horse owner consider when entering the game for the first time?** — Encino, California

Buying into a racehorse has got to be one of the most daunting endeavors anybody can ever undertake because it is fraught with uncertainty. I know how I feel when I venture out of my own area of expertise. The one thing I would caution anybody about is making sure they don't just jump in and make an impulse buy. Prospective owners should take their time before taking the leap. And it is a leap—a leap of faith. For anybody's first venture, I would suggest they enter into it with the idea of kissing the money goodbye and think of it as a learning experience. If something comes back, so much the better. But in this game, you have to pay one way or another to learn enough to survive.

➤ **You seem to be the only prominent owner brave enough to sound your voice on what is going on. Further, you are the only one who backs opinion up with viable, and attainable, pre- and postrace protocols that would effectively level the playing field. What will it take for racing to embrace your ideas?** — West Dundee, Illinois

Somebody in a position of power has got to get mad enough to get the FBI involved in racing because only this outfit has the tools and the motivation to attack the trainers and owners that use performance-enhancing drugs. I think fewer high-profile trainers seem to be cheating than four years ago.

➤ **Should there be a mandatory urine test for drugs (steroids, bronchial dilators, et cetera) at two-year-old sales?** — Alberta, Canada

I think the market is responding to the sales companies and the consignors by doing business only with reputable outfits. Buyers are tending to shun suspect consignors and rely on ones with good reputations.

➤ **Team Valor often buys horses that have established some serious form. What is your thinking on juveniles-in-training sales, with all their fast works, medication issues, and the like?** — Lexington, Kentucky

I have had a love/hate relationship with the two-year-old sales. On the one hand, they do come up with runners. On the other hand, buying at a sale is like walking through a minefield. I probably will not attend the two-year-old sales this year, choosing instead to buy yearlings.

➤ **How do you feel the emergence of synthetic racing surfaces will impact breeding in the U.S.?** — Acton, Massachusetts

This is the single most interesting question in the game today. Speed is anathema to racing on synthetic surfaces. All of the speedy bloodlines that have come to the fore are about to be washed down the drain. This is going to have an incredible impact not only on racing and bloodlines, but [also] on the two-year-old sales. Personally, I do not like watching racing on synthetics because the horses look like they are swimming and their action is not beautiful. On the other hand, however, horses come back sounder and, more important, they bounce back quicker. For those clever enough to figure out which bloodlines will dominate on the synthetic surfaces, there are going to be some fantastic rewards in the short run.

➤ **I'm a college freshman and have a deep passion for the Thoroughbred industry. I do not have any strong connections to people in the industry and I keep hearing that it's a hard business to break into unless you "know the right people" or are "from the right families." Can you give me any advice?** — Georgetown, Kentucky

Well, I don't happen to buy your story. When I came to Lexington in 1969, this town was pretty much as you described it. But not anymore. People that operate at the top of the horse business hire anybody that has a passion for the sport. I come from a completely nonhorse background. When I went to *The Blood-Horse*, I was not looking for a job. I was looking for a road map to the farms. I got to chatting with the advertising manager, who then brought me in to [see] editor Kent Hollingsworth. I told him that I was a writer and loved racing. He offered me a job on the spot. And it is even easier today. People respect young folks with passion. Try what I did. You may be surprised.

TALKIN' HORSES

BARRY IRWIN

➤ **You've enjoyed a lot of success purchasing horses overseas for racing in the U.S. What attributes do you look for when assessing tried horses in foreign racing jurisdictions?** — Lexington, Kentucky

Style first [and] turn of foot second. A horse that can lay handy and finish fast is what I look for.

➤ **Do people in the partnership retain any rights to a horse once its racing career is over?** — Pleasantville, New York

Participants in a partnership own 100 percent of the horse and any breeding rights, as long as they continue to own the animal in question. When a filly is sold, her breeding capabilities are passed on to the new owner. [It's the] same [thing] with a colt. Our partnerships are designed as racing, not breeding, enterprises. When a filly is retired, she is bred and sold. When a colt is sold, we have sometimes retained a small amount of breeding rights. In a few instances, we have sold half a stallion and retained a half. But by and large, we buy horses to race and sell them when they are finished running.

➤ **With so many integrity issues [in racing], where would you begin [with reforms]?** — Grove City, Ohio

Gambling makes racing. No gamblers, no sport. Gamblers won't bet unless they have a level playing field. This is where it all starts. Everything else flows from there.

➤ **Can you name a few things about handicapping that you've learned as an owner that you didn't know as a horseplayer?** — Buffalo, New York

I learned enough to give up serious betting. The most important lesson I have learned is that horses need a lot of time to recover from hard races. My best advice for horseplayers is to wait to make your biggest gambles on horses that, for one reason or another, were unable to show their best form in their last start. You cannot keep a good horse down.

➤ **You don't really see many female trainers—let alone in the limelight. What words of wisdom would you have for any female thinking of becoming a trainer or [who] is a trainer?** — Michigan

I do not distinguish between the sexes when it comes to horsemanship.

We have used female trainers in the United States, Europe, and South Africa. If there is a pitfall for a female trainer, it probably is with other women, not with men, so I would advise any female interested in training to be as professional as possible in their relationships with their male clients.

➤ **As an owner, what sort of punishments would you support if your trainers were found cheating? For example, if one horse is caught, [perhaps] the entire barn is suspended. Agree?** — Lexington, Kentucky

I do not agree with your punishment. I divide cheaters into two categories: a) ones who try to take an edge, and b) those that don't. When a trainer purposely gives a horse something that is prohibited, he deserves the full wrath of the law. When a trainer winds up with a positive [test result] that is a result of a contamination, I think that prudence is called for. We had one trainer who was suspended for administering a substance on race day and he was suspended. We agreed with that call. We have had another high-profile trainer recently who was suspended as a result of a contamination, and we wholeheartedly disagree with that ruling. I think that trainers who try to take an edge and are caught should be ruled out of the game.

➤ **What is the one quality you find integral to the success of any trainer?** — Herndon, Virginia

There are two things that I admire in a top trainer. First is the ability to win races. I know that sounds silly, but in this game, there is a sharp divide between winners and losers. Stark as night and day. I had a trainer named Gary Jones who took some time off, came back with a barn full of maiden $32,000 claimers and within weeks he was the leading trainer. He was just a winner. Secondly, I like trainers who tell me the truth about my horses and tell me the moment something bad happens to one of my horses. In this regard, Neil Drysdale is the best trainer I've had.

➤ **Should Lasix be banned?** — Ft. Lauderdale, Florida

Definitely [it should] be banned. It has been abused to an absurd degree. In human athletics, Salix is classified as a "masking agent" by the World Anti-Doping Association. Horses that bleed severely need to be rested, trained differently, or retired. If that means less racing, then so be it. This nation has led the way in breeding bleeders into its horses because it has relied on bleeder medication. Other countries try to rid their stock of this disease. And make no mistake about it, bleeding is a disease and it is hereditary.

➤ **The illegal practices certain trainers get away with is making it difficult for honest horsemen and their owners. When these "cheaters" are caught they simply hand over "the plan" to the assistant trainer. Why doesn't racing suspend the owners who support these trainers?**
— Keedysville, Maryland

Suspending owners who support trainers that cheat is a good idea. What racing really needs to do, if it ever decides to get serious, is to get the FBI involved in policing the game. Using their expertise and surveillance techniques, it would take about thirty days to put most of these owners and trainers where they belong, which is behind bars.

➤ **I have come across some partnerships at the low end of racing that require no expenses and are 65-35 or 40-60 splits. Do you think that arrangement will ever catch on at the high end of racing and would it attract more investors?** — Saddle Brook, New Jersey

We have tried every form of compensation, and the one we have now seems to work the best for our clients and us. When we were experimenting with different forms of compensation in 1997, our partners requested that there be no mark up, that we should only be compensated if the horse we sold our partners did well. The first and only horse we tried that with was Captain Bodgit. He became so successful that our compensation from 25 percent [on the] backend participation nearly equaled the cost of the animal himself. Our partners then asked that we mark up our horses up front and take a smaller kicker at the end if successful. We operate that way now.

TALKIN' HORSES
WITH
MAGGI MOSS

Maggi Moss was the leading owner in North America in 2006 by number of wins. Racing a stable comprised mainly of claiming horses—those at the lowest end of the racing ladder—Moss was leading owner at race meets at Churchill Downs, Fair Grounds, Aqueduct, Belmont, Presque Isle, and Prairie Meadows in 2007. An attorney in her native Des Moines, Iowa, Moss graduated from the University of Kentucky and is a lifelong horse enthusiast.

➤ **Congratulations on another great year. You are an inspiration to many. Do you have anyone who helps you keep track of all of your horses?** — Nashville, Tennessee

Thank you, it has been a lot of hard work and exceeded my dreams. I find myself working on the horses seven to eight hours a day, and it is now a full-time job; hence the continued leave of absence from [my] law practice. The passion I used to feel for the law has now transferred to the horses. I enjoy managing it myself and keep track of the horses by lists, by trainer, and/or track. The computer is a wonderful asset, and I review [the status of all my] horses every day and talk to trainers every day.

➤ **How did you get started in horse racing?** — Lexington, Kentucky

I immediately fell in love with horses at an early age; I started riding hunters and jumpers when I was ten and spent the next twenty years competing at horse shows. I started in Pony Club and learned the basics and went on to judge horse shows. I went to college at the University of Kentucky, and we spent a lot of time at Keeneland, but it seemed like a sport "out of reach" or beyond what I could ever imagine doing. I came back to Iowa to law school, and a girlfriend of mine owned part of a racehorse; I went with her to the track at Prairie Meadows and just fell in love with horses again. I approached a trainer by the name of Dick Clark in 1997 who seemed to have the best-looking and healthiest horses and asked him what it would take to own a racehorse. I claimed my first horse with him, Apak, who went on to set a track record, and I was hooked. I still own him, and my stable has expanded each year.

➤ **How do you manage owning racehorses and being an attorney?**
— New York, New York

For many years I concentrated only on my trial practice and worked long and hard hours. When I started getting more involved in the racehorses, I found myself [working in the law office] all day and [working with] the horses all night, and ended up slighting both professions. I simply got exhausted and took a leave of absence from the law in August 2006 and was supposed to return on January 1, 2007. It struck me that, for as long as I can remember, I never have stopped working, with very little life other than work. Therefore, I just recently became "of counsel," but I am not practicing law right now, [although I've] left the door open. I am just trying to have some quality of life, but [I'm] afraid I am not making much progress there; [I'm] only working harder with the horses.

➤ **What sort of barriers did you have to break through in such a male-dominated sport?** — Georgetown, Kentucky

I think the hardest part is gaining respect and being treated the same as men. From trainers to jockeys to owners, it seemed male dominated and at times, a sport of kings, not queens. I think it stems from a business that is extraordinarily expensive and like corporations or big businesses, that seems to be controlled and dominated by men.

The barriers are being able to stand up and be heard when I think something is wrong; to earn respect without spending what others might; and to break through barriers in a sport that, unfortunately, has been dominated by the very wealthy, who (usually) seem to be males. I have encountered difficulty at times in communicating with folks and in earning respect for what I do or how I do it. To simply be referred to as "a claiming operation" or not spending huge sums of money at sales should not be a measurement of success in this business, but it is.

Racing is and should be about success and winning the big races, but it needs to be proportionate to how and at what level you can gain success. A horse that can win a $10,000 claiming race is just as gallant and as exciting in this sport as [any horse]. It's perhaps easy to spend a great deal of money trying to buy the one big horse and winning that one big race, but perhaps much harder to do it by hard work and more meager means. The media controls many of our attitudes and thoughts in many ways. I would like it to be not just the "sport of kings" but a sport that is measured by hard work, integrity, and success. I think it has been dominated by wealthy and successful men, and I just don't see why it can't be equally as reachable by women.

➤ **With all your success in the racing side of our sport, do you ever see yourself joining the breeding aspect of our business?**
— Opelousas, Louisiana

I do find myself loving what I am doing, much like the law and trial work. I love studying patterns, trainers, tracks, numbers, replays, and the work that goes into it. Most of all, I just love horses and being around them. Ironically, one of my favorite places is the barn and not the track. I have one mare and a couple of babies and I have loved that. I think I would love all the intricacies of breeding but simply do not have the patience to do so. I have to run this operation on overhead versus profit/loss, and breeding does not fall into that business plan. Having had two [equine] babies, I just fall in love with them and racing becomes irrelevant; [I] never want to part with them, [which is] not a good plan for me unless I marry a billionaire next week!

➤ **Will you acquire your stock by way of the yearling sales more than claiming?** — Louisville, Kentucky

I have found the hardest thing is to really get much respect dealing with claiming horses. Perhaps that is where the glass ceiling is, or the inability to break into this game, unless you are a very wealthy person or have unlimited resources. I have made private purchases and bought yearlings and two-year-olds with little success. I simply can't justify the prices or the overhead of yearlings or breeding and still stay profitable. I have met many that have attempted to be successful in this business by sales, and their goals are to win the graded stakes or get to the big races.

TALKIN' HORSES

MAGGI MOSS

To run an operation that concentrates on the sales, especially yearling sales and the low percentages that even make it to the track, yet be able to win, is sometimes a staggering statistic. Add the overhead in raising, training, and vet costs, and I have to ask, is that type of financial loss worth winning the big races?

I just know I love the horses and seem to be better and more profitable in the claiming ranks. I am diversified in that I have bought two-year-olds and have yearlings and will continue to try to upgrade yearly. I guess the reality is I hope we are all in this for our love of the animal itself. It's a very tough business no matter what way we go. I am hopeful of doing it well and trying to earn respect in how I manage the horses, [whether that's] claiming or buying or sales.

➤ **What do you look for in a claiming horse or do your trainers pick them out for you?** — Des Moines, Iowa

There is so much that goes into this claiming game—it is fascinating and an excellent way for anyone who doesn't want to spend lots of money to enjoy racehorse ownership. It's quick and has great returns with less overhead. What motivates me in claiming horses is finding the ones that can go on to higher levels and become better [racehorses]. I enjoy the work that goes into it, and I enjoy the changes and successes in little things like stretching them out, or sprinting, or adding blinkers, or all the things you can do to make them happier and more successful. I pick out a lot of my own claims and do so by using the *Daily Racing Form* and Ragozin numbers, as well as patterns in tracks or trainers, replays, and many other factors. It's a lot of work, but I enjoy it.

➤ **Did your experience as a USEF hunter judge help you in selecting promising horses for racing?** — Ocala, Florida

I was very lucky to have a father who insisted that I join Pony Club and learn all about horses—shoeing, conformation, illnesses—before he'd let me compete or ride. He insisted that I know how to take care of a horse, not just ride them! The years of riding and judging taught me so much about conformation and horses; it has proven to be invaluable in picking horses and talking to trainers or vets. It is simply the most valuable asset I have. I have found going to sales still is like a continuing education, and there is just no end to how much one can still learn as I do every day.

➤ **When picking a trainer to care for your horses, do you go mainly by the trainers' winning percentages? Or do you look deeper into their operation than that?** — Farmington, New Mexico

It is much, much more than winning percentage. I have learned so much about picking trainers and have been on the really bad side of it and the best side of it. I think caring, trust, honesty, love for the horses and the care they get, and of course being good at what they do [are the best traits in a trainer]. I have been with trainers who have the best winning percentages and found that it can still be a disaster. I find it's more important to be with someone that I like, can trust, and understands me and can communicate with me and respect what I am trying to accomplish. I have heard that a great combination is a trainer "that is your good friend and can also be successful." And that is so true.

➤ **Do you have much power over choosing what is right for your horses, or is it always up to the trainer? Do you prefer taking the lead role in decision making, or do you prefer your trainer to do so?**
— Wilmington, North Carolina

It is a constant struggle and one of the hardest parts of what I have to deal with, quite frankly. I have many trainers, and the hardest part is dealing with the ones [with whom] I just do not have good communication. The best combination is an open communication about the horses and what is best for them individually, kind of like a good marriage. I have dealt with those trainers who really do not want to share all that I think is important in making the right decisions. It is a constant struggle and usually ends in a divorce. I have some trainers whom I simply adore, for each horse is discussed and I know when a horse should not run anymore and what is best for all of us. That is the way it should be.

➤ **Do you follow the careers of your horses after they've left your barn and do you have concerns about their lives after racing?**
— La Jolla, California

It is the hardest part of this business and the part that I question daily. The answer is "yes." They are all on my stable mail although, unfortunately, I have lost track of some and one in particular that I can't [locate]. When I broached the hardships of losing a horse, any horse, to a good friend and [said I] may be getting out, they replied that I'm "better in this business than out if I can just keep giving back." I quit giving to anything except animal causes a long time ago. I try very much to rescue the horses I can, and I actively support all retirement centers, including the one I co-chaired that opened in Iowa. I can't save all the animals, but I'd like to inasmuch as I'd like to save all the horses or [at least] not contribute to [their having] a bad life after racing. I just do as much as I can.

> **What are your views on the anti-slaughter movement?**
— Westfield, New Jersey

Three years ago I got a call at my office from a wonderful woman in Pennsylvania who had just rescued a horse that I had thought I had donated to a great farm. His name was U.S. Gold. When his racing days were over, I dealt with some individuals at Monmouth Park who told me about a wonderful riding academy in New York, with great pastures, where I could retire U.S. Gold; I made all the arrangements. A week later I got a call that he had been bought at a sale for $350 from the people who had bought him for slaughter. They saved him and that is the first I even knew about [the slaughter] sales or slaughterhouses. He was saved and is currently at the retirement center in Kentucky. I went on a rampage, literally, when I learned how it worked [the sales and the slaughter houses]. I contacted law enforcement about these folks and learned far more than I wanted to. Since then, I have worked hard against slaughterhouses by helping politically in every way I can.

> **What do you see as your greatest contribution to horse racing?**
— San Antonio, Texas

It hasn't been accomplished yet. On a small level I would like to show that you can be successful in this business as a woman without spending fortunes, and [that you] can do it with dignity and success, and that you can achieve goals in a sport thought of as only for the very wealthy. However, I think the greatest contribution I can give is my continued efforts toward life after racing for horses and better treatment of racehorses when their careers are over.

TALKIN' HORSES
WITH
JOSH PONS

Josh Pons is manager of his family's Country Life Farm near Baltimore, Maryland, and he and his wife, Ellen, a professional photographer, reside on the farm. They have two sons, Josh and August. Maryland's oldest Thoroughbred breeding farm, Country Life was founded in 1933 by Pons' grandfather Adolphe A. Pons. The family's racing operation, Merryland, is the state's oldest Thoroughbred training farm. In addition to operating the family farm, Pons worked for seven years as a writer for The Blood-Horse *magazine. He is the author of two books chronicling the daily diaries of a horse farm and racing stable:* Country Life Diary: Three Years in the Life of a Horse Farm *and* Merryland: Two Years in the Life of a Racing Stable. *Both books were published by Eclipse Press.*

➤ **Why would a breeder retire great horses in hope of producing another once-in-a-lifetime horse?** — Los Angeles, California

The most exciting racehorse in my lifetime was Secretariat. I was nineteen years old when he won the Triple Crown, and I remember watching Mrs. [Penny] Tweedy before the Belmont Stakes. She was eating Rolaids like they were mints. And he was retired after the end of his three-year-old season. So was Man o' War. It's not really a new thing in racing. There's that old saying, "If you keep leading them over there, eventually they'll get beat." Sometimes a horse has proven himself beyond doubt.

➤ **Do you believe overbreeding is a problem in the horse industry?**
— Yorba Linda, California

There are a lot of four-horse fields at tracks around the country. I'm not sure we're overbreeding racehorses as much as underbreeding racehorse owners.

TALKIN' HORSES

JOSH PONS

➤ **Do you believe in the nicking craze? Also, can you enlighten us small breeders on how you choose your matings?** — Cade, Louisiana

You like to see a pattern that has worked successfully. The best old-time breeders kept a split-page pedigree book and bred to what worked before. But they dug deeper than simply the sire line. They often returned the best blood of the sire back to him through the mare they selected. We like to match a mare to a stallion who suits her physically. When our stallion Citidancer was in his prime, we used to call him Jerry Rice, he was so fast-looking. We'd buy big old workhorse mares with plenty of bone and breed them to Citidancer, and he'd get about 9 percent stakes winners. You had to breed him to a mare with substance, regardless of the nick.

➤ **Will slots alone be the savior for Maryland racing?**

— Prescott Valley, Arizona

No [slots will not save Maryland racing]. Racing gets a failing grade in the hospitality business, but slots would help. Right now, these fine horse farms in Maryland are like family-style restaurants with no liquor license. Sure, our food is great, but all the cars are parked up the road at our competitors because they've got wine with their food.

➤ **Will slot machines actually help your racing partnerships, or is the current plan most beneficial to the breeders?** — Crooksville, Maryland

Most racehorses lose money. When purses are enhanced by slot machine revenue, you might get back what you've got in the horse.

➤ **If you could have three wishes granted for Maryland racing, what would they be?** — Baltimore, Maryland

A grandstand facility as nice as [the one at] Colonial Downs. A year-round educational effort on the importance of farms and racing jobs. A Maryland-bred fund that made it worthwhile to foal and breed in the state.

➤ **I know that Cigar was born at your farm. Can you tell us anything about what he was like as a baby?** — Mason, Ohio

I remember the day he cow-kicked my wife, Ellen, as she was leading him in with his dam, Solar Slew. Ellen was five months pregnant with our son Josh. She was just jumping in to help out at bringing-in time. He wasn't being bad. He just had an attitude. But that night, I told Ellen: "You're not leading any more mares and foals." I also remember the great foal photo Ellen took of Cigar standing beside Solar Slew. It was just another foal photo to include with the monthly statement to the owner, but it turned out to be a historic photo. It's kind of a lesson in trying to do things right in the horse breeding business. You never know when a champion is in your midst.

➤ **I loved *Country Life Diary* and now *Merryland*. [Do] you keep a diary every day or only when you are writing for publication?**
— O'Fallon, Illinois

I can't spell the word "cathartic" without stumbling. But I know what it means. Writing is cathartic to me, and I write something almost every day.

➤ **Why do horses race far less today than three or four decades ago?**
— La Grange, Kentucky

Year-round racing. Medications. Economics. When Merryland Farm was built in the 1930s and 1940s, horses came home for the winter. All those tendon tears and pulled muscles and pounded ankles had a chance to recover, regenerate. Now an $800 vet bill and a drop into claiming races is the quick fix, the exit strategy.

➤ **Is it unethical to buy young horses privately or at auction and then syndicate them for several multiples of the purchase price, or is this just part of the business?** — Darlington, Maryland

If the question is "what is a fair markup?" [then] add in the risk factor. If a promoter buys a horse and it bows a tendon or has colic surgery or cracks a cannon bone before it is placed in a partnership, that's a big loss. That's a big risk. We always retain a significant piece of every horse we put into a partnership, mostly fillies. The wholesale-to-retail factor is not that simple.

➤ **What are your favorite and least-favorite parts of operating a farm on a day-to-day basis?** — Lexington, Kentucky

My favorite part is like that aspect of horse racing that Munnings painted— the before and after; the mornings and evenings. In between are the headaches and the heartbreaks. I like walking the barns after all the help has gone home. I think they like it better too.

➤ **You have had great success with lightly raced stallion prospects. What [are] your criteria to choose a stallion? Has your thinking changed over the years?** — Brooklyn, New York

[I have] a gut feeling about brilliance unfulfilled. Amnesia about the failures is certainly helpful. My brother Michael and I have placed nineteen stallions into service since we took over Country Life in 1982. Only four could be qualified as successes: Carnivalay, Allen's Prospect, Citidancer, and Malibu Moon. The others just didn't have the run gene.

➤ **What is the best way to find out [our filly's] value as a broodmare, and who should we breed her with? Can you trust bloodstock agents?** — Dallas, Texas

The only true test of her value is the open market. A lot of mares have sentimental value, but the market is unforgivingly efficient. As to who to breed her to, you need to describe her physically. Find a stallion who has what she doesn't. I trust bloodstock agents all the time. Find a pro you like. You still make the final decisions.

➤ **Your family has been successful in every aspect of the industry from breeding to racing; what does it take to be successful in the horse business?** — Bayside, New York

Perseverance, mostly. Luck, certainly. The ability to take bad news without developing a persecution complex also helps.

➤ **What sire line would you most love to have at Country Life?** — Monrovia, California

In 1946, my grandfather bred Raise You, the dam of Raise a Native. In a business where the science of breeding is influenced so much by luck, sometimes sentiment carries the day. So I am partial to the Raise a Native line, through Mr. Prospector. Malibu Moon is out of a Mr. Prospector mare. Our fine stallion Allen's Prospect was by Mr. Prospector. You dance with them that brung you.

➤ **When did your grandfather give up working the farm?**
— Newark, Delaware

My grandfather bought Country Life Farm in 1933 at age forty-five. He had a stroke in 1939, which tells you something about running a farm. Then he [saw] all three sons all go off to World War II. I guess you could say he gave up working the farm on Christmas Day 1951. That's the day he died. None of my brothers or sisters or me was even born yet. He saved a way of life for a bunch of grandchildren he never knew. You didn't have to know him to know him, if you know this.

➤ **Should I breed my mare to the best stallion that I can afford or is there such a thing as breeding beyond the value of a mare?** — Paris, Kentucky

What's your goal? To race or sell? If you are breeding to race, then select a stallion you think will throw racehorses. If you don't want to be married to your broodmare, sometimes the only way out of the trap is to overbreed the mare and leap out on a limb.

➤ **What's more important in a stallion prospect—pedigree or race record?** — Cincinnati, Ohio

Pedigree. But you won't see an unraced stallion on the leading sire list—not since the 1950s, at least, when a determined breeder with a bunch of mares could start an unraced horse in the stud.

➤ **How early can you tell whether a stallion will be a success? Is it apparent when his babies are weanlings? Yearlings? Or do you need to wait until they begin training?** — Hillsdale, Michigan

You sure like to see nice-looking foals who take after their sire. I remember reading a quote from Bull Hancock about Buckpasser's foals. They sort of knew early on that he would be a spotty sire.

➤ **With the new racing surfaces being mandated in California and Kentucky, have any new trends in the types of sires begun to emerge?**
— Jersey City, New Jersey

You better have a sire who can go both ways. Suddenly a little grass action in the foals isn't the commercial drag it used to be for a sire.

TALKIN' HORSES
JOSH PONS

➤ **There are a number of partnership opportunities available. What do I need to consider to determine which one is right for me?** — Boise, Idaho

Go visit the promoter. Some racing partnerships can last longer than your kid is in college. You should know the college president.

➤ **For someone wanting to get started as a Thoroughbred owner, are partnerships the best way to start? What about claiming?**
— Lebanon, Ohio

Claiming is fine, but the sharpest minds in the training business are the poker-playing claiming trainers. I'd bet on them over a newcomer. A partnership spreads the risk. It doesn't eliminate it.

➤ **It seems like people are more critical of yearling conformation than stallion or stallion-prospect conformation. Shouldn't conformation be more important for stallions than for yearlings?**
— Georgetown, Kentucky

A stallion's success is measured on the leading sire list. Did you ever see crooked Mr. Prospector? Or tiny Northern Dancer? It's easy to be critical of a yearling's conformation unless you know what the sire looks like. Racing is not a horse show. It's a battle of wills. The best stallions impart that special fight into their runners, despite conformation.

➤ **Are your sons going to follow you into the family business?**
— Chicago, Illinois

I just hope they have a choice, that this business is vibrant enough for them to choose it if they want to.

➤ **Does it bother you as a breeder [that the medication issue and trainer suspensions] hurt the breeding industry?** — Atlanta, Georgia

I can't get beyond the steroid issue. A prominent Olympic sprinter [who was suspended] had yellow eyes from injecting his thighs with syringes of steroids routinely given to horses. If every Thoroughbred who came into the paddock on steroids had yellow eyes, maybe we'd have the push to outlaw such an obviously unfair and unhealthy practice. How many training accidents are caused by horses wild on steroids? A bunch.

➤ **I absolutely loved *Country Life Diary*; I'd love to know how the farm has changed since that book was published.** — Erie, Pennsylvania

Country Life hasn't changed very much since the first diary, which covered the years 1989 through 1991. Put new roofs on a bunch of the buildings. Re-fenced it entirely two years ago. That was a major undertaking. A locust post lasts about twenty-five years. I hope we're around to re-fence again. Thank you for your kind words about my book on this old farm.

➤ **Do you have a specific spot you like to go to think or write? Some location that inspires you, like a thinking tree or favorite chair?**
— Lexington, Kentucky

I have a limited retentive memory. I often talk to a digital recorder then sit down later and transcribe what I said. It triggers my memory. You can only write where it's quiet. It's a lonely art.

➤ **Do you think Maryland will go [to mandating] synthetic [track surfaces] and do you think it will help Maryland racing in the winter?**
— Scottsburg, Indiana

I don't think Maryland racing will go synthetic anytime soon. Magna just spent $30 million on its racing surfaces, and both the turf and dirt courses are Breeders' Cup-quality. If Pimlico went artificial, [the Preakness Stakes] would be the only classic [run] on it. I don't think it's the most important issue facing Maryland racing.

➤ **I am an aspiring writer and would love to combine that with my true love [horse racing]; any suggestions? If you could write any story about racing, what would you choose?** — Hudsonville, Michigan

Try keeping a diary. A story will emerge that is uniquely your own. Write what you know. If I could write any story about racing, I'd want to write about a homebred winning the Kentucky Derby. That's the Holy Grail in this eternally optimistic business.

➤ **What attributes are high on your list when looking at a stallion prospect that has limited race experience?** — Edgemont, Pennsylvania

Presence. A stallion that you are going to spend five years trying to prove has got to have presence. You can't describe it. But that presence gives you the enthusiasm to back him through the years of getting him going. It's a hard thing to describe, but you know it when you see it.

➤ **I bred and trained in the 1980s and early 1990s and am thinking about it again. Given the current state of the industry, would you advise a sixty-year-old to do it again?** — Bedford County, Virginia

Only if you are an obsessive-compulsive. The best trainers I know are hard-wired to remember and worry about every last detail.

➤ **How viable are Thoroughbred partnerships for people of modest incomes? I realize one should spend only what one could afford to lose, but what type of partnerships are the least risky?**
— St. Louis, Missouri

Partnerships? They are a great diversion for people looking for the adrenaline rush that comes with sports. There are lots of reasonable partnership opportunities around. No doubt the format will continue to be popular.

➤ **In order of importance, what are your criteria for selecting a broodmare with the goal of selling the foals at auction as yearlings?**
— Minneapolis, Minnesota

You better have ten broodmares with good conformation and hopefully some black type, because only three of their yearlings will ring the bell. The others will fall into repository hell, or die as foals, or run through the fence, or live long enough to grow into unmarketable conformation. Auctions will make a cynic of you quick.

➤ **I [understand] the financial need and benefits of slots, but how can the love of racing be reawakened?** — Florence, South Carolina

Big days bring big crowds. Look at our Maryland Million; 27,000 people packed into Laurel. To reawaken passion for horses requires some breakthrough afternoons. People are busy. You have to create events.

TALKIN' HORSES
WITH
J. PAUL REDDAM

Building a stable from a modest beginning, J. Paul Reddam has enjoyed the same success in horse racing he attained in the business world. Reddam was the founder of Ditech.com, a mortgage loan company that was among the pioneers of e-commerce and that he sold to General Motors in 1999. He is president of Cash Call, a California-based online consumer loan company and previously was a philosophy professor at Cal State-Los Angeles. He entered Thoroughbred racing with a 1988 claimer named Ocean Warrior and has built an operation that has horses distributed among trainers Craig Dollase, Doug O'Neill, Mark Hennig, Ben Cecil, and Jeremy Noseda. As a breeder, he owns a band of twenty broodmares maintained at Vessels Stallion Farm (California) and Kingswood (Kentucky) and a stable of Standardbreds based at Windsor Raceway and Sacramento's Cal-Expo. Among the top horses campaigned—in full and in part—in Reddam's name are grade I winners Ten Most Wanted, Wilko, Elloluv, Red Rocks, Great Hunter, Cash Included, and Swept Overboard.

➤ **Do you consider yourself a Canadian and do you have any horses here?** — Toronto, Ontario, Canada

Certainly. I am a Canadian citizen, so I think that counts as a Canadian. My parents and brothers and sisters all still live in Canada. Although I'm not sure the dreams and hopes of winning a Breeders' Cup race are a matter of patriotism, if I got lucky I would be sure to share that with my fellow Canadians. I just have a couple of harness horses racing at Windsor. I tried to get Craig Dollase to send a couple of horses to race in stakes at Woodbine, but something always happened before we could get there. Fearless Flyer won the 2004 Natalma Stakes, a grade III race at Woodbine, for me.

TALKIN' HORSES

J. Paul Reddam

➤ **Tell us some of the horses, with prices, you tried to buy and couldn't.**

— Lexington, Kentucky

I tried to buy Lost in the Fog for $2 million after his second start—no sale! I tried to buy a minority of Tapit before the [2004] Kentucky Derby at a $10 million valuation, but this didn't happen either. I thought he had stallion potential. In June I tried to buy Vacare for $500,000, but I didn't offer enough. The owners were right not to sell.

➤ **So many horses. So many trainers. How do you decide?**

— Paris, Kentucky

I have three terrific guys who act as bloodstock agents for me: Jamie McCalmont, Dennis O'Neill, and James Sternberg. Any horse that Dennis finds goes to his brother Doug. James works primarily with Craig Dollase. Jamie and I talk things over and then figure out where a horse should go.

➤ **Do you wager, and if so what is the biggest plunge you ever made? Did it pay off? If you don't want to answer this, I will understand.**

— Durham, North Carolina

The biggest bet I've ever made by far was $50,000 on Tapit in the 2004 Kentucky Derby. I tried to buy part of him and didn't get it done, so the bet was a hedge. When he ran up the track, I thought the $50,000 was probably the right end of the deal.

➤ **How much do you, as owner, affect the selection of future races?**

— New London, Connecticut

That really depends on which trainer it is. Doug O'Neill takes the most input. I have some horses with Mark Hennig, and he selects the races completely. Generally, I prefer to discuss the options and then come to a consensus.

➤ **How do you find enough time to devote to the horse racing business while you are running a large, successful corporation?**

— Fountain Valley, California

Most mornings I close my office door around 10 o'clock because that's when my trainers call. I will discuss things with them for forty-five minutes or so. In my spare time I try to read horse racing Web sites every day.

➤ **It seems that you have been very adept at identifying horses that would be successful in your program. How do you find them?**
— Dallas, Texas

The agents I work with have very different styles. Dennis O'Neill is wedded to the sheets. Jamie McCalmont pays attention to pedigree and who the current connections are. James Sternberg relies a lot on visual judgment. I like to bounce their respective recommendations off of one another before I make an offer.

➤ **Could you give an estimate of start-up money a person would need in the Thoroughbred racing game, say, at about the $15,000 level, particularly allowances?** — University Heights, Ohio

This game can be played at all financial levels. With $15k, I would partner with someone who has some successful experience to stretch your dollars further. It should be remembered that trainers are always overly optimistic, and they generally want another horse in the barn, so caution is important here.

➤ **Your horses seem to be running lights out lately. What made you decide to purchase Cash Included off her maiden win at Del Mar?**
— La Canada, California

Jamie McCalmont spotted Cash Included from her maiden win at Del Mar. He liked the way she fought from being down on the inside. James Sternberg actually represented me in the purchase as he was at Del Mar. I liked the fact that her pedigree said route but she won sprinting.

➤ **I am a big Corey Nakatani fan, and I know he rides first call on your horses. I have noticed that he has missed a lot of mounts over the past year.** — Las Vegas, Nevada

Corey has not ever taken off because of weight. Over the years he has had several injuries due to falls—racing or training—which take their toll. Riding at 119, he makes weight most of the time, and I don't mind if he is a couple of pounds overweight [if our horse gets assigned 116, as an example] because his skill is more important. I hope with the new artificial surfaces that the weight scale can go up so that our riders can maintain a healthy lifestyle.

TALKIN' HORSES

J. PAUL REDDAM

➤ **Do you rely on your own judgment when buying a horse at auction, or do you use advisers?** — Santa Cruz, California

I always have advisers. They give me their input, and I generally will make the ultimate decision. My guys are so important because I trust their judgment and experience regarding conformation, [an area] where I am a novice. I decide how much we should be willing to pay—we'll go back and forth together on price, and I try to handicap their level of conviction. It is an interesting dynamic, and I enjoy working with all of them.

➤ **Can you share any secrets to success that have enabled you to reach the upper echelons of both the horse racing and business worlds?**

— Lexington, Kentucky

Luck is my main secret. (It is probably my second secret, too, to be honest.) Beyond luck, what has worked for me is that, when I have trusted my own gut, things have worked out. I'll get expert opinions, but I am not afraid to disagree with them sometimes.

➤ **It seems that California racing is in a stretch of decline (too much racing, small fields, and so forth). Do you have any thoughts on how to stimulate fan interest and purses?** — Del Mar, California

Fan interest and purses go together since purses are based on handle and handle is based on people. I think we do a terrible job of marketing our product. Tracks and the business in general should bite the bullet and increase their marketing budgets several hundred percent. Even friends of mine are only vaguely aware that Santa Anita is running. Although spending so much on marketing would hurt the bottom line for the short run, it would eventually pay for itself and then some. Think about other products. Why do companies like Miller spend so much? Does anyone not know what a Miller is? They spend to keep their products in our collective consciousness.

➤ **How do you feel about online betting exchanges?**

— Yorba Linda, California

This is a product that is popular in England. I don't think it is legal in the U.S. at this time. It would be a great thing for American racing if the racetracks and the owners got the proper percentage of the takeout.

➤ **Many people I know are betting offshore to get rebates. Do the tracks understand they need to combat this and lower take-out or make rebates available to decent-size players. What are your thoughts?**
— Carlsbad, California

The tracks are afraid to be bold. The takeout splits that they agreed to years ago have the business model upside down. They sell their signal too cheaply and thus can't compete with things like offshore sites, yet they are afraid to cut them off because of the little bit of revenue they would lose. If they held ranks, they could fix this very quickly. Fans should be rewarded for making the effort to go to the races, not for sitting in front of a computer screen. A big crowd produces electricity, which is badly needed to keep everything rolling.

➤ **If horse racing is going to level the playing field, it needs to implement a national regimen where if a horse tests positive for a banned substance, the owner, trainer, and horse [would] be punished. As an owner, how would you react to such rules?** — Del Mar, California

The owner already gets punished since he or she loses the purse. I certainly think that the rules should be uniform as the system is lunacy now. However, horse racing is very political, and getting people on the same page is more difficult than you would imagine. Maybe your idea of punishing the poor horse would change some behaviors—but you would have owners filing suit because they didn't know what their trainer was doing, so why are they being punished, and so forth. Perhaps having people agree to certain conditions and punishments as the terms of entry would help.

➤ **What do you think [artificial tracks] will do to extend a horse's career on the track, thereby encouraging owners not to retire them to stud (for threat of injury) so early and giving the public more time to enjoy watching the really great ones develop?** — Marco Island, Florida

I think the new tracks are terrific. I was at Keeneland, and all of the jockeys were raving about how nice it was. Injuries are part of athletics, and so anything that can be done to cut down injury is a big positive. I am very disappointed that some venues have been slow to recognize this as the new surfaces will definitely extend racing careers. Although all of the breeders would howl, we might consider not allowing horses to breed until they are age five. People

J. PAUL REDDAM

would have no choice but to race the healthy ones in their four-year-old years. In turn, we could then market the true stars of our sport, the top horses.

➤ **Do you think there is a need for the Breeders' Cup to explore additional race options such as a filly and mare sprint, a turf sprint, or other possible races?** — Bossier City, Louisiana

There certainly is a gap for the three-year-old and older horses between the Sprint and the Classic. It's possible you could create another race in there—such as a mile and a sixteenth dirt race—but you have to be careful about overkill. I like the current eight-race format.

➤ **Do you ever have time to spend one-on-one with your horses? What is your favorite sport?** — Port Angeles, Washington

Horse racing is my favorite sport, followed by hockey. No, I don't get time to spend one-on-one [time] with the horses; I am not sure the trainers would trust me to be alone with a horse.

➤ **I wasn't familiar with your background; [it's] very inspiring. I hope to have a breeding and racing operation myself one day, but I'm worried, having gotten a BA in English, that I might've shot myself in the foot.** — Asheville, North Carolina

Thank you, you are very kind. Remember, I have a Ph. D. in philosophy, so the degree in English won't hurt you. It's important to use your imagination, which you have been trained to do. So go get 'em.

➤ **You've enjoyed a lot of success with Doug O'Neill recently. How did that union come about?** — Los Angeles, California

My friend and partner, Mark Schlesinger, had some claimers with Doug. Mark claimed Wacky American and later asked if I would like to be a partner. I said OK. Then Doug started calling me daily with the report on whether the horse was looking left or right out of the stall doors. Doug is a great guy, and I am honored to be associated with him.

Racing Officials & Others

ROGERS BEASLEY

MICHAEL BLOWEN

ED BOWEN

LARRY BRAMLAGE, DVM

TREVOR DENMAN

TOM DURKIN

ROBERT L. EVANS

TOM HAMMOND

STEVE HASKIN

SANDY HATFIELD

AVALYN HUNTER

DAN LIEBMAN

BARBARA LIVINGSTON

RANDY MOSS

BILL NACK

ALAN PORTER

DR. DEAN RICHARDSON

STEVE ROMAN

GEOFFREY RUSSELL

RIC WALDMAN

TALKIN' HORSES
WITH
ROGERS BEASLEY

Rogers Beasley was named director of racing at Keeneland in 2001 after serving nineteen years as the association's director of sales. Beasley, a New Orleans, Louisiana, native, graduated from Transylvania University in Lexington, Kentucky, and worked for several Central Kentucky banks before beginning a career in the Thoroughbred industry. As director of sales, Beasley was an instrumental force behind the introduction of preferred sessions to the September yearling sale, the creation of a repository to house X-rays and health information, institution of the wind arbitration process, and the inauguration of the April two-year-olds in training sale. Beasley's current job responsibilities include overseeing the condition book; developing new stakes races; finding new race sponsors; providing hospitality for owners and trainers; recruiting top jockeys, trainers, and horses for the race meetings; and maintaining the Keeneland training track. His online chat came prior to the first Keeneland race meet with the new Polytrack artificial racing surface.

➤ **While some very great horses have been able to handle both dirt and grass courses, it is commonly accepted that some are better bred for grass while others are better bred for dirt. Will we soon be adding a third category [of horses] that have breeding and conformation better suited to synthetic surfaces?** — Ventura, California

A great question and one that I do not believe we will have an answer for for another couple of years. There have been some statements that turf horses like this surface better than dirt horses—based on results from the September 2005 meet at Turfway—but I think that the horses in those races were better horses overall, so I reserve judgment until we have data from two or three meets under our belt. If turf horses do run better on the Polytrack, this could lead to a renewal of foreign champions being brought to stud in the U.S. When I became director of sales in 1982, some of the top sires were horses like Northern Dancer, Nijinsky II, Blushing Groom, Caro, and Lyphard. Would it be all bad to add a number of top European stallions to our rosters again?

➤ **Would you provide some suggestions of things that might be done to broaden the appeal of the game?** — Greenville, South Carolina

Racing as a whole does indeed need to do a better job of marketing itself, especially to younger fans. Keeneland is trying to do that via special promotions, such as our College Scholarship Day, where we give away ten $1,000 college scholarships throughout the race day via random drawings. It is the fastest-growing promotion we have during our meets. We need to improve parking, seating, and other amenities just as baseball has had to do to bring back fans.

➤ **Crowding has [become] a real problem at Keeneland on weekends. Is there any plan to open the infield to alleviate this?**
— Bloomington, Indiana

At this time there is no plan to open the infield. Over the past twelve years, Keeneland has spent millions of dollars on renovations to make our fans more comfortable when they attend the races. This included improving areas of the grandstand, doubling the number of bathrooms in the grandstand, improvements in the grandstand dining areas (as well as the patio behind the grandstand, by the finish line), enclosing the ground floor of the clubhouse, and myriad other additions. We realize that we need to do more and are working on the continuation of a master plan for the entire plant to accommodate our patrons. We believe that given more space for seating, wagering, and all the other amenities that our modern-day customers require, we could attract 40,000 on a Saturday.

➤ **What is the difference between other synthetic surfaces and Polytrack?** — Elmont, New York

The basic ingredients are very similar; however, we believe that some of the ingredients we use in Polytrack are far superior for handing ultraviolet rays or freezing weather, and that is a key element that puts us way ahead of the others at the end of the day. This is the only [artificial] surface to have been raced on in

Europe at all. Lingfield has [had Polytrack] for three years and Woverhampton for two, and so there is a proven durability there. At Newmarket this surface has been down for over ten years with exceptional results.

➤ **Keeneland has some of the best racing I've ever seen. To what do you attribute this: racing staff, money, or timing?** — Bowling Green, Kentucky

Howard Battle and Bill Greely really started this outstanding racing program at Keeneland, fueled by their knowledge of what horsemen wanted. There is no question that the timing is great, with everyone coming out of Florida, New Orleans, and California with an intense case of "Derby fever." My goal is to continue that education for all so that we will eventually have Keeneland grads across the country. The [purse] money is great, thanks to the total support of our board to ensure the highest quality of racing. As far as stakes go, we try to find niches that fit in well with other racetracks and develop those areas we think need to be addressed. My job is to keep everyone focused on the development of a good program for all.

➤ **Why are you running more claiming races every meet?**
— Florence, Kentucky

We have increased the number of claiming races in the fall to about 2.5 races per day. This was done for two reasons: 1) the number of quality horses in the fall was not there and 2) we feel that we need to take care of all our horsemen who race in Kentucky. We still believe that the quality of our card is second to none and will strive to maintain that excellence. Having said that, we have experienced a significant increase in our stall applications in the fall, and we believe that the field size in our maiden /allowance races will be on the rise. This still means that we have six maiden/allowance [races] every day and a stakes [race] almost every day.

➤ **Are additional race dates in the future for Keeneland?**
— Saddle Brook, New Jersey

We don't anticipate additional race dates for some very practical reasons. First, our fall meet falls between two of the largest horse sales in the world. That means we don't really have much flexibility in the fall. Second, our spring meet falls between the Turfway Park winter meet and Churchill Downs' spring meet.

In Kentucky, two Thoroughbred racetracks typically do not race at the same time. We own 50 percent of Turfway, and it is going great guns since installing Polytrack, so we have no interest in requesting some of their dates. We also doubt Churchill would be willing to give up the first Saturday in May! Lastly, we wouldn't want to change our short meets because we think the short, festival-type meets help make [racing at Keeneland] special.

➤ **Keeneland has had the reputation of being perhaps the most traditional racetrack in America. Do you find it ironic that Keeneland can now be viewed as a cutting-edge track? Is there one event or development responsible for this transformation?** — Austin, Texas

There are so many things about Keeneland that are rooted in tradition, but the single most important tradition we have is that the horse comes first. If you do what is best for the horse, all other things will take care of themselves. I have to laugh over that [traditional] reputation as we were the first to have a turf track in Kentucky, first in Kentucky with [an] aluminum rail, and first in the nation with the Visumatic timer. We also were the first to try a Pick 7 and the ten-cent superfecta and many years ago were the first in Kentucky to utilize that novel idea of betting and cashing at the same window, free parking, and so forth. We were the last to have an announcer, and we still require coats and ties for gentlemen in the clubhouse, a tradition I hope remains with us. To answer your original question, I believe that we have always tried to make the experience enjoyable and so err on the side of caution. I believe that, in my own experience starting with Mr. Ted Bassett and continuing with Bill Greely and now with Nick Nicholson, the goal has always been to take care of the horse and our customers in a first-class manner.

➤ **I have noticed [recent workout] times for the most part are very fast. I thought Polytrack times are slower. [To] what do you attribute the fast times? Do you think horses will stay fitter training over the traditional dirt or Polytrack?** — West Grove, Pennsylvania

The racetrack has some significant improvements over our training track, and we expect the times to be a little faster. I note that after our refurbishment of Turfway this summer, the times have improved and the last sprint stake was run in 8 and change. Having said that, the safety of the horse comes first,

ROGERS BEASLEY

and we will constantly monitor the times. As Mike Young, our maintenance chief, said, it will probably take a couple of meets for everything to settle and [for us to] have a good working knowledge of all weather conditions. In the beginning, we thought you would have to work horses harder as they appeared to move so easily over the Polytrack, but I am not sure that is true. We will find out more this fall as we have many trainers from across the country shipping in; we will get their thoughts while they are here. This surface will vary somewhat due to different weather patterns in their area and that could affect times. I do not think that horse racing will become too mundane with this surface.

➤ **When will the Breeders' Cup come to Keeneland?** — Whitewater, Wisconsin

For a long time, Keeneland has shied away from hosting the Breeders' Cup, as we think it is important to have it go to different venues across the nation in order to promote horse racing everywhere. Also, the capacity in our plant was not sufficient to do justice to the event. Having said that, never say never.

➤ **Will we ever see distance races [over 1¼ miles] again in the United States?** — Chicago, Illinois

While we do have a sufficient number of stakes races at those distances, the day-to-day filling of races for most racetracks dictates that you need at least eight horses for bettors to become interested. Hopefully, surfaces like Polytrack [will] keep horses sounder so that we can attempt an increase of those distance races.

➤ **How do you think that the current trend toward all synthetic surfaces will change the big races at Keeneland? Are you worried about [the Blue Grass Stakes] losing its importance as a prep for the Derby as long as that race is run on traditional dirt?** — Ann Arbor, Michigan

Remember one thing: By 2008 there will be three Derby preps—the Lane's End at Turfway, the Blue Grass, and the Santa Anita Derby—on synthetic surfaces. Also, please remember that since the refurbishment of Turfway, they just ran six furlongs in 1:08 and change and it was won by the mare that won the Princess Rooney Stakes [on dirt] this summer. I believe we will learn from each one and make them better.

➤ **Are you surprised at how fast owners and trainers have declared that Polytrack is the ideal racing surface, considering it has only been in use for one year in this country at an actual racing facility?**
— Lexington, Kentucky

Not at all; they understand that the safety of the horse is paramount to all of us. [Breakdowns] are one of the major reasons that people either get out of the game or never enter!

➤ **What are your thoughts on the progression of Internet wagering across the industry, particularly with respect to betting exchanges?**
— Austin, Texas

I believe that racetracks are going to have to take matters into their own hands and form their own ADWs [advance deposit wagering systems] in order to return a fair share to the owners and trainers who put on the show. We also need to get into the twenty-first century, technology-wise, to help our bettors and introduce new ones to our sport. Fixed odds are something we are looking into, and I believe hope is on the horizon.

➤ **Who is your favorite racehorse and what is your most memorable race?** — Washington, D.C.

Personal Ensign's Breeders' Cup [Distaff win in 1988]—never to be forgotten.

➤ **When you meet someone who is interested in investing significantly in the industry and has both the money and interest, what are your suggestions to finding the right people in terms of agents, farms, and trainers as advisers and consultants?** — Lexington, Kentucky

Contact the Thoroughbred Owners and Breeders Association. The important thing is to interview five or six people for every aspect of your plan. This is a tough business, and you need not only [to find people you can trust] but also enjoy the good times with, and commiserate the bad times with. [It's] the same group. This is not a business for the unemotional. Remember, there is no such thing as a dumb question. All of us learn every day in this game; that is what changed the sales: [the introduction of] new people and new ideas—some good, some not; but the thought process goes on.

TALKIN' HORSES
WITH
MICHAEL BLOWEN

Michael Blowen, founder and president of Old Friends, began working as a volunteer groom at Suffolk Downs during the 1990s and eventually raced a small stable of claiming-level horses before leaving his position as arts and entertainment reporter and film critic for The Boston Globe *to become operations director for the Thoroughbred Retirement Foundation. In that capacity Blowen gained an even greater appreciation for the plight of older, displaced Thoroughbreds, which led him to the idea of creating a permanent retirement home in the Bluegrass for horses. From its initial twenty-acre portion of Afton Farm, Old Friends has grown to a fifty-two-acre site known as Old Friends at Dream Chase Farm. Among the top retired horses who have resided there are Bonnie's Poker, Creator, Fortunate Prospect, Narrow Escape, Ogygian, Popcorn Deelites, Precisionist, Riva Way, Ruhlmann, Special Ring, Sunshine Forever, Swan's Way, and Taylor's Special.*

➤ **How realistic would it be to bring back Brian's Time and Forty Niner from Japan when their stud careers are done?** — Montreal, Quebec, Canada

We are very fortunate that Megumi Igarashi of Narvick International is keeping track of all our American champions in Japan. Since the devastating news about Ferdinand, we have worked with all the Thoroughbred breeding farms in Japan to transform a tragedy into something positive.

Virtually every farm [in Japan] is supportive of Old Friends. Brian's Time, a son of Roberto, as is Sunshine Forever, and Forty Niner, would be welcome at Old Friends when their breeding careers are over. Megumi Igarashi knows this, and I'm very confident that they will eventually join Old Friends when they're done breeding. The Japanese farms have been very cooperative with our efforts to bring the champions home, and we're confident that will continue.

➤ **Do you find it more difficult to care for stallions than for mares and geldings, and are there any precautions you need to take with the stallions?** — Haskin, New Jersey

When stallions are racing and breeding, they need to be controlled by their human caretakers. They are strong and willful. After they retire, they're the boss and they become easier to deal with. Ruhlmann is a case in point. He was an aggressive stallion when he was first retired to Old Friends by Ann and Jerry Moss. (He's the only retiree at Old Friends who is completely supported by his owners). But he's really settled down because he's the boss. We are just his servants. He is still not a pussycat and precautions must be taken, but he does understand that he's the boss and as long as we do his bidding, he's fine.

➤ **Do any of the former trainers or jockeys that have been connected with these horses support you in any way?** — Roswell, Georgia

Bill Mott, who trained Taylor's Special and Fraise, is very supportive. Jerry and Ann Moss have been very generous. Mr. and Mrs. John Amerman are extraordinarily generous, and we don't even have one of their horses. Chris McCarron was at the farm to visit Precisionist just a few hours after he arrived. Madeleine Pickens donated $65,000 to bring Fraise and Ogygian home. Michael Paulson donated Estrapade and money. Mr. and Mrs. John Veitch have been to visit Sunshine Forever, and Jack Preston sent a sizeable contribution to support his horse, Special Ring. Also, jockey Jean Cruguet has been great. There are some very kind people in horse racing who firmly believe that these great athletes have earned a dignified retirement.

➤ **What got you involved in such a noble cause? Do you currently watch racing? If so, who are some of your favorites?** — Cedar Rapids, Iowa

I'm not sure about the nobility part, but I got involved in horse retirement because I saw plenty of athletes that ran their hearts, lungs, and legs out for people that were [then] being discarded as soon as they went from the asset pile to the liability pile. I'm certain a psychotherapist would see plenty of parallels between their careers and mine. I am very, very lucky to be able to sit on the top of the hill at our new permanent facility and see great champions such as Precisionist, Ruhlmann, Creator, Sunshine Forever, Taylor's Special, Ogygian, Fortunate Prospect, Bull Inthe Heather, Special Ring, and all the others including Popcorn Deelites—one of the horses that played Seabiscuit—and my old $4,000 claimer, Invigorate. I get goose bumps every day just looking at them, and I never get tired of telling the stories of their lives. [Precisionist was euthanized September 27, 2006, due to the infirmities of old age.]

I not only watch racing, I try to get to the Keeneland simulcast every Sunday afternoon for the last few races from the East and the first few at Hollywood Park. My favorite runners are invariably sons and daughters or grandsons and granddaughters of our retirees. I root for the Thoroughbreds owned by the farms and the owners who support us. While my handicapping has suffered irreparable harm using this method, my enjoyment of racing has increased many times over.

➤ **If horsemen were serious about providing a dignified retirement for racehorses, [why not set up] a pension fund, perhaps a percentage of the betting income or the purses?** — Joppa, Maryland

It seems obvious. These great Thoroughbreds earned all the money. It only makes sense that they should have a 401K plan or social security system. But they don't. We're working on a plan that would dedicate a small percentage of their earnings to their retirement. I mean, they earned millions; they shouldn't be left penniless. It would also be good public relations if we could show that these horses earned their retirement. After all, without the athletes, where would the sport be? Let me know if you have specific ideas, and we'll work on them together.

➤ **What do you think about the bill in Congress aimed at stopping the slaughter of racehorses?** — Howard Beach, New York

It's horrible that the United States allows the slaughter of horses for exportation. But that's not the worst of it for racehorses. As my love of horses and horse racing evolved, I spent a lot of time at county fairs. This is the end of the road. If horses can't win here, they can't win anywhere. While spending time there, I saw killer trucks pull up and drag horses off to "riding academies" in distant states (there must be 500 riding academies in some of these areas to meet the demand). There should be a national law that no horse can leave a racetrack without a vet certificate stating that the horse is fit to travel. The trip is often more horrible than the destination.

➤ **What can be done to prevent such a crime [Ferdinand's slaughter] from happening again?** — Marco Island, Florida

The Japanese breeders were also devastated by Ferdinand's awful death. They are resolute in making sure it doesn't happen again. We've brought back four great Thoroughbreds from Japan: Sunshine Forever, Creator, Ogygian, and Fraise—with the cooperation and support of Japanese racing.

➤ **Do the expensive real estate prices in the Lexington area make it difficult to expand an operation like yours?** — Owensboro, Kentucky

We can only expand at the rate that we receive donations. One of our long-term goals is to keep Old Friends at Dream Chase Farm our permanent, boutique tourist farm and establish another location in Kentucky where the land is cheaper so we can retire some of the Thoroughbreds that deserve it but [who] wouldn't be tourist attractions. Got any space in Owensboro?

➤ **Who was the first horse you owned and who sold it to you? Also, what were the three golden rules you learned at "Figueroa University"?**
— East Boston, Massachusetts

[The writer of this question] is an old friend from Suffolk Downs, familiar with my mentor, trainer Carlos Figueroa. I'll try to keep the story short. One nasty, cold, icy February day at the Suffolk Downs simulcast, I bet $20 on a horse from Gulfstream Park at 8-1. I also keyed him in the trifecta with a plodder at 40-1. He won and the plodder finished third, with a 35-1 shot in the middle; I was sitting on about $5,000. They DQ'd my horse. I went for a long walk under the grandstand to settle down and ran into Carlos. In my deranged depression, I thought I could become a better handicapper if I learned more about the horses and suddenly blurted, "If I came to work for you, would you teach me about the horses?" I could tell by the sly look in Carlos' eye that I had been transformed into an all-day sucker. He told me to show up on Monday at 6 a.m. When I asked about pay, he withdrew in astonishment. "Paid? Paid? You are going to Figueroa University and you are on scholarship. But you need to pass the test."

"What test? I haven't even started yet."

"I will tell you the answer. What are the three things you need to know to survive on the backstretch? Lie, cheat, and steal."

At the time I thought he was joking. Years later, Ray Roy, treasurer of the

147

Thoroughbred Retirement Foundation, and I were at Rockingham Park convincing trainers to retire their old horses to the TRF. Ray was authorized to pay about $250 per horse. Carlos had a maiden Two Punch mare named Wedding Punch that was never going to win a race. She was doomed, but Carlos wouldn't give her up. I took him aside and offered to supplement the TRF offer with $500 cash of my own. He agreed. We put Wedding Punch on the trailer, and off she went. Ray handed Carlos the check and the veteran trainer asked me for the cash. I looked at him with a wide grin. "Lie, cheat, and steal."

➤ **I have aspirations of running a horse rescue. Do you have any advice?**
— Wilmington, Delaware

Start an Old Friends in the mid-Atlantic area focusing on retirees that made an impact on your area. People will come to visit; it's like [the movie] *Field of Dreams*—except it's nonfiction. I'll be glad to provide all the details and help you in any way I can. We want others to start Old Friends facilities all over.

➤ **Is it true that Creator was rescued from stallion fights? What is that exactly?** — New York, New York

When we first started Old Friends, we focused on bringing Sunshine Forever home from overseas and several of our early supporters heard about Creator and wrote saying they'd heard that an illegal cartel was setting him up for stallion fights (like cockfights). Since they only bid $3,000 for Creator, we knew he wasn't going anywhere good. We bid $5,000 and got him. That's the important thing.

➤ **Any news on when Alysheba [is] coming home?** — Orange Park, Florida

Alysheba is living like and with a king in Saudi Arabia. Dr. Jeff Pumphrey and Emmanuel de Seroux are working on our behalf to bring Alysheba back. Chris McCarron is very excited about bringing Alysheba home. The great son of Alydar is currently being bred to Arabian mares, but we have received indications that, when his breeding career is over, he will probably return to America. But the important thing is that he's being treated very well.

TALKIN' HORSES
WITH

ED BOWEN

Renowned racing historian Edward L. Bowen appeared as a "Talkin' Horses" guest shortly after the release of his book about the great Bold Ruler. The book was the final installment in the Thoroughbred Legends series. Included among the eighteen other books on horse racing written by Bowen were the Thoroughbred Legends profiles of Man o' War, War Admiral, and Nashua. Other books Bowen has written include Matriarchs: Great Mares of the 20th Century; Dynasties: Great Thoroughbred Stallions; *and* At the Wire: Horse Racing's Greatest Moments, *all published by Eclipse Press. Bowen, who lives in Versailles, Kentucky, near Lexington, also serves as president of the Grayson-Jockey Club Research Foundation, which funds equine research.*

➤ **One of the things people talk about today is how horses don't carry much weight. What is your view on this?** — Huntington, West Virginia

I think the trend away from asking horses to carry high weight is very regrettable. It eliminates one of the benchmarks by which we have traditionally evaluated American racehorses. Carrying weight, and conceding weight, is a challenge the great European horses seldom have been asked to meet, and now we are losing a unique way of testing our horses, too. At the same time, handicaps are beneficial to the business aspects of racing, especially when they create an intriguing betting proposition while also testing a horse. I admire the owners of Cigar and Skip Away, who were among the few recent horses tested with 130 pounds or more.

➤ **Bold Ruler was managed so well at stud. How good would he have been with books of 100 mares?** — Frankfort, Kentucky

His percentages of stakes winners would likely have been lower because by having many more mares the individual quality of mates would not have been sustained at such a high level. Nevertheless, he would probably have been even more influential than he was because more of his offspring would have been spread to other racing countries. It could not be proven, but I believe if he had been at stud in the era of Danehill and Sadler's Wells and [been] managed similar to them, he would have had similar numerical success as they have.

➤ **What tools would you like to see used in the electronic media to link the past with the races of today to bring a better appreciation of the sport to the casual fan?** — Berea, Ohio

The recent retouching of old footage of World War I action is an example of how modern technology can enhance old film. If this were done in a very high-class style, having colorized versions of great horses of the past would similarly enhance the modern viewers' appreciation of them. Also, in a much less high-tech area, I think it would be beneficial to viewers young and old for races to be put into context more frequently. For example, when the Woodward Stakes is shown, reviewing the champions which have run in it in the past would be easy and perhaps help new viewers have more appreciation for what they are about to see. And, of course, we old guys would soak it in gleefully.

➤ **Bold Ruler was from an era where horses ran more than they do today. Why do they run less today? Why can't we have iron horses like we used to?** — Grass Valley, California

Horses are probably capable of running more frequently than they do, but you cannot support forcing a trainer to race them more often if he/she is convinced that it would be physically wrong for the animal. One trainer told me that he is convinced the "stress per start" is more than it used to be. By that he included the speed work coming up to a race and also the fact that races are run so fast these days. It is so common for the first half-mile in a race today to shade forty-five seconds. What confuses me is that the claiming horses have undergone a decline in average starts per year similar to the decline in action for the more fashionable echelons. It is a subject that probably involves many things, including the sensitivity of trainers to their win percentages and the ease with which a horse can be scratched today. I hope the [Grayson-Jockey Club] Foundation can be a leader, or at least a catalyst, in developing some answers.

➤ **Besides Secretariat, did Bold Ruler ever sire a horse who could get a distance of ground? I remember the skepticism about whether Secretariat could do so prior to the Triple Crown.** — Lutherville, Maryland

The Bold Ruler offspring that excelled at 1¼ miles included Lamb Chop, who won the Coaching Club American Oaks, as well as Batteur, Successor, and the handicap champion Bold Bidder. The doubts about Bold Ruler getting a classic horse were introduced by his own failure in the Kentucky Derby and Belmont and then by the failures of some of his early sons, such as Bold Lad and Stupendous, in the Derby. The prejudice tended to linger even in the face of the successes of later sons and daughters. I was always baffled that, years later, his rider Eddie Arcaro lapsed back into saying Bold Ruler never was successful at 1¼ miles even though he himself had ridden him to three very important victories at that distance! He never got the Derby out of his mind, I guess. Having said that, it is only fair to mention that Mr. [Ogden] Phipps, whose mother bred and raced Bold Ruler, told me he regarded him as a brilliant miler who could get 1¼ mile under the right circumstances.

➤ **[Is Bold Ruler] underrated as a racehorse?** — Secaucus, New Jersey

I would agree that he is slightly underrated, but one also has to concede that 1¼ miles seems to have been his limit. If you could lift his career out of the 1950s and place it in today's context, he would be hailed as an even greater horse than he was back then. The fact that he did not succeed his only time at 1½ miles would have less impact on his reputation than it did then.

➤ **[Are] horses of today more fragile than the Bold Rulers, Nashuas, and Man o' Wars [of yesteryear]? If so, why?** — Detroit, Michigan

I think other factors besides soundness—or lack of it—enter into the decline in average number of starts for Thoroughbreds over the years. However, I think soundness is certainly one of the key issues. Concentration on speed has been a hallmark of breeders—especially American breeders—for more than a century, and speed is consistent with light bone. Since the skeleton is essentially dead weight that the muscles, ligaments, and so forth have to propel, the lighter the skeleton the less mass [that] has to be moved. Of course, you can reach the point of diminishing returns where the bone structure is sufficient to "house" the rest of the animal but cannot stand the pressure of bearing the force of high speed. I am afraid many of today's Thoroughbreds lack sufficient bone to withstand what we ask them to do. Fortunately, this can be offset to some extent by increasing scientific knowledge of how [bone development] seeks to respond to what is asked of it. A proper training regimen can go a certain distance toward preserving the soundness of horses, but it is quite an art.

➤ **What Thoroughbred was the best of the best?** — Salem, New Hampshire

I have danced around it by saying I "guess" Man o' War was the best because it really is just a guess. If you accept that he, Citation, and Secretariat are the most logical horses to be put at the very top (and there is no certainty even of that), then you have to determine for yourself which qualities trump which others. Each did something the two others did not. Man o' War did not win the Triple Crown whereas the others did; only Citation among the three raced after his three-year-old season. Secretariat was the only one of the three not to carry high weights in handicaps, and so forth. I have the sense that Citation's failure at stud might work against how he is treated historically although I try not to count that in my own thinking. So, I still hold by the answer that I "guess" Man o' War was the greatest.

➤ **Who is the most influential breeder of all time?** — Flint, Michigan

On this side of the Atlantic, I would regard Claiborne Farm as perhaps the most influential because of the large number of other breeders who benefited from their horses and the length of time that influence has lasted. Calumet Farm had a more dramatic era, but the lingering influence isn't quite the same. Overseas, I would have to say Federico Tesio and Lord Derby, at least from the standpoint of the twentieth century and up until now.

➤ **Who is the greatest racehorse you ever saw and whom do you consider the greatest Turf writer or sportswriter who covered horse racing?** — New York, New York

Among horses that I actually saw compete, I'll go with Secretariat. He had some baffling flaws and a series of defeats that needed excuses, but his performance in the Belmont Stakes even now seems unbelievable. I did have some bad luck in that the only times I saw Buckpasser, Dr. Fager, and Kelso run in the flesh, they all were beaten! As for the greatest sportswriter who covered racing, my old boss Kent Hollingsworth gets a sentimental call I can't resist. Attempting to be more objective, you could make a case for Red Smith. He was an all-sports guy but had a reverence for racing. Joe Palmer would be the choice of many, perhaps most, who are familiar with him, but there was a tendency towards flippancy first in some of his writing that I can't get away from.

➤ **What modern-day mares would make your list for a volume two of Matriarchs [available fall 2008 from Eclipse Press]?** — Yuma, Arizona

Toussaud would be one who comes to mind and Hasili, dam of Intercontinental, Banks Hill, and so forth, would rate a look. Miesque would also be appropriate and probably Tamerett. Personal Ensign also would qualify and the results of these [mares] are still coming in.

➤ **What racehorses do you wish you could have seen in person but never got to?** — Louisville, Kentucky

I have been fortunate to have seen a great many champions since the early 1960s. That means I just missed seeing Bold Ruler, Round Table, Gallant Man, and Gen. Duke in the flesh as racehorses although I saw the first three as stallions. So those horses stand out since it was almost possible for me to have seen them. As far as horses of long ago eras, I would have loved to have seen Man o' War, of course. Citation and Native Dancer also are high on that list while overseas I would have loved to see Hyperion, Ribot, and Sea-Bird in action.

➤ **How did you get interested in horse racing and how did you get started as a racing journalist?** — Dixiana, Alabama

My interest in racing was a merging of three influences as a child. My father loved horses although he cared little for racing, so we had riding horses and ponies when I was very young. Then, my aunt began sending the *Black Stallion* series of books to my brother for Christmas—seems like they came out once a year for a while. The final [influence] was that in the early 1950s, contrary to many complaints about racing shunning television, we got both the Wednesday and Saturday stakes on TV from Hialeah and Gulfstream Park. (I grew up in Fort Lauderdale, Florida.) So, I was an avid fan by the age of ten.

As for journalism, I looked on it as a possible way to get involved with Thoroughbred racing. English was a subject I did pretty well in, in high school, and I worked part-time one summer for the sports department of what was then a very small, fledgling newspaper, the *Sun-Sentinel*. I was in my third year at the University of Florida journalism school when there was a shake-up in the staff of *The Blood-Horse*. I had discovered the magazine on a family trip to Lexington and had been reading it for several years. I applied, hoping to be considered the next year after graduation, but they needed someone right away. I had worked one summer at Ocala Stud and one summer as a groom at Monmouth Park and Atlantic City, so they took a chance despite my not having a degree. I still thought of it as a way to get to a hands-on horseman's career of some sort, but I found the journalism aspect, along with the history, so beguiling that I stayed at it for many years and felt fortunate to do so.

> **When you were covering races for *The Blood-Horse*, are there certain ones or certain horses or people that stand out in your memory?**
— Poughkeepsie, New York

My first Kentucky Derby was won by Northern Dancer, and I feel like all Turf writers have been writing that story ever since. The Woodward Stakes that included Damascus, Buckpasser, and Dr. Fager was my first trip to New York and is never to be forgotten, of course. Once I was assigned the primary responsibility for coverage of the Triple Crown races for *The Blood-Horse*, starting in 1971, the most memorable horses were Canonero II (in part because of the difficulty of having a Derby winner with no English-speaking connections!), and, of course, Secretariat, Seattle Slew, and the Affirmed-Alydar series. The people who seemed the most fascinating to interview included Robert Kleberg of King Ranch, the Aga Khan, Paul Mellon, and, from a somewhat different aspect, trainers such as Woody Stephens, Neil Drysdale, Shug McGaughey, and John Russell. The real plum of a memory, though, was the opportunity to interview W. Averell Harriman on his early days as a horse owner. Here was a gentleman who by [the time of our interview] had dealt with World War II, had been governor of New York, adviser to a half-dozen presidents, and in one sentence he was back in the 1920s, still stung that Crusader beat his Chance Play in the Dwyer. How many great statesmen of the twentieth century would likely remark to you, "Chance Play was hard to rate"?

TALKIN' HORSES
WITH
LARRY BRAMLAGE, DVM

During his years as a member of the American Association of Equine Practioners' "On-Call" program for television viewers of the Triple Crown and the Breeders' Cup World Championships, Dr. Larry Bramlage has become a familiar figure to racing fans. A world-renowned veterinary surgeon who has practiced for more than thirty years, Bramlage is a partner in the prestigious Rood & Riddle Equine Hospital in Lexington, Kentucky. Bramlage has perfected a surgical technique to repair fractured fetlocks, a procedure called arthrodesis. Bramlage graduated from the Kansas State University College of Veterinary Medicine in 1975. He did an internship at Colorado State University and a residency at the Ohio State University College of Veterinary Medicine. He received a master's degree in veterinary surgery from Ohio State in 1978. He became a member of the American College of Veterinary Surgeons as a diplomate in 1983. In 1989 he moved to Lexington and joined Rood & Riddle. He is a past president of the AAEP and is president of the American College of Veterinary Surgeons. Bramlage is a "Distinguished Alumnus" of Ohio State University, a member of The Jockey Club of America, and a recipient of The Jockey Club Gold Medal for contributions to Thoroughbred Racing and the Joe Palmer Award from the Turf Writers of America in 2007. He is a member of the board of directors of the Grayson-Jockey Club Research Foundation and chairs its scientific advisory committee.

➤ **What advice could you give a breeder on avoiding the problem of contracted tendons in the newborn foal?** — Hebron, Kentucky

The only answer is to keep your horses as healthy as possible. Most causes of contracted tendons are undetermined, but those that can be determined are mostly nutritional or viral. So, healthy horses are less vulnerable.

TALKIN' HORSES

LARRY BRAMLAGE, DVM

➤ **What are the most popular types of corrective surgeries being done on sales horses?** — Lexington, Kentucky

There are two basic categories of surgical procedures: growth acceleration via periosteal transection, and growth retardation via transphyseal bridging. Both are used to correct conformation faults, but both require an actively growing physis (growth plate) to work.

➤ **[Do you have] any advice of what a young person like myself should do next after interning at studs in Kentucky, Ireland, and Australia but [who has] no college degree?** — Lexington, Kentucky

People with college degrees are actually a minority in most horse operations. Find a spot you like, work hard, and you will work your way up. Many young people don't realize the value most businesses place on good employees.

➤ **[Has] overcommercialization of Thoroughbred breeding contributed to the apparent decline in racing soundness?** — Miramar, Florida

To some degree the production will follow the demand. But I think it goes one step farther back. We no longer select for longevity, so why should we expect it? We select for brilliance in a few very prominent events. That is what people buy, or at least the potential to be brilliant, so that is what the market will produce. This is a free market economy like most of our society.

➤ **[Could] an amputation plus prosthetic leg have saved Barbaro's life? What would have been your approach?** — Shell Beach, California

It is my opinion, though not universally held, that amputation will never be very practical in the horse. In people it is the prosthesis/stump interface that requires continual attention and care. People sleep with their prosthesis off, horse can't. Horses will always [have] a problem where the prosthesis and the limb interface.

➤ **How effective is the practice of treating tendon injuries (bows and so forth) with stem cells? Can you describe the process and cost and [describe those] horses best suited by it?** — Louisville, Kentucky

Stem cells are the newest of all the treatments for tendonitis that don't work very well when one compares the treatment of tendons to other orthopedic procedures in the horse. Much of the information you ask for is unavailable. There are many ways to use stem cells, many different concentrations of stem cell treatments that are being called stem cells, [and] many cost variables that relate to the technique you choose and the product you employ. Perhaps one day, stem cells will rise to the top, but to this point it has not produced results that improve on some other methods.

➤ **[Do] you think that the advancements in equine surgery have had any negative effects on the overall soundness of the Thoroughbred? Also, is there any laminitis research that you believe to be particularly promising?** — Auburn, Alabama

The only way that you can credit advancements in surgery to weakening the breed is if you prefer the ultimate in natural selection and advocate that we fix nothing, and that only the strong survive long enough to be the stallions and mares. But if that is the premise, we should not vaccinate, not palpate mares to breed at the opportune time, [and] not treat a sick foal. We should not trim the feet, nor, for that matter, train much. We should just round the horses up in time to get them to the post and run to the finish line. Eventually, disease and injury, as well as diminished reproductive soundness, would weed out all the weak by Darwinian selection. With tongue in cheek, I took a few liberties with your question. We have to have a little fun.

➤ **It seems that horses started to break down more regularly, [even] with lighter schedules, in the late sixties. How do you feel about horses that were not that sound themselves being hot property in the breeding world?** — Maple Shade, New Jersey

Please refer to the earlier question on weakening of the breed. We don't place a premium on longevity or soundness in the market. Because the market does not pay a premium for it, horses are not selected for soundness, just extreme ability. Extreme ability comes at a price. A bigger engine with a lighter undercarriage is lighter and faster if it is a car or a horse. Data shows that even though horses race fewer times, the training and the races are tougher, so the demand is higher than fifty years ago. So many factors weigh into this analysis we could discuss it for a long time, but it does not mean that we should accept anything that we can modify for the better as unchangeable. That is why the new nationwide documentation of injury is so vital, important, and promising. It is time we critically assess each injury.

➤ **Is any type of biofeedback used on Thoroughbreds? If yes, what type, and how are the results beneficial?** — Palm Beach, Florida

This depends on what you define as biofeedback. If you are referring to the type of analysis and modification that is used on human Olympians, the application is limited because technique modification is difficult, and horses are so highly evolved over centuries of breeding that there has been little success in monitoring training through the sophisticated laboratory techniques used on people.

➤ **How much [influence] does an equine mortality insurance company have when it comes to the decision on putting down an insured horse?** — Ventura, California

Insurance [coverage] is a contract; the decisions are spelled out in the contract. Any owner can euthanize their horse anytime they want, but the insurance company is only responsible for payment when the conditions meet the contract agreed upon. The [AAEP] has a time-honored and well-accepted set of guidelines that help with humane euthanasia decisions. Most insurance companies accept these as valid guidelines.

➤ **How do you feel about the current policy of upper airway evaluation at public sale grounds?** — Lexington, Kentucky

The premise of the public auction is to establish value. Data has shown the examination of the airway to be superior to sound alone, but it also gives information that is unimportant and can be misinterpreted. So the experience of the evaluator is important to minimize falsely penalizing a good horse. Since the direct visualization is the superior information, it should be superior in establishing value in experienced hands.

➤ **What would happen to field sizes if United States racing were to go to absolutely no race-day medication?** — Lexington, Kentucky

My opinion [is] nothing [would happen]. The average field size has decreased less than one horse per field in the last sixty years. When we calculated the average field size, it went from approximately 8.9 horses/field to 8.1 horses/field in sixty years. The leveling influence in the field size is that there is not a lot of demand to run tenth through fourteenth. If you enter and the field comes up very tough, the current mentality is to scratch and run the next opportunity. That is not how it is supposed to be, but it is the reality, partially driven by the cost of keeping a horse in training and the need to be competitive when you run. We raise five times more horses each year than we did in each year in the 1950s. The number of racing opportunities is about equal. We have fewer tracks, but they have more dates. This means that if each horse was run in about the equal proportion to what they ran in 1950, the average field would be forty horses. Field size is most closely linked to the opportunity to be competitive.

➤ **I am an equine surgical resident. During your career, what has been the hardest thing to learn and do?** — Columbus, Ohio

Tough question. Surgeons are egotistical and usually driven people. Without those qualities it is tough to have the mentality to open a horse's abdomen or try to fix a horse's fracture when common sense says that you don't have much chance. Each of us will be different, but for me the tough thing to realize is that clients don't expect you to be perfect or to always succeed. They expect you to give them an honest appraisal of what their chances of success will be. When you do that, you are in the case together, and the surgeon does not have to carry the burden of success alone.

➤ **What horses have been memorable both in terms of being at the vet hospital and also in terms of being a teaching tool or learning a technique that has benefited other horses later?** — Nauvoo, Alabama

The premise of this question is what most people feel; it is that progress is made in leaps and bounds on a particular horse. This is not the case. Progress is made in small steps on multiple unknowns or forgotten horses that contributed bits of information that eventually benefited horses years later. Techniques become polished over time. Memorable horses in my career include Noble Dancer, the first million-dollar winner (actually just a few dollars short of a million) that I did a fetlock arthrodesis on. He had a twenty-year plus career as a stallion. Saratoga Six, the most valuable horse (insured value at the time) I ever fused an ankle on. Personal Ensign, the best athlete I ever fixed a fracture on,

LARRY BRAMLAGE, DVM

and maybe the best female equine athlete of her century. Grindstone, my first Kentucky Derby winner, as well as Strodes Creek, and Menifee, both of whom finished second in the Kentucky Derby.

> **Do you think [synthetic surfaces] really help prevent catastrophic breakdowns or are we just trying to gloss over problems within our breeding industry?** — Shawnee, Kansas

The data is pretty strong that catastrophic injuries have decreased. The jury is still out on routine injuries. I don't think they decrease nearly as much. It is not the track that presupposes that a horse is at risk for injury. It is the fact that each Thoroughbred must design and build the perfect skeleton for him to use as a racehorse. This is done with training. The yearlings are not born with racehorse skeletons; they have to mold their skeleton into [one] that will carry their weight and their mechanics competitively around the track. This is done by progressive, small episodes of overload, and then over-repair. This is training. The overloads are small stress fractures that result from training and cause the bone to over-repair and get stronger. These small stress fractures make bones vulnerable to uneven loading. This is where the track comes in. An even, consistent surface does not present the uneven foot plants and abnormal stresses that an inconsistent surface does. That is where the artificial surfaces have an advantage. They are consistent for the top seven inches or so. Dirt tracks are layered, and the cushion and base can vary more readily, leading to uneven landings for the horse's limbs at high speed. Most of the time the horse can compensate for these uneven spots, but sometimes the uneven spot, the horse's balance, fatigue, and the presence of a small stress fracture combine to result in failure of the bone. We could race draft horses over nearly any surface, and their bones are strong enough [so that] it wouldn't matter. But the Thoroughbred maintains only the minimum skeleton that is sufficient to carry them around the track. Excess skeleton is added weight and penalizes the horse's speed. So, the light skeleton is a speed advantage, unless it gets too light to carry its owner, and then it fails. This is why we will never eliminate injuries totally. Success is predicated on the fact that our athletes carry the minimum skeleton necessary. They run right on the edge of their physiology. But we have the obligation to mitigate anything in our power that may make it safer for them. Artificial surfaces may do that, but they have to stand the test of time. Remember when artificial turf came into sports? It was lauded as the ideal surface only to be cursed a few years later when many sprinted back to grass fields. This is a long answer, but questions about artificial surfaces are a hot topic right now.

➤ Is unsoundness any more prevalent in males vs. females?
— Dormont, Pennsylvania

No different. Both sexes have to train their skeleton to be a racehorse skeleton (see the question on artificial surfaces), so both are subject to the same forces that can precipitate an injury.

➤ I have read reports that young horses' bones fatigue during the early part of conditioning due to the lack of enough silicone in their system. Do you believe more silicone is required for proper bone development in a young horse [being conditioned]?
— Hayward, California

The addition of bio-available silicone has been shown to be beneficial to the young training horse. I think it is likely useful, not earth shaking, but useful. There is no data that shows the same for an injured site to this point.

➤ People say Lasix prevents bleeding during racing—Lasix is a diuretic. Shouldn't Lasix only prevent the pulmonary edema after the bleeding has occurred? — Riverside, California

No, Lasix has a well-documented primary effect. The mechanism is still debated, but it is the best we have [for a] reduction of the blood in the air spaces.

➤ It seems that breeders and consignors are selling X-rays as much as they sell horses. Do you think vets are becoming too conservative when evaluating joint X-rays for end-user clients and flunk horses that have imperfections that, in all probability, will not affect the horse's performance on the racetrack? — Reddick, Florida

There are variations from normal, and there is pathology when reading radiographs. The difficulty is that, in most instances, only experience will sort these out effectively. Inexperienced evaluators can unduly penalize a horse, as can consignors that carry around books of horses that they market as the one that buyers should buy because they have no marks on their pages. Rightfully, you should evaluate each horse on a combination of whether there is pathology and whether it is significant for this particular horse. We get into trouble when we try to shortcut the cerebral decision.

➤ **What are your thoughts as the industry wrestles with abolishing use of anabolic steroids as Keeneland and Fasig-Tipton [have] at sales, [and] several states [have] for racing horses?** — Seattle, Washington

As with most things, anabolic steroids are useful tools when used appropriately. So, I think they can be very valuable in treating some problems, in people and in the horse. But the problem comes with abuse, in people and in the horse. The short answer is that I don't think it is appropriate to have any anabolic steroids in the system of a sales horse when they are presented for sale. I think you could make a case for not having anabolic steroids on board for any stakes races and for any filly races. Geldings are a tougher problem. Castration removes the natural source of anabolic steroids for the training gelding. They sometimes need it. That makes a case for use but not abuse. The key will be in setting some logical level of use that is appropriate. That is what the RMTC [Racing Medication & Testing Consortium] is working on right now. This is how steroids are different in horses and in people. We don't castrate people to make them easier to handle.

➤ **[Assuming] finances aren't a factor, what is the ideal age to place a racehorse in training?** — Wynnewood, Pennsylvania

This answer is easy and well documented by science. The best age to train a horse is to start right at the end of growth and maintain the bone formation mechanism that has been doing the growing, and just shift it to responding to training. So, late yearlings and early two-year-olds train better, last longer, and make more starts than horses that wait until later to start training.

➤ **Do you support disclosure of all surgeries for weanlings, yearlings, and two-year-olds sold at public auction, and is a medical passport using a microchip [usable] to track such records?** — Los Angeles, California

I could answer this easily if you would insert the word "major" into your question right before surgeries. I'd say yes. The problem comes when you say "all." That creates a clerical nightmare. If you let us define "major surgery"—which would include all joint surgeries, abdominal surgeries, and so forth—we could do it practically. When you say "all," that includes lacerations, umbilical hernias, periosteal transactions, and things that I don't think are that important, and that creates clerical nightmares and potential for litigation that I would like to see us avoid. We already disclose joint and abdominal surgery. The ones up for debate are the limb-straightening procedures, where a few people are adamant they be disclosed, and most don't care because you can look at the horse and see the result. Thankfully, the invention of digital radiographs largely makes this point moot in relation to the use of screws and wires and transphyseal screws to correct conformation faults. Those who care can just check the radiographs to see if the horse had screws inserted. The scars are visible on the higher-detailed digital radiographs. I do support microchips, but largely for other reasons as the surgery argument is largely one of passion, not logic.

➤ **What factors do you consider when determining whether or not a bone chip should be surgically removed?** — Concord, New Hampshire

There is only one. Does it have the potential to create degeneration in the joint? This is a pass-fail decision. Degeneration in a joint is a permanent change; a joint will never be the same if it loses significant amounts of articular cartilage. All adults survive the rest of their lives on what they have when they finish growing. So you have to consider site, size, use, and anatomy, plus other factors.

➤ **As an expert in equine medicine, what are your thoughts regarding the health of Thoroughbreds used in racing?** — Milaca, Minnesota

It seems your premise is that horses are unhappy. If you spend any time around the racehorse you come to understand that they are so fit and so healthy, and they have so much energy they just do what the horsemen describe as "jump out of their skin." Each day I do lameness exams I marvel at them as physical specimens. I wish that at some time in my life I would have ever felt that good. Maybe I did and just can't remember. When they are sick, or when they become sore, they begin to lose that glow, but most of the time those horses are sent for a break because they are not competitive in the racing

Larry Bramlage, DVM

venue. If you stand by the rail and watch hundreds of horses train each morning at the track, you begin to understand how good they feel about what they are doing. So I don't accept your premise that horses are unhappy. If they are sick or injured, they need care, and they shouldn't be kept in training, but for most Thoroughbred horses, I believe they are happier training and getting all that attention than at any other time in their life. Why do human athletes like to perform?

➤ **Has significant progress been made in repairing fractures in Thoroughbreds? Has your arthrodesis surgery been successful in the vast majority of horses that had it done?** — Orland Park, Illinois

Yes, we have made great progress. The arthrodesis has progressed to where we save many more than we lose, but variations in the injury, such as loss of blood supply, opening of the skin, and exposure to infection, still present major hurdles.

➤ **Do you feel you are doing more corrective surgery on foals today then maybe ten years ago?** — Arcadia, California

Yes, we have more stallions that produce conformational faults. Unfortunately, some of those stallions also produce exceptional athletes as well. That is why the industry tolerates them.

➤ **I admire your ability to deal with breakdowns and tragedies on the track. Where does your strength come from to deal with these happenings?** — Boise, Idaho

Information and understanding make people comfortable with reality. That is how I approach my day-to-day work and how I try to portray the reality of sports injury when I am doing the "On Call" telecasts.

➤ **I understand how Barbaro developed laminitis, but I have always wondered how Secretariat and Foolish Pleasure became victims of this awful condition well after they were retired to stud.**
— Nottingham, New Hampshire

Laminitis is the end result of many systemic and local diseases. That is why it is so difficult to deal with. Virtually any sick horse is at risk, and many horses with no signs of disease come down with it though they may have had some unidentifiable subclinical problem.

➤ **[Is] there an increased risk for injury to a horse who trains and races on one surface and then switches to another?** — St. Croix, U.S. Virgin Islands

When horses move from track to track during the year, they will often get minor soreness after they train on the new surface for a while. The adaptation of the skeleton is work specific, and, therefore, they adapt to the type of stress they see in training. When they switch tracks, they see different stresses. This only happens after a while, not when they just change tracks for a race. The majority of the time it is not serious injury, just various overstress problems they are not adapted for.

➤ **How prevalent is OCD [a major bone disease in young horses] in racehorses? Does anyone keep track of this type of information? Is OCD a contributing factor in Thoroughbred breakdowns?**
— Christiana, Tennessee

OCDs are more common in big, fast-growing colts, but so are the fastest racehorses. There is no central clearinghouse, but there are various studies on a smaller scale that verify this fact. OCDs usually cause degenerative arthritis, not catastrophic failure, so the answer to your last question is "no." We normally say that we like to see the bone formation problems on a farm under 15 percent.

➤ **Do you believe if toe grabs, caulks, and bends were banned that it would have a positive impact on lessening the number of breakdowns?** — Saratoga Springs, New York

As with most things, this is neither black nor white. An absence of stability or traction is bad, as is excess traction. A stable, confident foot plant is a good thing for a horse. Tendon and ligament injuries tend to go up with slipping and sliding foot plants because muscles dampen the load when they can anticipate the forces that will be seen. When surprise loads are encountered they tend to create excess loads or uneven load application. This results in sprains and tears in supporting ligaments such as the suspensory branches, sesamoidean ligaments, and the cruciate ligaments of the stifles. Excess traction devices increase the jarring forces and torsion forces when the foot plant is too stable.

TALKIN' HORSES

LARRY BRAMLAGE, DVM

Recent data shows the stopping action of the foot hitting the ground is the excess force, rather than the force generated by the push off. I would favor elimination of all excess traction devices such as caulks and stickers. I would allow very low toe grabs, queens plates, and bends but not turn-downs.

➤ **What rules do you feel need to be changed or enforced, for example, Lasix and steroids?** — Scottsburg, Indiana

I happen to favor Lasix and phenylbutazone in therapeutic doses. I think they protect horses from more serious injuries and more aggressive treatments. I think we spend too much time, get too much bad press, and waste our resources on honest mistakes such as slight overages of these medications and, therefore, rob the resources from finding the people who are trying to cheat. I happen to think the owner, and the veterinarian who gave the illegal drug, should join the trainer in the responsibility for violations, and I think they should have penalties that are stiff enough that they can't be circumvented. We are trying to move this way as an industry.

➤ **What do you think has been the greatest advancement in equine orthopedic surgery in your career?** — Versailles, Kentucky

If you asked me for only one, I would say the realization that we could not take human techniques and just apply them to horses. When we started developing techniques of treatment, and then eventually implants designed specifically for horses, we began to make great strides. That, of course, was aided and paralleled by advancements in general anesthesia for horses, better understanding and availability of antibiotics, advancements in first aid, and others that all moved along with the advancement of veterinary medicine.

➤ **Since the synthetic track installations and the perceived future health of our Thoroughbreds will improve on the track surfaces, do you feel that Triple Crown tracks will be reluctant to change (in spite of the health of the horse, [to maintain the] history of the event)?**
— Ashland, Oregon

I don't think anything will overrule the health and welfare of the horse. But I think we should realize that synthetic surfaces as we know them are not an insurance policy preventing injury. They have some good aspects and some warts. I remain skeptical that we should make wholesale changes until we understand them a little better. In instances where they negate the huge variability in weather conditions, I think they were rightly installed.

➤ **Are there any publicly available stats on training and/or racetrack injuries or fatalities?** — Washington, North Carolina

Yes and no; yes, there are published studies in the veterinary literature that detail injuries over time in individual states. The trouble with these studies is that the entry points were defined differently, the results were tabulated differently, even the description of what is an injury was different. This means they can't reasonably be compared. That is why the injury reporting system that grew out of the Racetrack Injury Summit, sponsored by the Grayson-Jockey Club, is so important. Headed by Dr. Mary Scollay, this system will allow direct comparison of data for the first time.

➤ **What has been your most challenging surgical procedure in your career?** — Eddyville, Kentucky

Alydar's hind limb fracture [because of the] complicated situation, bad patient, [and the] bankers and lawyers everywhere. It was not the toughest individual surgery, but [it was] the toughest situation.

➤ **It seems [racehorses break down] more often now. [Are there] more horses or have we gone wrong in our breeding practices?**
— Crestwood, Kentucky

Injuries appear to have gone up some, but the press [coverage] has gone up exponentially, and the game has become national. Combine that with the instant news mentality and the desire to show the wrecks, not the fantastic finishes, in the popular press [coupled] with the fact that there are three views of each inch of every race on videotape or digital media and the injuries make primetime viewing. Every station wants to be bigger and better than the other in what they show. When was the last time that you saw the cleanest lap of the Indianapolis 500 vs. the one with the wreck?

TALKIN' HORSES

WITH

TREVOR DENMAN

A native of South Africa, Southern California track announcer Trevor Denman has become known for his distinctive voice and race-calling style that have served him well for more than three decades. Denman, who began his career in his native country at eighteen, relocated in 1983, and became the official announcer for the Breeders' Cup Thoroughbred Championships in 2006 when the ESPN network began broadcasting the races. Denman hosted "Talkin' Horses" during the week leading up to his first experience as the Breeders' Cup announcer. In addition to his career, Denman has also become involved in the issue of how horses are treated and is an ardent opponent of the use of the whip in horse racing.

➤ **You've seen a lot of horse races. Who are some of the standout horses that impressed you?** — Salina, Kansas

Wow! There are so many, and I am sure I will leave out a few here, but my best would include Cigar, John Henry, Sunday Silence, Estrapade, Precisionist, Best Pal, Alysheba, Bien Bien, Kotashan, Bayakoa, Lure, Winning Colors, Manila, Ferdinand, and A.P. Indy. I may have to add Bernardini after Saturday's Breeders' Cup Classic. [In the November 4, 2006, BC Classic, Bernardini finished a close second to Invasor.]

➤ **How do you think calling your first Breeders' Cup will rank among the milestones of such an accomplished life?** — Nevada City, California

After thirty-five years of calling the races, I have reached my apex with the Breeders' Cup. I told my wife that this is definitely the cherry on top of a cake I have been building for fifty years. I became interested in horse racing at age five; my most treasured possession is an album of newspaper clippings I have from that age. The cover reads, "Trevor's Horse Book June 1957."

I starting out calling the races aged eighteen in South Africa—where racing was huge. It was like calling *Monday Night Football* here—it was a great challenge. But the transition from South Africa to America was, by far, my greatest challenge. It had never been done before and the obstacles were obviously enormous.

➤ **What do you remember most about calling the 1989 Preakness [between Sunday Silence and Easy Goer] live as the Pimlico track announcer, and have you ever watched the video of Secretariat's Belmont and thought about how you would have called it?**
—Tustin, California

The 1989 Preakness is one of the most memorable races I have ever seen. The two horses were never more than a neck apart from the half-mile pole to home. I can't say what I would have said in Secretariat's Belmont; however, it is etched in the brain as a golden moment.

➤ **What do you think is the job of the race caller in relating the action of a horse race that makes it something that not everyone can do well or with distinction?** — Marco Island, Florida

Being a comment maker, or, as they are called in Europe, "commentators," is not just a matter of "joining the dots" and naming the horses in a race. One must paint a picture. Distances behind the leader are vital for a listener. Pace changes in the middle of a race are crucial. Types of trips and unexpected movements must be instantaneously spotted. From the quarter pole [to] home, don't waste time on horses who are going nowhere, concentrate on the contenders. Think like a jockey in a race. And, of course, make it exciting. Every race is someone's Kentucky Derby.

➤ **Who are your current favorite announcers, and who from the past are your favorites? Which do you prefer, announcing the Breeders' Cup or analyzing the Breeders' Cup races?** — San Diego, California

Jim McGrath was one [of my favorites]. I grew up in South Africa and we listened mainly to England's announcers. Sometimes, [we listened to] Australians, New Zealanders, and Irish announcers. Bill Collins, an Australian, had the biggest influence on me, followed by Peter O'Sullivan of England. I never heard an American announcer until I visited California at age twenty-four. Unfortunately, we had no connection to America in South Africa. We knew of [jockey] Bill Shoemaker and [trainer] Charlie Whittingham and that was about it. Communications were so different back then—remember, South Africa did not have television until 1976. So I cannot rate American announcers. However, the "old style" of calling races like a chart caller is all but defunct nowadays, so the old American announcers would not have influenced me.

Calling the races is a 10; analyzing them, a 1.

➤ **Have you ever been so overwhelmed by the performance of a horse during a race that you are either close to tears or speechless?**
— Denver, Colorado

The adrenalin sure does flow and I have had goose bumps in races. The only time I am speechless is when there is a bad accident in a race. Those are horrible moments.

➤ **Do you own any horses yourself for pleasure riding and, if so, what are the breeds and what riding discipline do you enjoy?**
— Los Angeles, California

No, I don't own any horses in America, but my wife and I do own an unraced two-year-old in South Africa who will run later this year.

➤ **You should be in the horse racing Hall of Fame. Do you think you'll ever call the Triple Crown races?** — Phoenix, Arizona

Unfortunately, announcers cannot get into the Hall of Fame in racing in America. I have no idea why. Famed English announcer Peter O'Sullivan was knighted in England, but we can't get into the Hall of Fame. With ESPN moving into the big races now, I think I have a good chance.

➤ **Why are Thoroughbred horse racing fans not attending live racing today as much as fifteen years ago?** — Lake Wylie, South Carolina

Competition has killed us. There is so much on TV and the Internet these days that the younger generation can't be bothered with handicapping or having to spend a day at the track. Horses just are not part of the culture anymore.

TALKIN' HORSES
WITH
TOM DURKIN

As track announcer at Aqueduct, Belmont, and Saratoga, Tom Durkin has become the voice of the Belmont Stakes and one of the most familiar symbols of Triple Crown racing on the airwaves today. Durkin splits his time between New York homes in Floral Park and Saratoga Springs and estimates that he's called races at more than fifty tracks in at least six countries around the world. A Chicago native, Durkin began his career by calling races at county fairs throughout Wisconsin during the early 1970s. He then became a "call taker" for the Daily Racing Form *and moved on to become track announcer (and sometime line maker and director of publicity) at tracks all over the country, including Cahokia Downs, Florida Downs (now Tampa Bay Downs), Commonwealth Park, Quad City Downs, and Balmoral Park. By the mid-1980s, Durkin was track announcer at Florida's Hialeah Park, the Meadowlands, and Balmoral. By the end of that decade, Durkin was also serving as host of* Racing from the Meadowlands *and* Thoroughbred World TV Magazine *while also working as a race caller, analyst, and feature producer at ESPN. Durkin also began his stint as analyst and race caller for NBC-TV and the Breeders' Cup World Championships in 1984. Durkin's appearance [on "Talkin' Horses"] came about two weeks after Barbaro's tragic injury in the 2006 Preakness Stakes.*

➤ **How difficult was it for you to finish the call of the [Preakness] when you, as a lover of horse racing, were no doubt consumed with concern for Barbaro?** — Cleveland, Ohio

Things happened very fast there, probably faster than I was able to think. There were two stories to tell. First, Barbaro. Then the Preakness. Once I was able to let people know as much as I knew about Barbaro, then I went on to the race.

TOM DURKIN

Unfortunately, this has happened before, so it was not a new experience. Once you know you have two stories to tell, you just proceed. One thing that was in the back of my mind was the possibility of the field racing into the stricken horse after the finish line. But Barbaro was safely out of the way, and it was a small field. Had the field been the size of the Derby, we would have had a real postrace problem.

➤ **How do you memorize all the horses' names before a race? I am twelve and would like to learn how to call races.** — St. Paul, Minnesota

First thing you need to do is develop a way to memorize things. You being twelve, I would say studying and doing your homework is the best way to prepare for a race-calling career later on. But what I do is associate the names of the horses with the colors the jockeys are wearing. Then repeat. Repeat. Repeat. Repeat. Now, hit the books!

➤ **What was the toughest race you've ever called?** — Bel Air, Maryland

Some would think the Arc de Triomphe with twenty-six horses and with the field disappearing behind a small forest for a while. But in those cases I use— shall we say … hmmmm … poetic license (making stuff up). But seriously, the hardest race to call was the 1990 Breeders' Cup Mile. The race after Go for Wand's [was] very difficult to concentrate [on]. [Go for Wand suffered a catastrophic breakdown in the stretch of the 1990 Breeders' Cup Distaff.]

➤ **Which is the most satisfying and exciting Kentucky Derby commentary you have given, and which was your favorite Derby winner?** — Burlington, Ontario, Canada

[The] most exciting Derby I have called … I suppose Barbaro. Huge effort. Sublime was the word I assigned.

➤ **What major race was your best call, and which was your worst call?**
— Lexington, Kentucky

I wouldn't say which was best. But among the worst was stating that Monarchos had won the Derby tying Secretariat's record. The track was playing incredibly fast that day. I thought the record could be broken. So I went back over the charts of Secretariat's Derby and wrote down on the bottom of my program the fractional times and final time. I wrote on the program 1:59.4 as the final time. Monarchos ran in 59.4; but Secretariat's time was 59.2. I didn't realize until a few months later how I could have made such a bonehead mistake. I needed reading glasses!

➤ **When did you start calling Funny Cide "the gutsy gelding"?**
— Hockessin, Delaware

When preparing for the Derby that year, I was trying to find a word to describe him. His Wood Memorial was very courageous, as were some of his earlier races. I thought "gutsy" was a good word. And in the Derby, it just came out "gutsy gelding."

➤ **Can you speak of the narrative of a race call and how it is perfected into a style?** — Marco Island, Florida

Well, each race is a different story. Some stories are more important than others. The Derby is more important than the fourth at Aqueduct. But the fourth at Aqueduct is pretty important to a guy who is alive in a pick three. So you need to find a "tone" for each race. And you need to give each horse at least one call. And getting a "feel" for a race … how pace scenarios develop, interaction between horses and jockeys. Most important—be accurate and energetic. And don't try too hard at style. Let that take care of itself. Horse races are innately exciting. Just describe it accurately, and you'll be fine.

➤ **Which one was more exciting to call—Probe and Park Avenue Joe or Victory Gallop and Real Quiet? Did you think there was a dead heat in both instances before the photo?** — New Hyde Park, New York

Probe and Park Avenue Joe [running a] dead heat in a match race—an unbelievable, unimaginable result. Victory Gallop and Real Quiet. Real Quiet wins the Triple Crown three inches before and three inches after the wire.

Which was the more exciting? I'd say "dead heat."

➤ **We love having you call at Saratoga racetrack. Do you enjoy being at the Spa?** — Gloversville, New York

I love the Spa. In fact, I just bought a house a half mile from the track. I close this week and can walk to work now. I love the Spaaaaaaa!!!

TALKIN' HORSES

TOM DURKIN

➤ **Do you bet on the races?** — Miami, Florida

[I] used to. But about a year ago, the folks at NYRA said they didn't want employees betting. So I don't.

➤ **Do you have any prepared phraseology that you are saving just in case a "Secretariat-at-Belmont" performance happens, or do you prefer to keep it completely spontaneous?** — Niceville, Florida

The calls for big races are not totally spontaneous. I do write down pages of stuff to say. If they pop out of my mouth during the call, fine. If not, fine. I just like to be prepared. I have a book of phrases and words I refer to constantly. I just transcribed them to a new file and did a word count; it's 8,708 words.

➤ **What do you consider to be more of a challenge to call? The Derby (due to field size) or the Breeders' Cup (since there are so many races)?**
— Omaha, Nebraska

No doubt the Breeders' Cup is more challenging—eight races, a hundred horses.

➤ **If there was a race of all eleven Triple Crown winners and you owned one of them, who would it be and who would be your jockey?**
— Ft. Lauderdale, Florida

[My] horse would be Citation. He won the Jersey Derby between the Preakness and Belmont. [My jockey would be] Chantal Sutherland; hey, I'm a guy, what can I say.

➤ **Do you think the Kentucky Derby would be a fairer and safer race if the number of horses is limited to fourteen or fifteen? Looking back at previous Kentucky Derby races, 1947 through 1968, most races were fifteen or fewer. Only one, in 1951, had twenty horses. How and when did the limit of twenty horses become a rule?** — Greenville, Ohio

I think they should completely abandon the rule that limits the field to twenty. As the announcer, I say limit it to … four or five horses. Actually, I think twenty is a good number. It adds greatly to the spectacle and, well, you'll get that occasional Giacomo who would have never gotten in if the field were limited to fourteen. Three-year-olds can get very good very quickly, so I think a small field would not be fair. As I recall, the 100th anniversary of the Derby when Cannonade won there were something like twenty-three or twenty-four; that was too many. A few years after that, they limited the fields to twenty.

➤ **Is there a place in horse racing for Hialeah?** — Conklin, New York

Horse heaven. What a shame to see her just sitting there. I always thought it would be perfect as the permanent sight for the Breeders' Cup. Won't happen, though. Hialeah was my first big job. I love that place.

➤ **[Have you] ever given any thought to [books on tape]? Does anybody ever recognize your voice when you're not at work and figure they know you from somewhere?** — Nashville, Tennessee

I'd love to do [books] on tape. I really enjoy doing voice-over work. Most of it is limited to horse racing commercials and [from] when I used to produce feature pieces on ESPN. I wish I could do more of that. Once in a while someone will recognize the voice, usually when I am up in Saratoga. Thank goodness I have a good, clear voice—what in the television business we call "a good face for radio." In the realm of do I know you from somewhere? When I first started working at the Meadowlands back in 1982 or so, I was taking the elevator and this fellow starts looking at me. And he says I know you … hmmmmmmmmmm … I know you … don't tell me … you're … you're … you're not Dave Johnson!!

➤ **If you had the place, are there two or three retired Thoroughbreds you'd like to adopt?** — Portland, Oregon

Evening Attire is one of my favorites. I think he is close to retiring. And a maiden named Conflictofinterest; she's the first horse I ever owned. What a thrill when she finally got on the grass and ran third.

➤ **If a Triple Crown is on the line, is preparing something to say sort of like writing an Oscar speech where you feel silly having it already written (like you're presuming victory) but feel even worse being caught unprepared should the big moment arrive?**
— Raleigh, North Carolina

Actually, I am pretty sure if and when a horse wins the Triple Crown I would not try to be too poetic. I think just simply "so and so wins the Triple Crown" is

TOM DURKIN

all [that needs to] be said. Those simple words carry with them a great deal of passion and history. To handle it otherwise would be gilding the lily, I think.

➤ **If you could call a Belmont of the past, what would you like to have called or even just witnessed? Are there any horses you'd like to have seen?** — Miami, Florida

Well, it sure would have been fun to call [Secretariat's race]. When Smarty Jones was trying to win it, I went out the day before and measured the spot where thirty-one lengths is and marked it on the rail. That is how confident I was that day. Oh, well. That's racing.

➤ **Is there something you'd recommend for a first-time Belmont attendee [to] make the experience particularly special? (You can totally tell a "best-kept secret"—just between us, we promise!)** — Atlanta, Georgia

Come to my house afterwards for the annual post-Belmont party. I live 200 yards from the track; [it's] a good time. But I kick everyone out at midnight. [I have to go to] work the next day. Ask the folks at *The Blood-Horse* for my e-mail. I'll give you directions.

➤ **Have you any role models from the past, or is this your own style?**
— Florence, South Carolina

I never made a conscious attempt at "style." The calls are a reflection of my own view of the game, my vocal dynamics (what I can and can't do with my voice), and my sense of taste. What I think sounds good. But my inspiration as a race caller comes from the inimitable Phil Georgeff of Chicago, my childhood hero. It was his enthusiasm that inspired me to be a race caller.

➤ **Before you call a big race like the Belmont, do you picture a pace scenario in your mind beforehand?** — Conshohocken, Pennsylvania

I plot out several scenarios and what I think will be a pace that would be too fast or too slow. For instance, in the Derby any horse that runs faster than 46.1 usually has no shot. So I plot out the call accordingly.

TALKIN' HORSES
WITH
ROBERT L. EVANS

After a long and distinguished career that included successes in the technology, manufacturing, private equity capital, and Thoroughbred industries, Robert L. Evans was named president and chief executive officer of Churchill Downs Inc. in August 2006. Evans succeeded Tom Meeker, who retired after twenty-two years at the CDI helm. Not long after Evans' appointment to the Churchill Downs position, the track-operating company announced it was entering into some joint ventures with rival Magna Entertainment Company. Evans previously held senior executive positions at Caterpillar Inc., Mazda Motor of America Inc., and Accenture Ltd., and top leadership positions at international technology and private equity capital companies, including Symphony Technology Group. Evans is also involved in the Thoroughbred industry as president and founder of Tenlane Farm LLC, a 260-acre commercial breeding operation in Woodford County, Kentucky. He has owned, bred, and raced Thoroughbreds for more than two decades.

➤ **Why are the Kentucky Derby and Kentucky Oaks limited to twenty runners per field, in contrast to other major group I races in Europe?**
— Montreal, Quebec, Canada

Safety is the primary reason why we don't exceed twenty runners in the Derby and Oaks. Many European courses have different layouts, generally with turns that aren't as tight and the course can handle more runners.

➤ **What are your thoughts on the Jockeys' Guild?** — Ferndale, California

I'm all for the Jockeys' Guild. From time to time, I'm sure we'll have differences of opinion, but I imagine those differences can be resolved amicably. In addition to working directly with the guild on raising funds for the Permanently Disabled

TALKIN' HORSES

ROBERT L. EVANS

Jockeys' Fund, we just settled our legal claims with the guild to the satisfaction of both parties, and we are glad to be moving forward in our relationship with the guild under its new leadership.

➤ **As a commercial breeder, do you have concerns that there are too many people breeding for the market or pinhooking for the market and [there are] not enough end users?** — Lexington, Kentucky

Every time a horse we've bred walks into the sales ring, I worry about whether there will be enough people [who are buyers].

➤ **What do you say to racing fans who are agitated every time they hear or read "The Kentucky Derby, presented by Yum! Brands"?**
— Louisville, Kentucky

I say Yum! Brands Inc. is a great, Louisville-based company. We're proud of our association with them. Yum! and its employees have done much to support, promote, and help us grow the reach of the Kentucky Derby during the many years we have been corporate partners. And, if there really are people who are agitated by that, then they might consider worrying about other, far more important things.

➤ **Can you compare the pari-mutuel industry to other industries that currently or in the past had similar difficulties?** — Jacksonville, Florida

It's always the same: innovate or die. I've worked a lot in the technology sector where the time between significant innovations is measured in months. Imagine trying to sell a 2005 cell phone in today's market. Obviously, Thoroughbred racing is running on an innovation cycle that's much longer than "months." But we better pick up the pace if we expect to succeed.

➤ **The last Breeders' Cup at CD [Churchill Downs] was in many ways a fiasco for patrons. Considering that, should CD be eligible to try again soon [to host the Breeders' Cup]?** — Paris, Kentucky

I agree that there were some customer service issues at the last Breeders' Cup at Churchill Downs; some we caused [and] some problems were caused by others. Regardless of who caused the problem, it's not acceptable to me. The Breeders' Cup has asked for proposals from tracks interested in hosting the event in 2008, 2009, and 2010. We're still thinking about what, if anything, we might want to do at Churchill Down Incorporated tracks.

➤ **What is your take on slots as a savior [to racing]? Also, what was your take on the track bias at the [last Churchill Downs hosted] Breeders' Cup?** — California, Maryland

If we have to compete with another gambling operation for the consumer's dollar, then we should have the same rights as anyone else to offer those consumers whatever games our competitors can. That's only fair. And we are making the investment to incorporate alternative gaming into our Fair Grounds operation since we have been authorized to do so by state and city officials. As far as slots being racing's "savior," I doubt that very much. Ultimately, racing needs to stand on its own feet financially. To your second question, we do everything we can to prevent track bias and make each race a fair contest. And we're pretty good at it. But given all the variables involved, I doubt it's ever completely eliminated, even with synthetic track surface materials.

➤ **What new wagering products is Churchill Downs considering? Do you see comingling of Asian pools in the future?** — Lexington, Kentucky

We're looking at a number of different wagering products and hope to introduce some of those (pending, of course, the requisite legislation and regulatory approvals) in the next year. We are also looking at how to increase the level of internationalization of Thoroughbred racing, and comingling wagering pools is one thing we're considering.

➤ **Why did CDI spend hundreds of millions of dollars on renovation at Churchill Downs and the average customer is still sitting on rusted metal chairs?** — Louisville, Kentucky

I'll take a look tomorrow and if we have rusty chairs, we'll get them replaced. In fact, we're in the process of replacing about 7,000 folding chairs around the track. But, know what? I've been fortunate to attend a lot of different sporting events in my life and I've had the chance to stand in the infield at the Derby and sit in the most expensive seats. Please don't spread this around, but the infield's more fun! The great thing about our clubhouse renovation is that you don't need a big bank account to experience the new and improved areas. We have a brand new food court, two sports bars, and large simulcast wagering areas—in addition to our trackside seating areas—that are open to all patrons. If you want to spend a little extra to sit in one of the dining rooms, Millionaires Row, or go all out and rent one of the Jockey Club Suites, you can do that too.

➤ **[Please respond] to criticism that both Churchill and Magna (the industry leaders) have been too slow to embrace improved technology [regarding] synthetic surfaces?** — Davis, California

I can understand your perspective on synthetic racing surfaces, but if you look closely at the experiences of other tracks that have installed synthetic surfaces—and some of the issues they've faced—I think you'll agree that there are still a lot of unknowns. We'd like more than just two years of data—preferably data we collect on our own at one of our facilities—before determining whether synthetic surfaces are the way to go at all of our tracks or just Arlington Park.

➤ **After years, it looks like things may be becoming a little more towards making a buck or two [with Churchill Downs' stock]. Should I buy, sell, [or] hold?** — La Costa, California

My job, and that of every Churchill Downs Incorporated employee, is to try to increase the value of our shareholders' investment in the company. If we're successful in doing that, the value of the company should increase over time. It's against our company policy to give out investment advice, and I don't think the SEC would approve of that, either.

➤ **Millions of wagering dollars have been lost by tracks due to archaic, wait-in-line, on-track betting systems. Why continue to live with such massive losses when handheld account wagering systems (or something similar) are available for serious players, leaving the long lines and pari-mutuel clerks to the neophytes?** — Lexington, Kentucky

I like mutuel clerks. Great people. They are part of the wonderful experience of wagering at the track. But I think you correctly see the future in that people will increasingly adopt technology-based customer service solutions if and when they perceive that it's a better experience. That's why we're launching www.twinspires.com.

➤ **How about giving online players the ability to make deposits/ withdrawals at local banks rather than driving to Churchill?**
— Louisville, Kentucky

Interesting idea. The U.S. Department of the Treasury is currently working on new regulations related to how financial institutions can manage customer accounts related to online wagering. Let's see how that turns out, and then we can consider your idea.

➤ **What more can we expect out of the cooperation between CDI and Magna? Will you work together to get the most out of your stakes schedule and fit it more into a TV schedule?** — Wall, New Jersey

Both Churchill Downs Incorporated and Magna Entertainment Corp. are interested in using TV in different ways to promote racing to those who currently play the game and to those who have yet to find out how much fun our sport can be.

➤ **How would a potential bankruptcy of Magna Entertainment affect the industry? Would [CDI] be willing to buy MEC tracks?**
— Del Mar, California

It would be terribly disruptive. We're looking primarily at ways to grow our business without acquiring additional tracks. As a public company, we can't speak to any specific development plans, including potential acquisitions, until they reach a point of substantial completion. We are interested in it to take the bidding to a price where we can operate at a profit.

➤ **Like many bettors, I'd like to get the rebates formerly offered by Pinnacle in a legal way. Why are you not selling your signal to legal domestic operations like Premier Turf?** — Chicago, Illinois

Premier Turf is undergoing the due diligence investigation that we require of all ADW (advance deposit wagering) providers, including those that offer rebates. This is a primary function of TrackNet Media Group, which we launched with Magna Entertainment Corp. earlier this month.

TALKIN' HORSES
WITH
TOM HAMMOND

Tom Hammond, who went from being a $35-a-week racing reporter for a local radio station to one of the premier sports journalists in the business, dreamed of being a farm manager or racing his own Thoroughbred stable. A Lexington, Kentucky, native, Hammond graduated from the University of Kentucky with a master's degree in animal science. Among the events he has covered for NBC have been the Triple Crown races, Breeders' Cup World Championships, Olympic track and field, the World Ice Skating Championships, NBA and WNBA basketball, college and arena football, and Southeastern Conference basketball. Hammond participated in an online chat prior to his television coverage of the 2006 Kentucky Derby.

➤ **You had wanted to become a farm manager at first. How did you end up as a newscaster?** — Weston, Connecticut

As a teenager, I worked at several Central Kentucky horse farms, including Spendthrift. Then, to round out my practical equine experience, I worked at the racetrack for three summers. When I graduated from college, I couldn't get a very good job so, out of semidesperation, I went to graduate school. While in grad school, I began doing pedigree research for Tom Gentry. One of his friends, Dave Hooper, worked for the *Racing Form* and also had a fifteen-minute nightly radio show, giving race results. These were the days before Internet, TVG, and the information explosion. When the *Racing Form* transferred Hooper, Gentry suggested I take over the radio show. I'm sure I was awful, but I did take it over for the princely sum of $35 a week. Once I had that foot in the door, I guess I found my calling. I volunteered for every news and sports event the station had, moved to local TV for ten years, became a Thoroughbred sales announcer, and co-founded a video production company with Ron Mossotti that specialized in horses. In 1980 I began doing regional SEC basketball telecasts. In 1984 I was hired for the first Breeders' Cup on NBC and after that signed to an NBC contract for year-round events. Whew! Now you know more about me than you could ever have possibly wanted to know.

➤ **Please tell us about that one horse race you witnessed that stands above all others.** — Miami, Florida

It's tough to pick just one, but I can narrow it down to two. The first and, I guess, top race I have seen in person would be the Belmont Stakes in 1978. I was in the track announcer's booth at Belmont Park, standing next to my friend, the late Chic Anderson, as he called the race for both the track and TV. You know the story: Affirmed and Stevie Cauthen going for the Triple Crown against their rival Alydar. They engaged on the backstretch and raced head and head to the wire, Alydar taking a short lead, but Affirmed somehow willing himself to victory. It was thrilling and now in hindsight, even more so since that was our last Triple Crown winner. The other race that really thrilled me was the 1988 Breeders' Cup Distaff at Churchill Downs. Personal Ensign, in her final race, was trying to remain unbeaten against Winning Colors, who was returning to the track where she had her greatest moment, winning the Derby. A few yards from home, Personal Ensign seemed beaten—the streak ended—but again, somehow, she found a way to victory and entered the books with her perfect record.

➤ **I was wondering if you get caught up in having a favorite on race day?**
— Seattle, Washington

I guess I'm kind of old school as far as remaining neutral. I just think that the host should remain neutral, at least in appearance. But I have had plenty of experience with that in my career. Being a University of Kentucky grad and living in Lexington, everyone expects me to be partisan when broadcasting a UK game, but I'm just not. In fact, opposing fans think I am biased toward Kentucky, but UK fans think I bend over backwards to be unbiased and actually favor the other team. I figure that must put me somewhere in the middle. The same thing applies to Notre Dame football; since NBC does all the Irish home games, again, I just try to play it straight. Same with the Olympics when a U.S. athlete competes. So, I've had plenty of practice, and it's really not difficult to stay neutral in racing or anything else.

TALKIN' HORSES

TOM HAMMOND

➤ **You worked the horse sales for years. Do you miss it and is there any chance you would do them again?** — Nebo, Kentucky

I started as the sale announcer at Keeneland in the early 1970s while I was sports director at WLEX-TV in Lexington. I was hired by the legendary auctioneer George Swinebroad. I was able to supplement my television income (which wasn't much) and stay in Lexington, rather than bounce around the country trying to get to a bigger market. I stayed in the stand at Keeneland for fifteen years or so and became somewhat of a sales-announcing specialist, first adding the Ocala Breeders' Sales and gradually expanding till I was working at auctions in about a dozen states. But when I began doing network television—first on what is now Jefferson Pilot for SEC basketball and starting in 1984 with the first Breeders' Cup on NBC—I gave up the sales announcing. I really don't miss it that much, especially when I see the sales lasting two weeks at a time. Man, those sales can wear you out, so I doubt I'll return to that.

➤ **What makes a great jockey, and who are some of your favorites as far as riding skills, courage, and—most important—heart?**
— Atlanta, Georgia

When considering jockeys' winning percentages, you have to remember that the jockey can't get off and push. He or she still has to be on a horse that is capable of winning and then help them do just that. A baseball player is a star if he gets a hit 30 percent of the time. I have great admiration for the courage of each and every rider, whether they get a leg up at the Derby or are riding somewhere in the backwaters of racing. They put their life on the line every time they go to the track. That's why racing needs to make sure they are adequately insured. I have always admired jockeys who had a sense of pace, that clock in their head. Living in Kentucky, I saw Pat Day nearly every race, every day, and thought his ability to get a horse to relax, to save energy for later, was amazing. I marveled at the way Steve Cauthen and Cash Asmussen could go to Europe and effectively change racing with their ability to judge pace. I grew up watching Don Brumfield, Steve Brooks, et al., and remember seeing Eddie Arcaro, Bill Hartack, and all the great ones of that era. When I worked summers in New York [during] college, I used to enjoy talking to John L. Rotz, whom I considered a thinking man's jockey. I have great admiration for all of them.

➤ **What was the most exciting race you ever covered?**
— Pittsburgh, Pennsylvania

I think the greatest race I have covered at NBC would have to be the aforementioned 1988 Breeders' Cup Distaff, Personal Ensign over Winning Colors. As for the NBC coverage of the Triple Crown, it was such a thrill for a lifelong Kentuckian to host the Kentucky Derby that you can imagine the feeling I had in 2001. Then, the race was won by Monarchos, [who was] trained by John Ward, [who has been] a friend through high school, college, and beyond. Then, when Smarty Jones was going for the Triple Crown in the Belmont Stakes, the buildup was incredible. I think the whole country was paying attention and then stopped for a moment when the race was run. It reminded me of what it must have been like when Seabiscuit faced War Admiral. And last year, Afleet Alex winning the Preakness. As I said on the air, "breathtaking."

➤ **It's nice to see and hear about the human side of racing on the big telecasts, but very little time is devoted to showing the horses. Is there any chance that for this year's Derby we will see more of the horses?** — Syosset, New York

One thing you will never see on NBC is the shortening of the post parade; in fact, we usually devote so much time to it that we are playing catch-up for a while. I have always felt, especially at the Breeders' Cup, where you are dealing with so many races, that every horse deserves a mention and a bit of information, and often the post parade is the only time they get that mention. I am not sure how other television entities feel about it, but that's my take. You have to remember that these telecasts, especially the Derby, are geared to attract a general audience. To your average viewer, the horses all look pretty much the same, but they can identify with the human stories and, thus, have a rooting interest. Ideally, the telecast is a mix of human and equine stories.

➤ **Is there really a future for the industry on TV in the run-ups before the Triple Crown and Breeders' Cup, or should the industry pursue other available media outlets to present its product to viewers?** — Berea, Ohio

ESPN has been the victim of some bad luck with Kentucky Derby prep races being cut short because the event preceding it ran long, and it has happened to us in the past as well. Anytime you are dealing with live sporting events, that risk exists, and there is really no solution that I know. Are you old enough to remember the "Heidi" game when NBC cut away from an AFL football game to show the movie and the audience missed a fantastic finish? You have to see every event to its conclusion, and you can't slide post time much for a televised race because of all the simulcast betting, and so forth. ESPN doesn't actually produce those racing shows. The NTRA purchases the time and does the production, so I don't know if that gives them less leverage or not. I doubt it; I just think it's bad luck. I think television is essential to the health of racing, and the NTRA—when it was founded—made increased television exposure one of its priorities. I don't know of any other media outlet that could take its place. Even though viewership of all sports on television is declining due to the expansion of cable, the Internet, and so forth, it is still the only medium where you can get that many people viewing a specific event. That's why television sports still command huge rights fee payments and huge charges for commercial time on the broadcasts.

➤ **What is your most memorable Derby, and were you there?**

— Richmond, Virginia

Because I was doing the network broadcast for the first time in 2001, that Derby would have to be up there, but there are some other candidates. In 2004, a half-hour or so before we went on the air, a cloudburst hit Churchill Downs— wind, hail, rain. The track looked like a lake, and I was up to my ankles in water. I didn't think there was any way we could get on the air; all the equipment would be shot. But we did, and Smarty Jones made it memorable as well. 1964 [was] the first Derby I saw in person. I had seen Northern Dancer win the Blue Grass Stakes at Keeneland and followed him to Churchill Downs to see him win the Derby. In fact, when he went for the Triple Crown, I was there to see him lose to Quadrangle, I believe. I had gone to New York for a summer job. The race was run at Aqueduct while they were rebuilding Belmont. I remember seeing Chris Schenkel in the paddock for the broadcast, little dreaming that one day I would be out there in front of the camera. In 1973, though there were doubts about Secretariat going a mile and a quarter before the race, at its conclusion you got the idea that you had witnessed greatness. In 1974, [I was at] the 100th Derby and the record crowd there to see Cannonade win the roses.

➤ **What do you do to prepare for the Kentucky Derby presentation? Do you have a favorite Derby moment? Who is your pick for the Run for the Roses this year?** — Cedar Rapids, Iowa

I'll take the questions in reverse order, beginning with a cop out, not picking a winner: [I have] three reasons. I would just hate for some owner or trainer that I have to deal with later to be upset about me picking or not picking their horse. Were I an analyst, I would expect to make a selection but, as host, I think I need to remain impartial. I'm just old-fashioned that way. As for the other two reasons, my past performances of picking winners are awful, and in this year's Derby, I'm totally at a loss. The preparations for a Derby broadcast really extend year-round. I don't feel horse racing is something you can cram for in the days before a broadcast. It has to be an ongoing process. So, even while I'm doing other sports, I'm keeping an eye on racing. It was made a bit tougher this year since I spent a month at the Olympics in Torino, Italy. As the major preps unfold, I try to identify the leading horses and all the relevant stories. I compile a file on each horse and on Derby history. We have a stats man who provides information, and then Derby week, I hit the barns to talk with the connections. I will have spoken with the producer, Sam Flood, and director, David Michaels, as we get closer, so we're all on the same page. In the last couple of days before the race, I'll confer with the feature producers and hash out a script, then add the narration. On Friday, we'll have a brief rehearsal and then, that night, a production meeting with about fifty people as we go over each aspect of the broadcast. Then on Saturday, I'll join a couple of hundred others from NBC for the actual broadcast, and usually about ten minutes in [to the broadcast] all hell breaks loose and we fly by the seat of our pants.

➤ **Which two horses—a colt and a filly—were the best you ever saw and why?** — Rochester, New York

For the reasons I've already mentioned, I'd have to say Secretariat and Personal Ensign. I didn't see Man o' War, but the old-timers at the track thought he was the best. One of those was Hall of Fame trainer Sherill Ward, for whom I worked during three summers. In fact, he told me that he was so taken by the length of his stride during a race at Belmont, that before they harrowed the track he went out with his pocketknife and made two notches in the rail to mark the length of his stride. The mention of Mr. Ward brings three other horses to mind that I admired. [One was] the great Forego, trained in his early career by Mr. Ward. [Another was] Kelso, who was racing while I was working at the track in the summers. And a filly that I helped groom in the summer at Belmont and Saratoga, Indian Sunlite. She was a huge gray, owned by George Humphrey. We called her the "big gray rabbit." She won several stakes in New York and Florida.

➤ **Do you think this is the year we'll finally see a Triple Crown winner? Any ideas why it hasn't happened for so long?** — Williamstown, New Jersey

I think the answer to why we have not had a Triple Crown winner for so long is a complex one, and one that includes just some plain old bad luck, since we have had some close calls in recent years. Chiefly, I think the American Thoroughbred is not as durable as he once was and [is] not bred for classic distances. In the heyday of the private stable, horses were bred with classic races in mind. Today, they are often bred with the sales ring in mind. American racing and breeding has been built increasingly around speed, not so much for a horse that can get a mile and a quarter. Add to that the fact that many of the best American bloodlines have been [exported] to Europe, the Middle East, and Japan in recent years. So, when you ask a horse to go classic distances on three different surfaces in a short span of time, it's a difficult task for our modern Thoroughbred. Ben Jones used to run in the Derby Trial on Tuesday and run in the Derby on Saturday. You wouldn't do that today. In many ways, the Derby is the tricky one. Because the field is so unwieldy, often with unreasonable speed, the best horse doesn't win. One other thought: In the past, the Triple Crown races were the top races in terms of money and prestige and, if you had a horse good enough, they danced every dance. Now, you see trainers passing one of the races and coming at you with a fresh horse later.

➤ **Did you approach the classics in 2002, 2003, and 2004 with any special preparation personally in the event of a Triple Crown victory?**
— Florence, South Carolina

If you know that you could be a part of history you need to think in advance of how you might handle it. After all, people could be listening to those tapes 100 years from now, so you better be able to match the moment with proper commentary. My style has often been to first let the moment play because if you have set it up properly, there is little you can say [that will be as] eloquent as the pictures. So, yes, in those possible Triple Crown years, I did have an outline of what I might say if it happened, much as I did in some of those Olympic moments [I covered]. You can't script it, but you can certainly give it some thought.

➤ **Who were your influences in broadcasting, in horse racing broadcasting?** — Andover, Massachusetts

Growing up in Kentucky, I had the luxury of listening to a couple of excellent broadcasters that might not be familiar nationally. I had no idea I would ever be behind a microphone, but just listening to them had to shape my style. Both Claude Sullivan and Cawood Ledford, who have passed away now, were among them. I was able to work with Cawood after I got into the business. The horse racing part of it, the sales announcing and broadcasting the races, had to be influenced by the late J.B. Faulconer, broadcaster and longtime P.R. director at Keeneland. He was one of my mentors, as was Dick Enberg once I got to the level of network television.

➤ **What would you name as the two or three greatest races or calls of your career?** — Portland, Oregon

Certainly the 1988 Breeders' Cup Distaff with Personal Ensign and Winning Colors and the Classic that same year with Alysheba charging out of the darkness. A couple of Cigar's Breeders' Cup Classics rank up there, along with Sunday Silence versus Easy Goer. The 2004 Belmont Stakes with the Triple Crown on the line for Smarty Jones, and my very first NBC Derby, with my friend John Ward winning with Monarchos in 2001. But perhaps most of all, [my favorite was] the very first Breeders' Cup Classic, the rough stretch run with Slew o' Gold, Gate Dancer, and Wild Again. It was the perfect conclusion to the kind of day John Gaines had envisioned when he devised the Breeders' Cup. As we went off the air, Gaines saw me and gave me a bear hug, then Michael Weissman, executive producer of NBC sports, said to me, "We didn't realize until this week that we had a real broadcaster on our hands. Would you be interested in doing others sports for NBC, starting with NFL football?" My career was set.

TALKIN' HORSES
WITH
STEVE HASKIN

Steve Haskin, senior correspondent for the The Blood-Horse *magazine and an authority on the Triple Crown, has been the most frequent guest host on "Talkin' Horses." Haskin is an award-winning Turf writer renowned for his Kentucky Derby commentary, with weekly articles, Classic Spotlights, and the "Derby Dozen" all found on bloodhorse.com's special Triple Crown Mania section. Previously, during his nearly three decades at* Daily Racing Form, *Steve made a name with his "Derby Watch" columns. Haskin—who has won five Red Smith Awards for his Kentucky Derby coverage—is the author of* Horse Racing's Holy Grail: The Epic Quest for the Kentucky Derby; Tales from the Triple Crown; *and biographies of Dr. Fager, John Henry, and Kelso, all published by Eclipse Press. Haskin's frequent appearances on "Talkin' Horses" are usually timed to coincide with major Triple Crown races or the Breeders' Cup World Championships. Because many questions posed to Haskin during these chats are centered on specific horses and races, the questions and answers chosen for this book are those pertaining to Haskin's industry observations and opinions and those that are historical.*

➤ **[Should] the Triple Crown format be altered (e.g., shorten the distances and spread out the races)?** — Lutherville, Maryland

Although many people seem to be favoring that, I'm definitely not one of them. The Triple Crown has become an institution, something historic. Winning all three races is supposed to be extremely difficult, reserved for those few who have the greatness to accomplish it. It didn't prevent Seattle Slew and Affirmed from going on to have great four-year-old campaigns. If you make it easier and more horses start sweeping it, no one will care any longer and mainstream America [will lose interest]. Besides, people in general have a very short attention span. If you spread out the races, by the time the Belmont comes along, a lot of people will have lost interest. Also, many things can happen in between, and you'll find more Derby and Preakness winners who don't even make it to the Belmont. One more point, the majority of Triple Crown sweeps occurred in years when you had one great horse, and the rest as a whole were ordinary (Affirmed and Alydar were an exception). The Triple Crown fields back in the 1930s and 1940s were all pretty small. Now, with horses having to earn their way in to the Derby, you have to beat a full field of stakes horses, and the race is harder on the participants than in the past. But look how close so many horses have come since 1997. Sure, we'd love to see a Triple Crown winner, but be careful what you wish for. As long as no one does it, people will flock to Belmont, hoping to be part of history. Once a horse sweeps the Triple Crown, people will say, "OK, it's been done; now it's not that big a deal any more."

➤ **Do you think there is too much emphasis on the breakdowns of the horses during nationally televised races?** — Springfield, Pennsylvania

Not at all. It's a dark side of this sport that you cannot ignore. You have to address it and pour your heart out over it, and inform the public what happened and what is going to happen. But I'm not for showing it ad nauseam or showing anything too graphic. After all, racing on television does not need shock value. Every shocking sight is another nail in the coffin in terms of driving people away from the sport. I believe we have more animal lovers in racing than ever before. Just look at Barbaro. Racing got more publicity from his injury and subsequent death than any from any race, horse, or event in memory by far.

➤ **Will [artificial racing surfaces] earn industry-wide acceptance or, after a multiyear experiment, go the way of Astroturf?** — St. Louis, Missouri

Artificial surfaces no doubt will go on to earn industry-wide acceptance, even though the majority of the tracks who have them rushed into it without studying it sufficiently. There is still a lot of changing, tweaking, and experimenting with them. That should have been done before putting horses over them in competition. Only if horses continue to be injured on them will they go the way of Astroturf. That will render them useless. But as long as studies show they cut down dramatically on the number of fatal injuries, more tracks will opt to use them, partly due to pressure. As for the Triple Crown races,

STEVE HASKIN

the day they go to synthetic surfaces is the day we can throw away the history books, because racing as it was will cease to exist. Thoroughbreds were meant to run on natural surfaces, not rubbish, and I mean that in the literal sense, not the derogatory sense. We will never know what a true great horse is anymore if they have to run over tires and balloons.

➤ **[Is it] fair that most Eclipse awards go to Breeders' Cup [World Championship] winners without consideration of major stakes races over the rest of the year?** — Louisville, Kentucky

I definitely feel that it has hurt our sport. I love the Breeders' Cup. I enjoy it more than the Derby. I love the whole international aspect of it and seeing all the European journalists and horsemen. But, yes, there is too much emphasis on the Breeders' Cup races, which have turned everything else into prep races. Just look at the conservative approach by so many trainers this year. We lost Curlin in the Travers, Street Sense in the Belmont, Any Given Saturday in the Jockey Club Gold Cup, all because the trainers wanted to have a fresher horse come Breeders' Cup day. And we do not give the [winners of] races early in the year, such as the Santa Anita Handicap, the Metropolitan Mile, the Hollywood Gold Cup, and so forth, enough thought when voting for champions. It's become a mindless task for the most part. Voters need to start looking at the year as a whole and not just concentrate on one day of racing. Yes, it's supposed to be the World Championships, but it doesn't always work out that way, and you have to look beyond horses who win a BC race and nothing else.

➤ **Smarty Jones and Afleet Alex were clearly superior to the rest of their cohorts, yet neither won the Triple Crown. Is it still possible [to win the Triple Crown]?** — Cambridge, Massachusetts

Yes, it's definitely possible. Either one of them had the talent to do it; they each were physically ready to do it, but only one thing for each of them stood in their way. Smarty was too rank early and was ganged up on by three talented horses and three talented riders, all of whom I feel compromised their own chances of winning by pushing Smarty into a suicidal third quarter in :22⅘. The only reason Birdstone won was because Edgar Prado was the only jockey riding for second. Afleet Alex, in my opinion, "bounced"—as the speed gurus say—off his unnecessary route in the Arkansas Derby, and was a bit too close to that torrid pace in the Derby. Then again, who knows if his bounce in the Derby didn't set him up for his huge wins in the Preakness and Belmont. It just wasn't his day. But things might have been different had he won the Arkansas Derby by two lengths under a strong hand ride instead of being whipped several times with a six-length lead. Then again, Jeremy Rose's rides in the Preakness and Belmont were two of the best I've ever seen, so who really knows?

➤ **What do you think racing needs to do to its image to appeal to a larger audience and increase its fan base?** — Lexington, Kentucky

We need a much more aggressive marketing campaign, something clever other than a slogan. What good is a slogan if only racing fans hear it? We have to sell not only the equine athletes, but the jockeys, as the Japanese did with Yutaka Take. Having contests is fine, but having them only on racing Web sites is not going to do it. You have to make them public, like the old Irish Sweepstakes. Get the fans involved on ESPN and ESPN.com, in newspapers across the country. Give the sports fan, not just the racing fan, a chance to participate and win money. We have to get them involved in our sport and follow our athletes. We also need a governing body, and maybe a commissioner, to set rules and penalties, as they have in other sports. Right now, each racetrack governs itself and that won't cut it with the public. As long as there is no one to make rules, racing will remain splintered and at war with itself. To have TVG and HRTV competing, and all the infighting that goes on, is self destructive. Imagine if the original thirteen states governed themselves with no Congress to vote and set down rules. We'd be singing "God Save the Queen." (*Yes, I know that's an extreme comparison, but it sounded good.*)

➤ **How do you evaluate the current conflicts of various racing jurisdictions and their respective states?** — Williamsburg, Virginia

They're not only current [conflicts], they go way back. Racing has always had jurisdictions with their own rules, while keeping a closed eye and ear to the rest of the sport. Racing is a fragmented sport, with everyone out for themselves, regardless of the ramifications. [Unless] racing can get unified, which I don't see unless some messiah shows up, it will to be every track for itself. We need uniform drug rules and a governing body to make rules and issue penalties.

TALKIN' HORSES

STEVE HASKIN

➤ **If you can name only one strong handicapping method for a novice, what angle would you suggest?** — Delta, British Columbia

It's tough narrowing it down to only one, and it depends if you mean a particular handicapping angle or a system like Beyer or the Speed Sheets. One of my favorite angles was seen in the Breeders' Cup World Championships, and that is horses showing speed going a mile and then dropping back into a sprint, as Silver Train did. I also like [to see a] second race blinkers on, allowing a horse a wake-up race [the] first time with blinkers. As for a system, I believe Ragozin and Thoro-Graph are more thought out and far superior to Beyers, but they cost money. If you use the Beyers, make sure it's only one of several tools. Start by going to the paddock as often as possible and make mental notes of what you see, and then equate that to the horse's performance.

➤ **How loyal are you if you have backed a horse leading to the Derby but know you won't get much of a price come the big day?** — Louisville, Kentucky

I don't back horses monetarily in the futures, but I will bet on Derby Day. When it comes to money, I'm not very loyal to favorites. I will always try to find an overlay, some horse who will be a big value play. I'm not looking to make $100 in the Derby. I'm mostly a straight win bettor, so I need to find a horse long enough to give me a shot at making some big bucks.

➤ **Mr. Haskin, can you tell me your three or four most important factors you use to handicap a top race like the Derby?** — Midlothian, Texas

How the horses look and train (I like looking at how their coats change in the days leading up the race), class (who they've been running against), how much improvement they're showing, and pedigree. I'll add speed figures, and I like to see a horse who has been looked in the eye and responded to the challenge.

➤ **Why has the twenty-horse field become the norm? Often the best horse doesn't win, merely the luckiest who got the best trip. With the Belmont, and to a lesser extent the Preakness, you can be fairly certain that the horse who won was the best horse.** — Chapel Hill, North Carolina

The twenty-horse limit was introduced when there were twenty-three horses in the 1973 Derby. The Derby is so big and generates so much revenue, Churchill Downs is not going to keep horses out, so I doubt very strongly you're going to see the number lowered. It's not a true race on most occasions, but no one wants to deprive people of their only chance to run in the Derby. The uncertainty of it, because of the big field, makes it all the more fascinating. Ideally, it should be a one-gate field of fourteen. But that's not going to happen.

> **If you could only write about one thing you witnessed during your coverage of racing, what might that one event be?** — Tuscaloosa, Alabama

Wow, you mean one article? That's encompassing quite a lot. Oddly enough, just off the top of my head, I might have to say something that didn't take place on the track but in an arena. When Cigar was brought to Madison Square Garden by a police escort after his retirement and paraded and was honored at the National Horse Show, it was as emotional moment as I can remember. When Bill Mott walked him around the arena in the dark, with just a spotlight on him and the horse as a single trumpet played "Auld Lang Syne," it literally brought me to tears. I get choked up just thinking about it. And they had Bill Cosby there, and the New York Knicks cheerleaders, and the Clydesdales, and members of the Rangers and Knicks—it was a very special moment.

> **Would you enlighten me as to the importance of Native Dancer as a sire in Thoroughbred racing?** — Garland, Texas

Consider this: The Native Dancer sire line, mainly through Mr. Prospector, has produced Kentucky Derby winners Majestic Prince, Affirmed, Genuine Risk, Alysheba, Unbridled, Strike the Gold, Thunder Gulch, Fusaichi Pegasus, Real Quiet, Grindstone, Monarchos, War Emblem, Funny Cide, Smarty Jones, and Street Sense. And Barbaro traces to Native Dancer through Mr. Prospector on the female side. You can't get much more dominant than that.

> **As a traditionalist, what's harder to see happen: [Naming of the Kentucky Derby] Presented by Yum! [Brands] or synthetic surfaces?**
> — Lexington, Kentucky

Wow, that is a tough one. Of course, synthetic surfaces have a much more profound effect on the sport. I'm not against anything that prevents or lessens breakdowns, but I don't know that putting in a superior dirt track like the ones at Churchill Downs or Fair Grounds wouldn't have the same effect. And it's still too

STEVE HASKIN

early to say that synthetic surfaces are the cure-all. They have plenty of injuries and breakdowns that we never hear of, but at least the catastrophic ones seem to be down, and that's what's important. I just feel more time should have been spent studying them to avoid what happened at Del Mar and especially Santa Anita. As for Yum! Brands, what can I say? Tradition has been replaced by profits. As a journalist who writes for a publication that wants the Yum! [Brands] mentioned, my only recourse is to try to avoid mentioning the name Kentucky Derby altogether. But sometimes, that's not possible. I'm not against sponsorship, and I'm not going to criticize Churchill Downs for making money at the expense of tradition, no matter how ridiculous something sounds.

➤ **Would you give us your top three horses in the last decade at 1¼ miles on the dirt?** — Westerville, Ohio

Let's go ten years, since 1998. I'll say, in no particular order, Invasor, Skip Away, and Tiznow, only because they excelled at 10 furlongs on several occasions and for more than one year. So, I wouldn't include horses like Ghostzapper who only ran that far one time. I would rank Point Given, Barbaro, Street Sense, and Bernardini up there as well, but they didn't race at four. Curlin would join the top three with a big year in 2008. He's practically there already. He has the potential to be one of the greats.

➤ **Steve, which race is harder to win, the Kentucky Derby (with a twenty-horse field) or the Belmont with the 1½-mile distance at the end of a grueling campaign? Which horse was better, Smarty [Jones] or [Afleet] Alex, each losing one of those races by one length?** — Matawan, New Jersey

I believe the Derby is the hardest race to win, which is why the best horse usually doesn't. There are simply too many ways to lose, and you have to be extremely lucky. The Belmont is only hard to win if it exposes your weakness, which is generally the inability to settle and relax. Funny Cide and Smarty Jones both lost for that reason. Charismatic was too close to a strong pace. It would have been hard for War Emblem to win even if he hadn't stumbled at the start. If Afleet Alex had won the Derby, the Triple Crown would have been a piece of cake because you could do anything with him. I believe the main reason he lost the Derby was because his race in the Arkansas Derby was too good. Jeremy Rose shouldn't have allowed him to win by eight lengths and definitely shouldn't have hit him several times with the whip, with the horse having to come back and peak in three weeks. I think that took just enough of the edge off him to account for the one length he was beaten. I really can't compare Smarty to Alex. They both were spectacular horses in their own way and had greatness stamped all over them had they stayed around. I think Alex was the more exciting of the two to watch because of his tremendous turn of foot.

➤ **What things do you foresee in the next fifteen years in the horse racing industry that will have a major impact on the sport?** — Lake Forest, Illinois

Interesting question. I think you'll see major changes in the Breeders' Cup, possibly holding the event in a foreign country. If they're correct, it'll become a festival of racing. But they're going to need to do more than just keep adding races. They have to make it festive and get the whole world interested. I would love to say the Breeders' Cup will be run every other year at Hialeah, but that is dreaming. A negative change will be the further demise of racetracks. Who knows, maybe you'll be able to bet on football games and other sports at the racetrack. Maybe we'll have an Eclipse Award for Artificial Surface Horse of the Year for horses who race exclusively on artificial surfaces. This will keep them separated from dirt horses when trying to determine year-end honors.

➤ **Why are some horses never the same when they return from Dubai?**
— Murfreesboro, Tennessee

I don't know that they're never the same. Some take longer to get over the trip than others. The first World Cup winner, Cigar, was back in top form and winning stakes three months later, and there have been many since. English Channel and Honey Ryder both ran terribly there but were back in full force by summer. It's a long trip for a horse, especially early in the year when they're just coming back off a layoff. Sacrificing three months or more out of the year is the price one pays for the lure of big bucks. If it turns out to be a bust, then you've accomplished nothing other than to give up a quarter of the year or longer.

➤ **[Will we] ever get rid of handicap racing?** — Chicago, Illinois

Handicap racing is basically a dinosaur that is being kept alive. Racing people forget that handicaps were essential in the old days in order to bring a field of horses together and make the race competitive because there was only win, place, and show wagering, and one daily double. So, the betting public needed a fair shot to cash a ticket when you had an overwhelming favorite. Now, with exactas, trifectas, superfectas, late daily doubles, and pick 3s, 4s, 5s, and 6s you can use the favorite to your advantage and no longer need handicaps to make the fields equal. Also, back then, racing was a popular sport and pretty much sold itself. Nowadays, racing has an identity problem, along with its other problems, and requires more aggressive marketing. It's hard to sell your stars to the public when you try to get them beat. It's OK to have handicap racing in claiming, allowance, and maybe [grade] III stakes to keep the entries full, but they should be eliminated from [grade] II and especially [grade] I stakes.

➤ **Along with pedigree, what do you look for in determining whether a three-year-old will stretch out effectively in distance from his two-year-old sprint races?** — Bethpage, New York

I look at him physically. If he's a blocky, short-coupled horse, he might not stretch out despite his pedigree. Nowadays, as long as a horse has some stamina in his female family and looks the part physically, he should be able to go the mile and a quarter because we don't have too many horses left who are inundated with stamina, so most of the horses in the Derby aren't true stayers.

➤ **[Regarding] the lightly trained Derby horse vs. the three-year-old who has been more heavily run, is conditioning enough, or should they be getting more racing experience before Churchill?** — Mamaroneck, New York

Until a lightly raced horse—with only four career starts or only two starts at three or unraced at two—wins the Derby, I favor the horses who have experience and have been toughened. I prefer a prep three weeks out as opposed to four, but in a case like Giacomo, or Baffert's and Whittingham's Santa Anita Derby horses, if they have several long, fast works, that should help toughen them for the rigors of the Derby. Remember, Giacomo had been racing steadily for seven months prior to the Derby. Also important is using the race before the Derby as a prep more than anything else. Look what happened to three horses—Afleet Alex, Bellamy Road, and Bandini—who won their preps by a pole. The key is to peak on Derby Day, not three or four weeks before. You want the Derby to start you on a roll. It's no coincidence that the last three Preakness winners all romped after winning the Derby. Look how much easier Charismatic's and Real

Quiet's Preakness wins were compared to the Derby. If you go into the Derby the right way, it actually moves you up for the Preakness.

➤ **Which horse was the best you have ever seen?** — Hanover Park, Illinois

For an entire career, racing at two, three, and four, it was Spectacular Bid, simply because he could do everything. He set records, carried weight, won in the East, West, Midwest, and South at any distance up to a mile and a quarter, and defeated top horses. And how about this little known stat: In his walkover, he closed his final two quarters in :24 flat and :24⅕. That is sensational for a race, but a walkover? Also, I have to mention Dr. Fager for the single greatest season ever, and Secretariat and Damascus as the greatest three-year-olds I have ever seen. I also have to mention Forego as the most extraordinary horse I've seen. His feat of winning the 1½-mile Woodward, the seven-furlong Vosburgh, and the two-mile Jockey Club Gold Cup in a seven-week period was one of the most remarkable accomplishments ever. That year he won at one and one-half mile and two miles and was voted champion sprinter.

➤ **What can we do to breed soundness back into Thoroughbreds while still keeping their commercial value high enough?** — Frankfort, Kentucky

It's too late to start breeding soundness into Thoroughbreds because there is so little of it left. What we have to do is convince the racetracks to make their surfaces safer on horses and stop obsessing over fast times and track records. [Artificial surfaces], whether you like [them] or not, should help keep horses sounder and racing longer.

➤ **Is the "Dosage Theory" dead? Have we entered an era when inherent stamina is not a fundamental Derby-winning characteristic?**
— New York, New York

I think the word "dead" pretty much sums it up. There are simply way too many young stallions, many of them sons of prominent stallions like Storm Cat, and the chef-de-race list has not been updated to account for all these new stallions. Therefore, the dosage index figures are now way out of whack and have no bearing on a horse's ability to go a distance. Most of the old stamina/class stallions have faded into the fifth generation and have no bearing on his dosage any longer. The new formula is pretty simple: Forget the sire and check

STEVE HASKIN

out the dam for stamina influences. It seems nowadays that any stallion can sire a Derby winner as long as there is sufficient stamina in the dam. One of the reasons is that there are very few stamina-oriented stallions left, so no one stallion has that much of an advantage over another.

> **If I don't go into journalism in the horse racing field, I plan to go into equine business—breeding, bloodstock adviser, [or] something [else]. Could you suggest some [good schools] you know are successful?** — Concordia, Kansas

My advice is not to concentrate on journalism in the horse racing field as much as equine studies. Take it from me; you do not need to major in journalism unless writing is your passion and your priority. I did not attend college, going straight to Wall Street where I became a stock trader. I gave it all up to work as a copy boy for the old *Morning Telegraph* and it was only years later I found out I could write. Keep pursuing writing, but it is passion, knowledge, and the ability to tell a story that will serve you better as a writer in the racing field. You can always [earn a] double major in English and animal science and see how that works out. That's what my daughter did at Rutgers University, which has an excellent equine science program. Also, look into the University of Arizona.

> **During your coverage at Churchill the week of the Derby you always seem to comment on the "beautiful coat" of the horses you favor. Do you have some handicapping theory on coats?** — Moorpark, California

Believe me, it's not my theory. A radiant, dappled coat is a sign of good health and a happy horse, and that normally equates to a good performance if he's good enough, of course. In 2003 I could see Atswhatimtalknbout's coat blossom day by day after a skin rash until he looked spectacular. He finished a fast-closing fourth and may have been [the best horse of the group]. Must have been his name that got him beat. Of course, there are horses with beautiful coats who don't run well, but it's still a good tool in trying to find a horse who is going to run big.

> **Please give me your opinion of two-year-old first time starters on Lasix and bumping at the start of races.** — Syosset, New York

You hit a real sore spot with the first one. I've always been befuddled by that one. It just shows how totally inconsistent this sport is in everything it does, and that is because we have no ruling body to make, well, rules. Why does an older horse have to bleed before he or she can get Lasix when almost all two-year-olds get it? When did they bleed? In a workout? All of them? It's ridiculous. In regard to the bumping, if there indeed is more bumping, it could be because jocks know they're not going to get DQ'd [disqualified] for doing it ... at least not 99 percent of the time. Either that, or today's jocks are not as skilled as the ones of the past in getting a horse to break in a straight line. If they DQ a few of these, you'll see jocks a lot more awake in the gate.

➤ **Do you believe [any horses] won the races that they did due to their particular jockey's style?** — Franklin, North Carolina

I can remember more top jocks who did not fit a horse's style. I thought Gary Stevens was the perfect fit for Silver Charm. Jerry Bailey fit almost every horse, especially Cigar. And look at the roll he went on with Skip Away after taking over that mount. If he had ridden Skip Away throughout his career, the horse would have shattered Cigar's earnings mark. I thought Pat Day was a perfect fit for Lady's Secret. No one could nurse a horse on the lead like Day, and those two were a great team. Grass is another story because a horse can get into trouble a lot easier. So, it's more hit and miss. You're going to have more good rides and bad rides, or I should say good trips and bad trips.

➤ **You [wrote] an article on my Hall of Fame grandfather, trainer Max Hirsch, who trained Assault as a three-year-old through the Triple Crown, which he won in 1946. Could you [tell the story]? (Bill Hirsch)** — Floral Park, New York

Just so you'll know, your father trained my all-time favorite filly, Gallant Bloom. I was crazy about her and couldn't wait to visit her at King Ranch whenever I went to Lexington. The reason your grandfather had so many tough horses was because he culled all the soft horses early on. By training his horses hard, he was able to separate the ones who could withstand his training and the ones who couldn't. Many trainers back then trained that way. But they're much more conservative now. The closest we have now is Bob Baffert. Assault had a clubfoot and most trainers now wouldn't have anything to do with him. Your grandfather ran Assault in the Wood Memorial, which was two weeks before the Derby. He won that and then ran in the Derby Trial over a deep, muddy track, four days before the Derby, finishing fourth. That served as his

Derby tightener, and he came back and won the Derby and the Triple Crown. What people don't know is that, because he [fought] life and death to hold off Lord Boswell in the Preakness, he wasn't even the favorite in the Belmont. After sweeping the Triple Crown, Max ran him back two weeks later in the Dwyer, which he won easily. After losing six straight, finishing in the money in five of them, he won seven in a row, carrying as much as 135 and 133 pounds.

➤ **Which horse has disappointed you the most in terms of pedigree for the Derby?** — Troy, New York

That's an interesting and unique question. I'd like to use the word "surprised" rather than disappointed. All pedigrees have something there to give a horse credentials if you go back far enough. Many people were shocked Smarty Jones won the Derby, but pedigrees have changed dramatically, and you can't label a horse a sprinter any longer. I was surprised Bold Forbes won the Derby, but that was mainly because of how fast he was at two and how he looked like he was going to be strictly a sprinter. His sire, Irish Castle, was a fast horse who looked to be a sire of speed horses. But Bold Forbes did have stamina in his female family. Still, I would have thought you were crazy had you told me when he was two that he'd win the Derby.

➤ **[With respect to] the distance of the Belmont, is it better to be on the lead or a closer? If [it's] an early speed horse, who is the best one?**
— Kenosha, Wisconsin

It all depends on how relaxed a horse is. It's always better to be in the hunt at Belmont as long as your horse is nice and relaxed and you can keep a little bit of a loose rein on him. Smarty Jones and Funny Cide were never able to relax and that is what did them in, not a lack of stamina. Had Smarty been able to relax, he would have romped in the Belmont, in my opinion.

➤ **Why does the Horse of the Year not reward the animal who did the most for the total industry [such as Afleet Alex]?** — Barboursville, West Virginia

Because Horse of the Year is looked upon by most as an award given to the horse who accomplished the most on the track and is not based on the publicity he generated for the sport. Afleet Alex has indeed done more for racing, and in my mind is worthy of Horse of the Year. But Saint Liam was a grade I winner all year and won the championship race, and that is what most voters will look at. There are no rules as to the criteria for Horse of the Year, so it is up to each individual to vote the way they see fit. I believe many will agree with you and vote for Alex because of what he did for racing, and they have every right to. He is a special horse and did enough on the track to be a deserving Horse of the Year. But if the majority of voters vote the way they did last year, under similar circumstances, then Saint Liam probably will get it.

➤ **[The excitement over] Seabiscuit, Smarty Jones, and Barbaro [show] America is by no means done with horse racing. You'd think experiencing an incredible rush over two minutes would be tailor-made for modern America.** — Atlanta, Georgia

It is tailor-made for modern America, but it's not something that perpetuates itself. People are spoiled, and they want fairy-tale stories all the time. But when one does come along, they seem to embrace it more each time. Let's not forget Funny Cide; that story rocked New York like few sports stories have. Smarty Jones, Barbaro, and Funny Cide all were linked to the Triple Crown, and once that is over, people feel the great story lines are over until the following year. Seabiscuit was a different era when horses sold themselves, especially those with longevity. More than Triple Crown heroes [we need] the Seabiscuits, Kelsos, John Henrys, and Foregos so that people can latch on to them. The longer they do, the longer they are exposed to the excitement and beauty of Thoroughbred racing.

➤ **Has a horse that you thought looked poor in terms of appearance and works heading up to the Derby ever really surprised you with a huge performance?** — Philadelphia, Pennsylvania

The first one that comes to my mind would be Thunder Gulch in 1995. There was nothing about his physical appearance I didn't like, but when he worked in company with a filly, he continuously leaned in throughout his run down the stretch and refused to pass her. That was one work that I looked at in a negative light that obviously had no bearing on the colt's performance. Sometimes, in a case like Grindstone, I could not form an opinion because he came out every morning in the dark and I never once got a good look at the horse. I cannot say that any horse who looked poorly came back to run a big race in the Derby.

TALKIN' HORSES
WITH
SANDY HATFIELD

According to the Three Chimneys Farm Web site, the duties of stallion manager Sandy Hatfield consist of "one part stallion care, one part breeding supervisor, one part ambassador and press agent for the Three Chimneys stallions, and one part ambassador for the horse business to the thousands of visitors hosted at Three Chimneys Farm each year." Hatfield joined Three Chimneys in early 2000 after previously serving in a similar capacity at Gainsborough Farm, Calumet Farm, and North Ridge Farm. Among the stallions under her care at the Midway, Kentucky, farm are Kentucky Derby winner Smarty Jones, Dynaformer, War Chant, Rahy, and Flower Alley. Other popular stallions that previously stood at the farm were the late Seattle Slew and Kentucky Derby winner Point Given, who relocated to Japan. Hatfield served as the president of the Kentucky Thoroughbred Farm Managers' Club for 2000. A native of Oklahoma, Hatfield majored in animal science at Oklahoma State University and Murray State University. In addition to her professional interests, Hatfield has been on the board of directors of Big Brothers/Big Sisters of the Bluegrass since 1996.

➤ **I love Dynaformer as a sire. I know he has a reputation as a tough horse, but he must have some good qualities. How does his groom handle him?** — Nicholasville, Kentucky

Our approach to any of the stallions is to let them be who they are as much as we can. They are, after all, breeding stallions and some are tougher than others. Most stallions are like adolescent boys—they need to be "boys," but they have to have boundaries. It's all about patience, finding common ground, getting along, and then, of course, hiring good horsemen to put it all into practice.

➤ **How did you make it from Murray State University to [being] the stallion manager at Three Chimneys Farm? I am graduating and trying to get into the Thoroughbred racing world.** — Murray, Kentucky

I graduated with a bachelor of science degree in May and started mucking stalls in June. I wish there had been a program like KEMI [Kentucky Equine Management Internship] around at that time to help me get introduced to the Thoroughbred world and making those ever-important connections in the industry. If you're going to make it in farm management, you have to be willing to put in some sweat equity. I have worked in every area of the farm, and it helped me to better appreciate each phase of farm life. It's not just a job, it's a lifestyle. You have to love it to make a career out of it, but I'm so lucky to do what I love and get paid for it.

➤ **Out of all the stallions at Three Chimney's Farm, which one is the toughest? And which one is the gentlest?** — Cedar Rapids, Iowa

All of the stallions have their bad days, but I would say Capote and Dynaformer are the toughest on a daily basis. Seattle Slew had his share of tough days as well. Wild Again and Point Given are the easiest to get along with.

➤ **Do you believe that the number of mares stallions have been booked to in recent years is compromising the quality of the offspring?**
— Nashville, Tennessee

I don't think the number of mares a horse breeds has an effect on the quality of his offspring per se. I do think the market is being flooded with offspring of unproven sires and most people are breeding horses to sell, not to race. There are a lot of great racehorse sires that are getting overlooked in favor of the new "hot" first-year stallions. We limit the size of our stallions' books because we think that's the best thing to do for the breeder, the syndicate member, and the marketplace.

➤ **What do you think the most interesting part of your job is?**
— Hudsonville, Michigan

The most interesting part of my job is figuring out each horse as an individual—his likes and dislikes—in and out of the breeding shed. The most important part of my job is the daily care of these great stallions and making the breeding process as safe, quick, and efficient as possible. I also enjoy meeting people and being an ambassador of sorts for the horse industry to the people who visit Three Chimneys Farm.

➤ **Do you think that your stallions know that they are special and a select group?** — Saddle Brook, New Jersey

Most definitely. I believe their confidence on the racetrack follows them to the stallion barn.

➤ **What are some of the challenges of getting new stallions off to a good start?** — Portland, Oregon

When starting a new stallion, the best thing to remember is patience. It needs to be a positive experience for him, so being calm, quiet, and not in a hurry are important factors.

➤ **How is a stud fee set on a first-year stallion? I am sure that breeding, race record, and so forth figures into the equation. But what other factors help establish first-year fees?** — Baton Rouge, Louisiana

Breeding, race record, and conformation are all important factors. You also have to be a good judge of what the market will bear. We try to set our fees so that they are fair, and the breeder can make money.

➤ **For stallion and mare safety reasons, would it be beneficial to the Thoroughbred breeding industry if artificial insemination was accepted by The Jockey Club? Do you see this as an option anytime soon?** — Dana Point, California

Certainly, it would be safer if only one animal was present at a time. But that's not the only issue. You have to also think about the breed and the impact of AI upon the breed. I don't think artificial insemination would be beneficial to the breed as a whole as it would limit diversity in the gene pool. I don't see it happening in the near future.

➤ **With such an impressive group of stallions, which is your favorite personality to work with, and why?** — New York, New York

Getting to know each horse's individual personalities is one of the reasons

I was drawn to the stallion barn. The really smart horses are always the most challenging and interesting to work with; they make you think.

➤ **I understand that the arrival of Smarty Jones brought a huge influx of fans to the farm that continues to this day. How does that affect the day-to-day operations?** — Philadelphia, Pennsylvania

Smarty Jones has changed so many lives, including ours. We have enlarged our parking lot, built a visitor center, and have hired an additional person to help handle the increased volume of phone calls and correspondence and assist with the duties of the public tours we give five days a week.

➤ **What advice do you have for me and other females entering the Thoroughbred industry?** — Hamilton, Ontario, Canada

Find the right people to work for who will give you the opportunity to expand your knowledge. Then work harder than you have to. Don't get discouraged, and don't give up.

➤ **Do you feel that your stallions are better suited to produce [more successful horses for synthetic surfaces], considering their turf background?** — Lexington, Kentucky

Although not all of our stallions are considered turf sires, I do believe the jury is still out on that one. It's possible that the turf sires will do well, but there may be a new group come along that just do well on a synthetic surface.

➤ **Three Chimneys is well known for exercising its stallions under saddle as long as they can physically handle the work. Since stallion management is largely about keeping the horse happy, what [does] this contribute? [Can you] give us one other thing you've learned through your career about satisfying the demands of stallions at stud?** — Ewing, New Jersey

Having someone on their back, working with them from a whole different angle, is a big part of how the daily exercise keeps the stallions happy physically and mentally. I believe exercise is one of the most important factors in the horses' well-being and that outside turnout time is one of the most important factors in their happiness.

TALKIN' HORSES

SANDY HATFIELD

➤ **Who is the best-behaved stallion you have ever known, and who wins the bad-boy award?** — South Lake Tahoe, California

The Bart and Quiet American win the good-boy awards. The first bad-boy I ever handled was Liloy, and he taught me a lot about what to do and what not to do with a tough horse.

➤ **I understand one of your passions outside of the stallions at Three Chimneys is Big Brothers/Big Sisters. Do many horse farm owners and staff support this very worthy group?** — Lexington, Kentucky

Many of the horse farms and horsemen have been very generous in their support. We are planning a fundraising event just for the horse farms next year. I'm hoping *all* the horse farms will get involved in helping this great program that makes such a difference in the lives of children.

➤ **Now that [Smarty Jones'] first foals are officially yearlings, what [are] your impressions of them in general? [Have you] noticed any particular traits that Smarty seems to be throwing to a good amount of his foals, physically or temperamentally?**
— Naples, Florida

Smarty's babies are racy looking, good sized, well balanced, and have a very athletic walk. The ones we have at the farm have a good temperament. Mrs. [Pat] Chapman came last spring to look at all we could get her around to see, and she kept commenting how she could "see Smarty" in so many of them. We're excited about his offspring.

➤ **Would you ever consider working with stallions elsewhere in the world; if so, where?** — Sydney, Australia

I hope to one day be able to visit other countries and share my experiences with others.

➤ **Having worked with both Elusive Quality [at Gainsborough] and Smarty Jones, do you notice any similarities between father and son?**
— Midway, Kentucky

Although their personalities are very different, they are both very well-balanced horses with great conformation.

➤ **Which stallions get ridden in the mornings? How much does Point Given weigh?** — North Middletown, Kentucky

We ride Albert the Great, Flower Alley, Good Reward, Rahy, and War Chant. We recently built a covered walker that will allow us to exercise the stallions that can't be ridden. All of our stallions are weighed once a month, and in January Point Given weighed 1,486 pounds.

➤ **Since you have handled several large stallion operations over the years, have you been able to pick out any trait—conformation or disposition-wise—that gives you a clue that, "Hey, this is going to be a good one"?** — Marshall, Virginia

I wish I could say, "Yes," but if I knew the answer, I'd be rich and living on an island somewhere. It's easier to pick out the not-so-good ones. A lot of the ones that you think have all the right attributes and you are sure they are going to be the next superstar don't even get to second base. Some of the ones you aren't so high on jump up and do well. You just can't measure the drive and determination a stallion will pass on until his offspring have a chance to prove themselves after a few years on the track. All you can do is just like the old saying, "Breed the best to the best and hope for the best." It's all about hopes and dreams.

➤ **Is [Rahy] a small horse? I have never seen him in person but have had luck with his offspring. The only issue I ever have with them is some are very small.** — Medfield, Massachusetts

Rahy is 15.1 hands [a hand is 4 inches], not the biggest horse but neither were Northern Dancer, Blushing Groom, Nureyev, or Lyphard. I think you have to breed the right type of mare to Rahy and those that do their homework have had a lot of luck with his offspring, such as Dreaming of Anna.

➤ **What do you do on a normal day?** — Madison, Wisconsin

We get here at 7:00 a.m. and check in with the night watchman. The grooms check their horses and feed them and send any that exercise that morning to the jog track. I download the night watch scanner to make sure all the horses were checked during the night. Then it's time to get all the paperwork for the morning shed and get things set up. The first mares arrive around 8:30 and

TALKIN' HORSES

SANDY HATFIELD

the [breeding] session is usually over about 10:00 to 10:30. Once I get all the incoming paperwork from the mares and make all my notes, I take the finished paperwork to the office. If any clients are scheduled to view the stallions, this is the time I take them around. After lunch I might show the stallions again. Then the routine starts over again with the set up, mares arriving about 1:30 and the last mare leaving around 3:30, paperwork, and a visit to the office. I set up for the evening session at 6:00 p.m. and we expect mares at 6:30 or so and the day is usually over around 8:00 p.m. Of course, that doesn't include the work the other people do in the barn like turning the stallions out, cleaning stalls, bringing horses back up, grooming the stallions, and cleaning up the receiving barn, the breeding shed, and the stallion barns. And don't forget the daily tour at 1:00 p.m. It's a busy day for all of us.

➤ **I've noticed that Point Given as well as Albert the Great are very interested when you talk to them. Albert shook his head in an affirmative manner when we asked him some questions. Then he laid down on his back and moved his legs up and down like he was dancing when we started to walk away. It seems that both of these stallions love attention and are very intelligent.** — Cincinnati, Ohio

Most stallions do like attention. Don't forget they are prey animals in the wild and therefore think very differently than we do. The research that Dr. Sue McDonnell has done on horse behavior at New Bolton Center is really amazing, and if you ever get a chance to read any of her books, they are fascinating.

➤ **Is it typical to breed the same stallion/mare combination multiple times?** — Carlisle, Pennsylvania

People have differing opinions on that subject. A lot of people think that if it worked well once that it merits trying again. Just think what it would be like to have another horse that was similar to Barbaro, wouldn't it be worth it? How wonderful to be able to try to make your hopes and dreams come true.

TALKIN' HORSES
WITH
AVALYN HUNTER

A racing fan since Secretariat's record-breaking Triple Crown campaign in 1973, Hunter began studying pedigrees at age fifteen, beginning with Sir Charles Leicester's classic work Bloodstock Breeding, *which details the pedigrees of winners of the Derby Stakes during the first half of the twentieth century. Twenty-five years later, Sir Charles' book served as a model and inspiration for Hunter's first book,* American Classic Pedigrees 1914-2002 *(Eclipse Press). Covering the race records, antecedents, and descendants of the winners of the American Triple Crown races plus the Kentucky Oaks and Coaching Club American Oaks for fillies, the massive work took some two years to write and was released in May 2003. Since then, Hunter has continued to write extensively about Thoroughbred pedigrees and racing history in trade publications. A former Air Force officer, Hunter is a graduate of Vanderbilt University (B.A., psychology) and Southern Illinois University at Edwardsville (M.A., clinical psychology) and has worked as a mental health professional since 1993. She lives in Florida with her husband and two children. Avalyn has recently added to her busy routine the role of regular contributor of pedigree profiles to bloodhorsenow.com. Her second book, a biography of the great sire Northern Dancer, is titled* The Kingmaker: How Northern Dancer Founded a Racing Dynasty, *while her newest book release is* Gold Rush: How Mr. Prospector Became Racing's Billion-Dollar Sire, *both for Eclipse Press.*

➤ **How did you get interested in studying pedigrees?** — Waco, Texas

To tell you the truth, I'm not really sure how I got the pedigree bug. I can remember reading C.W. Anderson's book *The Smashers* and watching Secretariat's Triple Crown run when I was about twelve (yes, I know I'm dating

AVALYN HUNTER

myself), and curiosity took over from there. I was starting to fill notebooks with stuff about Thoroughbred bloodlines by the time I was fifteen or so.

➤ **Most high-priced yearlings don't turn out to be good runners. Why do you think that is?** — Boise, Idaho

It's mostly a matter of numbers. Even among the best-bred, most athletically built youngsters, the majority of them are going to be failures on the racecourse—that's just the nature of the game. There simply isn't any exact science to choosing yearlings, which is good news for those of us who don't have bottomless pockets. There's always the chance of coming up with a John Henry, a Seattle Slew, or a Spectacular Bid even if you don't have great wealth.

➤ **Reports show that horses make fewer starts. Why?** — Youngstown, Ohio

I believe there are several factors involved here. One is the shift from domination of racing by wealthy owner-breeders whose primary interest was sport to the modern commercial market, in which the business aspects of the sport now predominate. Owners like the Belmonts and the Whitneys had no particular incentive to retire a colt after one brilliant season: They didn't need the money, insurance costs usually weren't a consideration, and they would usually stand their champions at home—there were no big syndication deals in those days, at least none comparable to those in the modern era. Today, if a fashionably bred horse pulls down a grade I race, there's a lot of financial incentives to retire him to stud before he can do something that will diminish his reputation or make him less attractive. Geldings aren't subject to this, of course, and horses without fashionable pedigrees don't have as much of a financial push towards retirement. However, training styles have changed, and very few trainers now race a horse into fitness in the style of Ben and Jimmy Jones at Calumet or a lot of the other old-timers. Even the very best conditioners of the modern era depend far more heavily on workouts and less on prep races to get a horse fit for a big race than did the big-name trainers of the mid-twentieth century and earlier. I also believe medication has been an issue. Medications were supposed to help horses race sounder and longer, but it seems that in too many cases, medications have been used to substitute for "tincture of time" and may actually have contributed to breakdowns. This is an area where American social philosophy works against our horses: We're used to instant gratification and quick solutions, and given the choice between giving a horse months of rest followed by months of getting it back into racing shape and giving a horse a medication that will supposedly resolve the problem within a couple of days or weeks, which do you think a lot of trainers and owners will go for? I used to feel that the inherent soundness of the breed had also declined, and I do feel that excessively muscular bodies and lack of bone are perhaps more common than they were half a century ago. My colleague, Alan Porter, recently published another viewpoint, however. He pointed out that although the very best Thoroughbreds probably haven't improved in at least several decades— meaning that the breed has reached its genetic limits—the average horse of the breed has continued to improve, at least in terms of speed. Because of this, there is less of a gap between the top horses and the bottom level than there used to be, and Alan feels this results in most horses having to make a harder effort in each and every race than was the case fifty years back—and this causes most horses to need more time between races than they used to. It's an interesting take, and one that I'm still mulling over.

➤ **Are pedigrees overrated? Usually this happens: Two full brothers, one is a champion and the other can't win a $5,000 claiming race. Can you explain that scientifically?** — Pismo Beach, California

Many authorities hold that genetics makes up no more than 40 percent of what goes into a top Thoroughbred—nutrition, training, and a host of other factors make up the other 60 percent. On average, full brothers only share 50 percent of their genes, so there's quite a bit of variation there as well. But consider this: Let's say that a mare produces five full siblings, of which one is a good stakes winner, one is a modest allowance horses, one is a bottom-rung claimer, one can't win at all, and one never races—not an uncommon type of spread. Given that the breed only produces about 48 percent winners and 3 percent stakes winners, this hypothetical group of siblings would be well ahead of the averages. Pedigrees aren't everything, but they do count for something.

➤ **What [do] you recommend to someone who wants to study pedigrees to work at becoming an expert?** — St. Paul, Minnesota

Read, read, read—anything on Thoroughbreds you can get your hands on. Subscribe to at least one major trade publication so that you can get a feel for what's working in modern bloodlines; things can change a lot in just a few years. Go to stallion shows, auctions, and open houses when you can so that you can start developing an eye for what various lines tend to look like in flesh and blood.

➤ **With racing converting to artificial surfaces, will we see a new breed come forth?** — Lexington, Kentucky

There will undoubtedly be some shifts. So far, the best available data indicate that "turf" bloodlines are at a modest advantage in converting to the all-weather surfaces, but the advantage does not seem to be so great that the traditional "dirt" lines are going to go away anytime soon. My own hope is that a mix of dirt, synthetic, and turf surfaces will encourage a greater variety of stallions to be given decent opportunities at stud, which would be all to the good. Prior to these synthetic surfaces coming in, many a top turf runner has had trouble getting established as a stallion in the American commercial market; people may be more inclined to give "turfy" lines a chance now.

➤ **[Has] Mr. Prospector had as much of an impact on the Thoroughbred breed as Northern Dancer? Of the two, who do you think has impacted the breed more?** — Brockville, Ontario, Canada

As a group, Northern Dancer's sons were superior sires to Mr. Prospector's, just as Northern Dancer himself was a better sire in terms of percentages of stakes winners and number of champions. So as a male-line influence, I think Northern Dancer has impacted the breed more. Mr. Prospector, however, is a far better broodmare sire than Northern Dancer was and may wind up having an equal impact in the end, thanks to his daughters.

➤ **Why has the Mr. Prospector sire line gotten so many Derby, Preakness, and Belmont winners and only a few BC Classic winners?**
— Brick, New Jersey

The BC Classic has been dominated by older males, most of which seemed very genuine in their ability to get the mile and a quarter, and most of which were relatively slow developers. Brilliant juveniles and three-year-olds who show their brilliance in the spring usually don't last that long, partly because they are pushing for speed while they are still physically immature (a risk factor for injury) and partly because their commercial value as sires makes it unlikely that they will rehab for the track after relatively minor injuries, which in theory would not preclude further racing. The Mr. Prospectors as a group have tended to come to hand early, which is good from the viewpoint of the commercial market, not so good for the prospects of having a staying older horse. It's no coincidence that the BC Classic has an unusually high number of winners from less commercial lines, which are not as precocious but tend to have more stamina.

➤ **What particular physical trait made Native Dancer's tail-male lineage so prominent in Mr. Prospector?** — San Juan, Puerto Rico

Mr. Prospector possessed great physical balance combined with the power behind—which is necessary for success in American dirt racing. His balance and proportions made him a good fit for a large percentage of the North American mare population of the late twentieth century, and the strong quarters he usually contributed helped in producing offspring with the speed to be competitive in the racing environment of their time.

➤ **Are there any resources you suggest I get to learn more about what to look for when I buy my first horse?** — Darien, Connecticut

I don't consider myself an expert on conformation, but [I] am working to develop a better eye by going to stallion shows and open houses to see what all the terms used in conformation texts look like in the flesh. There are many excellent books and videos on conformation on the market, but if you're interested in racehorses, you'll probably want to look at the ones that are slanted towards Thoroughbreds.

➤ **With all due respect to Bold Ruler and Mr. Prospector, I feel [Northern Dancer's] influence on the breed was unmatched. Whom do you consider as the most likely of his great-grandsons to carry the Dancer line forward?** — Toronto, Ontario, Canada

That's a tough one. The Danehill branch is certainly going great guns in Australia and Europe but may be reaching a saturation point in the former region. Montjeu has emerged as a top classic sire in Europe and may maintain the Sadler's Wells branch of Northern Dancer in England and France. In the U.S., the Storm Cats have been all the rage commercially, but I think the long-term future of the Northern Dancer male line in North America may lie more with the Danzig and Deputy Minister branches.

➤ **How well do you think that stallions like Invasor and Candy Ride or even North Light and Hat Trick cross with most of the mares in North America since most of them all have Northern Dancer or Mr. Prospector?** — McArthur, Ohio

The big trick with foreign-bred stallions is determining how well they will match up with the North American broodmare population, which is distinctly different from the South American or South African populations. The latter tend to be more stamina-oriented and to have more of a European flavor. The presence of Northern Dancer or Mr. Prospector four or five generations back in a sire's pedigree is not going to matter nearly so much as what's in the rest of the pedigree. I'm certainly hoping that Invasor and Candy Ride do well here, but of the stallions you named, I'd say Hat Trick is probably the best fit for the market here, both because of his miler speed and because his overall pedigree is largely North American.

➤ **If you could have a filly by any active stallion out of any active broodmare to use as your foundation mare, who would the stallion and broodmare be?** — Ft. Lauderdale, Florida

That's easy—I'd take Rags to Riches as my foundation mare. She's by a great sire, A.P Indy, and her dam, Better Than Honour, was not only a good runner herself but hails from one of the best families in the *American Stud Book*. And if I couldn't get Rags, I'd take a sister of hers in a heartbeat!

➤ **The three major sires are—to me—Storm Cat, A.P. Indy, and Gone West, in that order. Each of them has Secretariat as the broodmare sire. [How could] a disappointing sire, such as Secretariat, become such a great influence as a broodmare sire?** — Minneapolis, Minnesota

Well-bred horses with good race records are usually bred to mares from strong female families. Even if their daughters don't quite live up to expectations on the track, their strong genetic backgrounds and the fact that their good pedigrees get them matings with good stallions give them a strong chance of success as producers. Secretariat, by the way, wasn't nearly as disappointing as some sources would have you think—he did get champions Lady's Secret and Risen Star and about 9 percent stakes winners from foals, which is about triple the breed average.

> **I am unclear on the meaning of the asterisk that appears before the names of some horses. [Could you] explain [it]?** — Cleveland, Ohio

The asterisk indicates a horse that was imported to North America. Its use phased out during the 1970s; the custom now is to put a code indicating the horse's country of origin in parentheses after the name—for instance, Invasor (Arg), with "Arg" standing for Argentina. In North American records, the absence of the code means that the horse was bred in North America. If the "=" sign appears in front of the name, it means the horse has never been in North America.

> **Many people consider Storm Cat the world's top sire, but A.P. Indy always ranks at the top of most statistical sire lists. Even in *The Blood-Horse*, most farms advertising stallions make references or comparisons to him. And he "nicks" well with the Mr. Prospector line mares. Where do you think he stacks up?** — Revere, Massachusetts

A.P. Indy is one of the best living stamina sires around and has succeeded in maintaining the Seattle Slew male line. I think he is likely to be quite an important broodmare sire as well in years to come as he has been bred to a superb pool of mates.

> **How do you think Invasor will do as a stud?** — Evansville, Indiana

It's difficult to say. Because of his ownership, he should get some very good mates in terms of previous production records and racing quality. The trick is figuring out which lines are most likely to be compatible with him because the bottom half of his pedigree is full of names that simply haven't had a lot of exposure in crossing to North American bloodlines. Based on what I have studied of South American bloodlines and the Blushing Groom male line, I would be looking for strains of Seattle Slew, In Reality (particularly the Relaunch branch), Roberto, and Nijinsky II in his mates. Mr. Prospector is a possibility, and I would also consider mares by Southern Halo and his son More Than Ready as possibilities. I am certainly hoping Invasor will buck the trends against South American-bred sires in Kentucky and do well because he was one of the most exciting and consistent racehorses I've seen in several years.

➤ **Has the prevalence of medications led to any "weakening of the breed" by compensating stallions that otherwise might be considered less valuable because of a tendency to produce genetically inferior offspring?** — Louisville, Kentucky

I think I covered this somewhat in the answer to an earlier question, but I do think that the use of medications may mask problems than might make a horse less attractive as a stud prospect. I'd prefer it if we followed the Europeans' lead in not permitting race-day medications, but I don't see that as happening anytime soon.

➤ **Have [Americans gotten] away from breeding for stamina and durability? What are your feelings about how young racehorses are whisked away to the breeding shed before they even reach their potential? Street Cry, sire of Street Sense, raced until at least four or five, so why the rush?** — Shawnee, Kansas

I'd like to see horses race longer, but as long as the big money is to be found in the breeding shed rather than on the track, the majority of top runners are going to head there as soon as they've made their reputations. There are still a few sporting owners who don't seem too inclined to rush a top horse into retirement—the Phipps Stable comes to mind, and the late Allen Paulson was another—but for most, the Thoroughbred industry is a business, and they're going to go where the biggest profits are.

➤ **Who do you think is the most influential broodmare sire right now? Of the past several decades? Of all time?** — Flint, Michigan

Right now, Mr. Prospector is clearly king of the heap in North America. He has nine broodmare sire titles under his belt and since his youngest daughters are foals of 2000, he should still be a force in the broodmare sire ranks for another seven or eight years. Buckpasser was, I think, the clear standout of the latter third of the twentieth century in this country. He was one of the very few sires to top 10 percent stakes winners from foals as a maternal grandsire, and I have no doubt that he would have added several more broodmare sire titles to his resume had he not died at the untimely age of fifteen. When you're talking about the best broodmare sire of all time, there are so many marvelous names to choose from that the mind reels. *Sir Gallahad III with his twelve titles in this area immediately comes to mind, but what of Lexington, whose daughters brought him lasting influence long after his sire line had died away? What of *Princequillo, an eight-time broodmare sire leader in an age with more competition than *Sir Gallahad III faced and the maternal grandsire of Secretariat? What of Man o' War, who despite a relatively small number of producing daughters figured no less than twenty-two times among America's top ten broodmare sires and has legions of top horses descended in tail-female from his daughters? And, if you go abroad, one must reckon with the likes of St. Simon and Hyperion, or further back still to old Herod, whose daughters crossed so effectively with the great Eclipse and his sons. The choices are many and a worthy case can be made for each one.

➤ **It appears that there are more soundness issues in horses who have Raise a Native in the broodmare sire line vs. their sire line. Is this just perception due to breakdowns of Barbaro, Pine Island, Union City, and so forth that happen during major racing events?**
— Eastwood, Kentucky

I haven't studied this particular angle, so I can't give anything approaching a definitive opinion. Speaking off the cuff, I think it's probably just perception because of recent events. Raise a Native is now five or six generations back in most pedigrees, so in evaluating a pedigree for possible soundness issues, I'd worry a lot more about the parents and grandparents Raise a Native's genes are coming through than about the old boy himself.

➤ *Kingmaker* **is far and away the most accessible book on Thoroughbred breeding that I have read for a long time. Mr. Prospector is only just beginning to have an impact out here in Oz. Is the gulf widening between American breeding (specifically for dirt racing) and the rest of the (Turf) world?** — Sydney, Australia

I think there has been a significant gap between North American dirt breeding and the rest of the world for some time, and the Land of Oz has been

TALKIN' HORSES

Avalyn Hunter

in a pretty good position to observe this because of all the shuttle stallions that have been coming from Kentucky. Most have been a lot less than spectacular with the change of the mare population base and the different racing conditions, although I understand there are some high hopes for Southern Image as he brings the Halo cross to all those Danehill-line mares—a very similar situation to that which greeted Sunday Silence when he went to Japan and saw all those mares by Northern Taste and his sons. It will be interesting to see if the parallel holds up. The one major racing country that has done very well with Mr. Prospector-line horses outside North America is Argentina, which is also one of the few countries I know of outside North America that has a substantial amount of dirt racing. I don't think this is coincidence. Chile, although it doesn't have as large a racing and breeding industry as Argentina, has also had some favorable impact from Mr. Prospector-line sire[s] and does have some dirt racing, but I think the best Mr. P horse down there has been Barkerville, who was out of a Nijinsky II mare. Those Mr. Prospector strains that have done well in Europe, Machiavellian and Kingmambo, both had female lines that suggested the possibility of turf success.

➤ **Assuming the sire lines of both stallions are "reliable" and both stallions have good conformation, would you rather see a stallion prospect with a solid, multigenerational quality pedigree and lower claiming level race record or one with a weaker quality pedigree but with a nongraded stakes-winning race record?** — Redding, California

I'd rather see neither, because both are quite likely to be flops even in a regional market. Generally speaking, the solid racehorse with the weak pedigree is likely to get a lot of small winners but not much quality while the well-bred racing failure may get a couple of notable successes but will have poor overall results because he is likely to pass on the physical or mental issues that negatively impacted his own racing career. (To tell the truth, relatively few colts with really fashionable pedigrees wind up in the claiming ranks; they usually get retired first due to injury or the owner's understandable desire not to have the horse's lack of ability fully exposed to the owners of potential mates.)

Of course, what constitutes a weak pedigree is somewhat in the eye of the beholder. Take Concorde's Tune, who has been a bargain for Florida breeders for the last decade. He never won or placed in a graded stakes and never even won a listed race though he did win three minor stakes. And you certainly couldn't call his pedigree fashionable (Concorde Bound—Parisian Tune, by Tunerup). But he was a tough, consistent sprinter who could handle dirt or grass, and he is a full brother to the very fast grade II winner Parisian Flight. He gets plenty of winners and has 6 percent stakes winners from his foals three years of age and older. Nobody's going to mistake him for a great sire, but for his $3,500 stud fee he definitely delivers the goods. And I will confess right here that, based on his race record and pedigree, I wouldn't have picked him as a successful regional sire when he retired. So much for the crystal ball.

➤ **Do you think that [Mr. Prospector's] ability to endow his offspring with speed is a function of Mr. P being "more" [a representative] of Raise a Native than a representative of his broodmare sire Nashua and his second dam sire (Count Fleet)?** — Miami, Florida

Blinding speed was certainly a hallmark of both Raise a Native and his sire Native Dancer, but don't discount either Nashua or Count Fleet in that department. Both were champion juveniles, and Count Fleet for many years held the record for the fastest mile ever run by a two-year-old. And, of course, Mr. Prospector is a direct female-line descendant or Myrtlewood, the American champion sprinter of 1936. All of these horses undoubtedly contributed to his considerable talent.

TALKIN' HORSES
WITH
DAN LIEBMAN

In October 2007, Dan Liebman became only the sixth editor-in-chief in the storied ninety-one-year history of The Blood-Horse. *Liebman joined Blood-Horse Publications in 1993 as research director and became executive editor in 1998. Prior to joining the company, Liebman was the Midwest deputy editor for* The Racing Times *from 1991 to 1993, and was a columnist for the Kentucky bureau of* Daily Racing Form *from 1984 to 1991. The native of Frankfort, Kentucky, is a graduate of the University of Kentucky.*

➤ **Have you ever owned a racehorse or broodmare? If not, your important position should require that you do.** — Lexington, Kentucky

Yes, I have owned horses. And, I have wagered on many. But I'm not sure I buy your premise. You can report on war without having served in the military. You can report on schools without having been a teacher. But there is a difference: You don't have to be passionate about education to report on it. Our employees are passionate about horses and about the Thoroughbred industry. I feel very strongly about this industry. Our job has many facets to it, including observing the industry and reporting and commenting on it. Being owned [by], though operated independently of, the Thoroughbred Owners and Breeders Association, Blood-Horse Publications is a part of the industry.

➤ **Where do you think the new racing fans will come from, and do you see any change in the way people see racing except as a place to gamble?** — Syracuse, New York

Many young people are drawn to things like poker, which involves gambling. Many of them are our future customers. There is much disposable income among many young people. Our product is the horse and we must remember that, but gambling is an integral part of the equation. Purses and handle are what drive the racing side. But, yes, we can draw them also with the majesty of the horses and through special events.

➤ **As a long-time reader and sometimes contributor to _The Blood-Horse_, I know you will take all the Blood-Horse Publications in bold, new directions, while preserving what is valuable from the past. [Are there] any new things to look forward to in the immediate future?**
— Portland, Oregon

Thanks so much, for the nice comments as well as the encouragement and faith in me. You know I take the ninety-plus-year history of _The Blood-Horse_ very seriously. I will work hard to continue the integrity we have displayed over those years. One new thing is video, which will really debut at The Breeders' Cup. I'm very excited about it. Other digital products will surely be in our future. You can even look for a "new" _Blood-Horse_ magazine. What I mean is that as we develop more digital products, the print magazine must also change. I look forward to you contributing to _The Blood-Horse_ again.

➤ **If there was one thing that you could change with the magazine, what would it be?** — New York, New York

If I could change one thing it would be to have more pages every week to tell the stories of our industry. This comes from the former executive editor, who [as the one] being responsible for the content always wanted more space.

➤ **Where does John Henry rank among the all-time greats?**
— Barboursville, West Virginia

He was among the truly great horses. Anyone who watched his races knows that. The Arlington Million with The Bart was a great, great race. Yes, he was quite the overachiever. We know his pedigree was not fashionable and he was not a pretty horse. But what a heart, what a personality, what tenacity. A true legend.

➤ **What can the racing public do when the local racetrack gets slots and forgets about the horseplayer?** — Springfield, Pennsylvania

Complain and complain loudly. These days we have two [types] of tracks: those that have slots and those that want slots. It could quite possibly be a short-term fix, but the have-nots simply want a level playing field. Imagine owning a track in Texas, Maryland, Kentucky, and so forth, where nearby states have slots, thus higher purses. You would want them, too. As I said, complain.

➤ **What is the most challenging aspect, both currently and in the near future, for you as editor-in-chief? And what is the most interesting?**
— Newmarket, England

The immediate challenge is only two weeks away, the Breeders' Cup, which is the first over two days and the first for us to post video. The future challenges are many, but a key [will be] delivering products geared toward the owners and breeders of our industry. The most interesting part of the job is that I enjoy being a journalist and love horses. This is a dream job for a horse-crazy kid from Central Kentucky.

➤ **Where do you see the future of the printed product, in this case *The Blood-Horse* magazine, headed in the next few years?** — Belfry, Kentucky

We know people get their information differently than just a few years ago. For a few years now, I have been stressing more features stories, something you have not seen online and that gives you a reason to sit on the couch and enjoy the printed magazine. I think we can find other features to similarly improve the print product.

➤ **What can the industry do to attract new owners who will remain in the business?** — Okemos, Michigan

We've been asking ourselves this question for a long time. Some of the answers are: Encourage existing owners to bring friends into the game; hope existing owners will begin partnerships; strive to get more racing on television; and promote events to get new fans to the races.

➤ **Racing is relying more and more on purse money from revenue from slot machines and other gaming devices. Can racing survive without an increase in self-generated handle?** — Hammond, Indiana

Handle has been increasing, but certainly in many locations you are right: Purses are what they are solely because of slots revenue. Racing can survive in this manner in the short term.

➤ **With matters of integrity and the public, is perception as important as reality?** — Elko, Nevada

Yes, perception is very important. You can't make a second first impression. Just like publishing a magazine, you are nothing if you don't have integrity.

➤ **Racing has been very tardy in identifying and testing for the drugs that have polluted every other major sport. If we don't act quickly, the integrity of our sport will be damaged beyond repair. What is your stance and what actions do you propose?** — Lexington, Kentucky

I covered my first convention of racing commissioners in 1984. They were talking about uniform medication rules then. I think our industry is finally taking some very real steps to address the things you mention. The Sales Integrity Task Force has come up with a list of recommendations. The Racing Medication group is making great strides. [Drug] threshold levels are needed. Indiana has recently become the first state to agree to out-of-competition testing, which will also take place prior to this year's Breeders' Cup in New Jersey. I agree that we have been slow to react but I am optimistic we are now addressing the issues.

➤ **Congratulations on the new appointment. In all of your experiences covering the sport of Thoroughbred racing, what has been your favorite moment?** — Shelbyville, Kentucky

My favorite moment was being named editor-in-chief of *The Blood-Horse*. Prior to that, it was seeing a foal being born for the first time, which I was invited to do at Airdrie Stud nearly twenty-five years ago. I realized how beautiful the animal is from its first breaths.

➤ **Does the Breeders' Cup need to consider subsidizing the travel expenses of foreign horses as is done by the Dubai World Cup and the Hong Kong Festival? Also, shouldn't the Breeders' Cup attempt to coordinate its date with the world's other important meetings so that the Arc is not a mere twenty days before our big day?**
— Wallingford, Pennsylvania

The Breeders' Cup program is different than the others you mention since it involves the nomination of stallions and foals. It is the championship event. If

Dan Liebman

horsemen want to run in those races, they will pay their way there. The others have created events to promote themselves, which requires subsidies. In fact, you may not know they also pay a portion of the expenses for journalists, which the Breeders' Cup does not, and should not. The Arc, of course, was established long before the Breeders' Cup. To be a championship event in the United States, it would be hard to run much later in the year. As it is, many horsemen have had to alter their training schedules to make the Breeders' Cup.

➤ **I really like bloodhorse.com; I read some articles but use it mainly to download past performances. Since I'm in horse racing only to win money, what does *The Blood-Horse* magazine offer to help me do this?** — Newark, Delaware

I began handicapping at age nine and found one of the most useful pieces of knowledge to be pedigree information. Within the pages of *The Blood-Horse* is where I gleaned bits and pieces of useful information, from articles and sire lists. Handicapping is one of the greatest cerebral challenges out there. The learning never stops.

TALKIN' HORSES

WITH

Barbara Livingston

Barbara Livingston, who has been photographing horse racing for more than thirty-five years, is widely recognized as one of the sport's top photographers. She has twice been recognized with racing's highest honor, the Eclipse Award for Outstanding Photography. Barbara's work has graced the covers of countless racing books and magazines, and she is a regular contributor to racing's top weekly, The Blood-Horse. *Barbara's work has also appeared in mainstream publications such as* Newsweek, People, Sports Illustrated *(including their two-page "Leading Off" spread),* ESPN The Magazine, GQ, *and on the covers of* TV Guide *and* Vanity Fair. *Her photos have also appeared on* MTV, MSNBC, CBS Sunday Morning, ESPN, HBO, *and* Entertainment Tonight. *Eclipse Press has published four books by Barbara:* Four Seasons of Racing *(1998);* Old Friends *(2002);* Barbara Livingston's Saratoga: Images from the Heart *(2005), and* More Old Friends *(2007). Barbara graduated with a BFA/Experimental Photography degree from Syracuse University. She lives in Saratoga Springs, New York.*

➤ **That wonderful photo of Afleet Alex reaching for all he was worth for that candy his jockey Jeremy Rose was unwrapping was absolutely great. Do you ask people to try things like that to get a good photo, or [do you] snap the photo before the moment's gone?** — Idaho

Thanks so much for your kind words about the Afleet Alex/Jeremy Rose photograph. The moment was a priceless one, and I was very fortunate to be there. Generally, I don't set up "tender" shots as they tend to be spontaneous, yet I always try to pay attention so I'll be ready if such a moment happens. In the case of Afleet Alex, Jeremy was being interviewed on a bench when Afleet Alex suddenly noticed him. The horse pushed his head over the fence begging for

TALKIN' HORSES

BARBARA LIVINGSTON

a treat, and Jeremy happily obliged. Sometimes, we'll set up a particular shot and a tender moment will happen as a result. For instance, we once set up a mare and foal for a portrait at Highcliff Farm. The mare suddenly turned to her foal and licked him several times. The shot was absolutely precious, showing the relationship between the loving mare and her young foal, much more successful than the standard "set up" portrait we took that day.

➤ **Why did you become interested in the older Thoroughbreds and recording their retirement with photographs?** — Woodstock, Georgia

I'm not sure exactly why I became interested in photographing the equine elders. Their life experience has provided them white hairs, knobby knees, and swayed backs. They are truly beautiful, like grandparents who have lived through many experiences. I also love the history that lives through these older horses. Visiting Freetex brought back memories of the day he won the Monmouth Invitational, while Genuine Risk's blazed face will always bring thoughts of a very special Derby. While my memory of these races is unique, many others also experience wonderful memories when these horses are remembered. It is fun to "share" those horses. Older memories, somehow, feel more sweet. Perhaps the first older Thoroughbred I photographed was, at least in part, responsible. At age sixteen, in 1977, I visited Lexington for the first time. Our first stop was Spendthrift Farm to see Nashua, one of the great racehorses of modern generations. I asked his groom, Clem Brooks, if Nashua could be brought out. Clem obliged, mentioning that Nashua could be a tough old boy. Then out came Nashua. The grand old horse was twenty-five, with a slightly swayed back. He paid attention to Clem and was a gentleman, yet he suddenly lifted his head high and stared into the distance. The look was overwhelming—I still remember his magnificence and power, all of these years later. It was truly the "look of eagles" and internal "flame" that I'd often read about in racing books. Nashua was living history, and with each passing year his history grew. I loved that about him, as I do about each horse.

➤ **Are there some [horses] in particular that you like to picture more? A certain color, build, and so forth?** — Harrisburg, Pennsylvania

It's funny, as my initial response would be to say gray horses such as Gander and With Anticipation. But then I think about a gorgeous red chestnut Class

Play yearling in morning sunlight, or the near-black Irish Actress with her dished face and bright star. Then there are the rare white Thoroughbreds, who look like horses of a dream world, and the kindly bay Riva Ridge—and it gets tougher to choose a particular favorite color. I'll say gray horses, but it's definitely a close race! I am passionate about photographing mares, as they aren't recorded as often as stallions. There are countless photos of Danzig, for instance, yet I'd guess photos of his dam, Pas de Nom, are rare. A shoot I'll always treasure was at Darby Dan, consisting of their four (!) living Queen Elizabeth II Challenge Cup winners together. Amazing. Regarding build and so forth, my initial response would be to say the old-timers. But then there are those spindly-legged foals peering out from behind their dams, and stallions in full glory galloping in their paddocks, and racehorses dancing on their toes in the paddock. I don't think I have a favorite build/shape or age. As I often say to friends, horses are just magic.

➤ **How has the Saratoga racing scene changed since you started attending years ago?** — Xenia, Ohio

The scene has changed over all of these (many!) years, for both good and bad. But considering how much the outside world has changed, it's remarkable how much has remained the same at the track. I miss the days when Mack Miller and others sent out their morning sets, when the riders wore matching outfits in the stable colors. And I miss the old paddock or, rather, the lack thereof. Long ago, the horses were saddled for races under the trees, with no fence separating them from the spectators. While it must have been an insurance nightmare, it certainly made for wonderful close-up photos, including a few unplanned action shots. The building (grandstand and clubhouse) itself hasn't undergone many noticeable changes, which is great. It feels sacred—imagine, the hoofbeats of Man o' War resounded through that building! I love imagining what the grandstand, complete with old wooden trusses, has seen during its long, quiet vigil.

It was easier to wander around at the races, and the town, when I first attended (in 1971). The crowds were much smaller back then. It also seemed there were more "core" racing fans in those days, who knew the jockeys by name and understood the game.

Yet I'm very grateful for all of Saratoga's (many!) visitors now, as they obviously help keep our sport going. Many still know the jockeys by name, and some will become lifelong fans. There are still countless wonderful photographic opportunities to be found, but there is a longer line at the food stands.

➤ **I was wondering if any of your photos are cropped at all, or do you catch the moment exactly as we see it in the photograph?**
— Portsmouth, New Hampshire

It varies although a good percentage are full-frame. I try to see the entire image when shooting. Truebreadpudding worked out wonderfully and she, fortunately, filled the entire frame edge-to-edge. My other Eclipse Award shot, Turnback the Alarm, was also a case of a full-frame photo, which worked out.

For races, especially, I often do some cropping. Horses, from the tip of their tail to their nose, tend to be much longer than they are tall (even with the jockeys up), so there is often spare room at the top and bottom of photos. I crop out that dead space. There are also occasional times when the action happens somewhat far off, such as one morning at Saratoga when Point Given reared as he returned to his barn. I was relatively far away, but took photos. I was able to crop them later to work well, although I wouldn't have wanted to try to enlarge them any bigger than 8 inches x 10 inches!

➤ **Who are some of the more memorable racehorses you've photographed (and "met") in terms of personality or presence or beauty or temperament?** — Ohio

Of the extra, extra special ones, I've never met a kinder, gentler mare than Sugar and Spice. The old Calumet grade I winner's name fit her perfectly. Raja Baba was a delight, and so easy to be around—what a professional he was in all that he did during his very long life. And the great Cigar—well, I (like so many) sure grew to love that white-rimmed eye and his knowing glance. A true champion! In my opinion, Flag Down was the most beautiful horse I've ever photographed. The bay colt was truly elegant, and "breathed fire." Cormorant is another favorite due to his very strong will and presence. Cormorant's son Gander is also a wonderful model. His solo trip to "win" the 2002 Saratoga Breeders' Cup (after losing Mike Smith) made for a fun photo that appears in the new book. I love the powerful, light-gray With Anticipation with his white European-trimmed tail, and the aged, dark bay Freetex peering hesitantly from behind his long, untrimmed forelock. My all-time favorite horse was Sip Sip Sip, whom I only met once. His photo appeared in a 1971 *New York Times* when he won the first race at Aqueduct (they used to run those photos). I loved his name, and clipped out the photo. I was ten at the time.

I followed him for years and photographed him at Saratoga in 1974. In 1977 I visited Belmont Park and trainer Sid Watters allowed me to meet Sip Sip Sip—just before [he went] out to compete on smaller circuits. A groom gave me carrots to feed to Sip Sip Sip, and I got my picture taken with him as well. That day, I learned that Sip Sip Sip was blind in one eye. Since an eye surgery as a child, I've had monocular vision, so that made Sip Sip Sip extra special.

➤ **Not that anyone could duplicate [your skill], but what kind of camera do you use?** — Everett, Washington

I use Canon cameras, both digital and film. With film, it's the Canon 1-V, and my main digital camera is the Mark-II. Both offer many frames-per-second and are really easy to use. Given the option, I prefer using film for really important events, such as photographing Genuine Risk or a Travers' finish. I used film for most of the shots in my new book, for instance. But for the quick turnaround photos, such as many race finishes, digital is easier. Both have their definite strengths and weaknesses. My favorite lens is the Canon 70-200/2.8 lens, which I use for a large portion of my shooting.

➤ **Who has been your most difficult horse to photograph? Who was the biggest ham?** — Marietta, Georgia

Ah, the most difficult; what an interesting question. The two stallions who came with the "worst press" were probably Personal Flag (in his earlier days) and Compliance. In both cases a groom brought a bat or hose out in one hand as they led the stallion with the other. As each was posed, the groom waved the bat/weapon around to keep the stallion's attention. The stallions did indeed pay attention although Compliance stopped enjoying the photo session after a few minutes. When he stopped enjoying it, we promptly put him back in his stall. Cormorant was difficult to stand for photos as he is a tough son-of-a-gun. Eventually, he made for a wonderful model. I'm very patient with horses as I understand what we're asking them to do doesn't make sense. Interestingly, now that I think about it, there've been quite a few difficult horses—horses that

BARBARA LIVINGSTON

took an hour or more to photograph. But most eventually tolerated the silliness of our photo shoots (although they probably thought very bad things about me at the time).

The "biggest ham" award might go to Cigar, who certainly knows a camera click means some adoring fan is nearby. He strikes a pose and says, "Look at me!" which we are happy to do. Other excellent models include All Along, Sugar and Spice, Affirmed, Dahlia, Cozzene, Empire Maker, Alivida, Gander, Flag Down, Lure, Sightseek—the list could go on all day.

➤ **What is your opinion of the quality of digital cameras and do you think they will ever replace the traditional film SLR cameras?**
— Ottawa, Ontario, Canada

Digital cameras have improved dramatically in the past few years, and many of the issues I had with them just one generation back have been fixed. Today, a top-quality digital camera is certainly capable of taking a photo that can be enlarged to a substantial size without noticeable image "breakdown." The color can still be a bit odd, in that a blue sky sometimes seems exaggerated or red silks might get a color cast. But their ease of use, and not having to go to a photo lab, are definite advantages. I primarily shoot digital nowadays.

I still shoot lots of film for many "extra special" occasions. I have a fear of digital images some day being unopenable, whether it's due to CDs or DVDs or Photoshop changing or disappearing. I still like the look and feel of film/prints. I think, for the most part, digital will eventually replace traditional film SLR cameras. It seems they're heading that direction fairly quickly! But I believe (and hope) top-quality film cameras will be available for generations, primarily for fine artists and fashion/commercial photographers.

➤ **You seem to examine your subjects carefully, which helps you choose the correct lightning, angle, movement, and look. It seems like only a few years ago track photography was a man's world. How did you ever persevere at such a young age?** — Queensbury, New York

I was fortunate to grow up near a horse farm, where the owner kindly gave me free rein with his horses. Long before I picked up a camera at age ten, I was a fearless rider and groom. I studied horses at every possible opportunity—drawing them, learning equine anatomy, reading every book I could find.

Horses, and racing, meant the world to me, as they still do. One day I discovered that, with a camera, I could record the horses. What a wonderful thing.

It was really difficult to become a professional photographer, but I'm not sure if my gender helped or hurt me. In recent years I was told by a farm secretary that she had to talk a horse owner into letting me take their stallion photos. He felt a male could do a better job. But when I'm at the track and a nice male groom sees me trying to get a good photo, they take pity on this lady and try their best to help.

➤ **What horses of former years do you especially wish you could go back in time to capture on film?** — Springfield, Missouri

I always wanted to photograph Man o' War. I can't imagine how it would feel to see the horse who was "as near to living flame as horses get" (Joe Palmer). Others include White Beauty, the first Jockey Club-recorded white Thoroughbred, Hastings, and Display. The latter two were said to be very bad actors, and I think they'd be fascinating to photograph—as long as I could photograph them with a long lens!

➤ **Where are the best "spots" for the average fan to get great shots at Saratoga, especially in the mornings?** — Bristol, Connecticut

Mornings at Saratoga can be tough, especially when you're on the front side/breakfast, and the sun is strong. Every horse galloping by will be annoyingly backlit, and difficult to expose correctly. If you do want to photograph horses galloping backlit, be sure to overexpose your camera (if you shoot film) so the film will read the horse more than the sunny background.

I'm always happy when horses walk through the paddock on their way trackside in the morning; Affirmed used to do that, and Bill Turner would take Seattle Slew for a few spins through the paddock. The lighting there is often all shadow, which makes for even, nice lighting. But for most morning shots on the front side, the only really well-lit shots are when horses head the wrong way. As they jog toward you, the sun hits their fronts and that makes for a pretty shot. In the afternoons, I love to photograph the horses as they come up the paddock walkway toward the track. There is a track entry (the clubhouse entry) where there's a gap for people to cross. Right there, on the side that has the sun against your back, great shots can be found if you stand up against the rail near that tent. Basically, for most ease in shooting I usually try to have the sunlight behind my back whenever possible, so it is bright on the horse. On cloudy days, lighting is less of an issue. I like cloudy days.

➤ **Can you describe your early photo experiences?**

— New Haven, Connecticut

Some of my early, published photos weren't exactly stellar, and I still cringe to think of some photos that have my credit line. In my first few years shooting, one of my shots of a sales-topping yearling was published. Now, it really was a bad photo as the horse was completely squared off. Tony Leonard, considered the master of conformation photography, came up to me, took my arm, and looked me in the eyes. He quietly said something like, "Barbara, your work is very good. But you really should try to always show four legs of a horse in a photo, rather than just two." That stuck with me, and I learned something I'd recommended to others: Do not allow a photo to be published that isn't good. People will notice your name on that photo much more quickly than they would a great shot.

The first foal shoot I did was pretty bad, too. Now, I should have known that the cute, golden-chestnut foal with the four white stockings was all splayed out, but I was so nervous about the mare being nervous and the grooms being unhappy that I just clicked away quickly. I didn't want to take up too much of their time. When I got the photos back, I'll be darned if the shots didn't look just like that foal did—his bright white legs heading "easty-westy." I made that pretty cute foal look, well, not so cute. Those were both quick lessons learned, I must say!

➤ **You have taken many pictures of The Bid [Spectacular Bid]. Was he one of your favorite subjects?** — Holmes, New York

It seems you and I share a favorite in Spectacular Bid. He was magnificent! I never saw him at the track as he was due to run at Saratoga but didn't. But [once he was retired from racing] as a stallion, I visited him often. From 1991 on he resided at Milfer Farm, just two hours from here. They were kind enough to allow me to visit when I wanted, such as on his twenty-fifth birthday when we baked him a cake. (Sadly, he didn't care for my cooking any more than people do.) Bid knew just how to pose, and how long he had to be a polite subject. He was great to work with, but he didn't care for too much fussing and could nip if he got bored. I loved that about him.

My favorite thing about the Bid, I think, was his tail. It wasn't just gray, or white, but was instead a beautiful, glowing silver, traced with gold. He is a model in *Old Friends*, but I don't currently have any plans to publish a book about him. He is definitely deserving, however!

➤ **Hey, tell the truth—are those shots you take of a fog-laden Saratoga technically enhanced, or are they for real!** — Lexington, Kentucky

They're not enhanced nor do I use filters as Saratoga has some incredible mornings. There's a catch nowadays, however: Digital images, in my opinion, generally look a bit more saturated than photos from film. As such, the color seems a little brighter than what appeared before my eyes; but some other photographers have disagreed with me about that. Saratoga sunrises, with their rays of sun and dense fog, can be absolutely breathtaking ... surreal.

➤ **What kind of advice do you give to someone interested in getting started in equine photography?** — Newtown, Pennsylvania

It's difficult to become a professional racing photographer nowadays, as so many people want to be one and opportunities (at least paying ones!) are somewhat limited. But I always give the advice that worked for me: Choose your own road, learn from your mistakes, and just keep trying. Learn as much as you can about the equipment you're using, and, most important, enjoy your time out there. In the past, when people interested in photography have assisted me, I found myself getting distracted while trying to help them learn. As such, I have several long-term assistants whom I use at my shoots, people who pretty much know what to do all on their own. For people interested in helping out equine photographers, in order to learn the trade, I recommend contacting track photographers who might be seeking assistance. They might not pay, but the experience could be very helpful.

➤ **Have you ever had problems from male photographers who thought the finish line was their turf?** — Del Mar, California

That's a humorous question at face value, but it actually has been a struggle at times. At times my character has been questioned, and I've been buffeted

BARBARA LIVINGSTON

about—both physically and mentally. While that could happen to anyone, it's happened at the hands of male photographers. Of course, most racing photographers (at least back in "the old days") were male, so perhaps it was sheer coincidence. I learned from that (possible) coincidence, however, to fight harder. After all, if I gave up, they'd win—and my family has a stubborn streak that's way too strong for its own good.

I can't imagine what it would have been like to photograph racing, as a female, back in the truly old days, and off the top of my head I can't even remember the names of any female racing photographers prior to 1970 (my first early female influences included Inger Drysdale and Katey Barrett). While Virginia Slim felt we've come a long way, baby, I think things will become more equal in the future (although there still seem to be some male photographers who, on some level, feel the finish line is their turf). That's not to say there aren't any up sides to being a female racing photographer!

➤ **Seattle Slew is my favorite. Was he as temperamental and spirited in his older days when you took his picture?** — Rural Valley, Pennsylvania

I think "king of the paddock," or perhaps "king of the world," would describe Seattle Slew very well. It's funny: He was always completely classy whenever I saw him—stood like a statue, walked where asked, professional as could be (from 1977 at Saratoga through 2001 at Three Chimneys). Of course, they didn't ask anything really unusual of him as, well, as [he] was Seattle Slew.

His handlers, and especially his longtime groom, Tom Wade, knew very well that he commanded respect, and they gave it to him in abundance. Perhaps he was a bit "hotter" in his youth, but he still had that incredible, "I am Seattle Slew" appearance into his old age. I still miss him.

➤ **You're an amazing writer as well as photographer. Did you study journalism in college or does it come naturally?** — Indianapolis, Indiana

What a nice question; thank you so much. I'm not sure where my love of writing comes from although I began writing horse stories by the time I was ten. Those stories were direct C.W. Anderson rip-offs, I must admit: child gets unwanted, injured racehorse; child nurtures said racehorse; said racehorse wins a big race and child gets trophy and money. Oh, and horse gets carrots.

One of my older sisters is a writer, and my father has authored several books.

I took a writing course or two in college and enjoyed them, but I was so focused on becoming a racing photographer I didn't really give any thought to writing. I enjoy writing tremendously, however—assuming it's a subject I'm passionate about. These horses make writing easy.

➤ **How difficult is it for you when you cast the net so wide and get to know and photograph so many of your old friends only to lose them seemingly on a weekly basis?** — Arlington Heights, Illinois

Wow, what a kind question. It's actually quite difficult at times, depending on how close I was to the particular "old friend." Although Gato Del Sol had health issues in recent years, for instance, his death was somehow shocking to me. I just figured he'd be grazing out in his Stone Farm paddock forever, his silver coat rich in the deep green and gold grasses, with Staci Hancock bringing him carrots. His death actually brought tears to my eyes.

I learned of another remarkable horse's death just yesterday, a horse featured in *More Old Friends,* and I immediately felt that familiar sadness. But the feeling passes when I remember the great, long, rich lives these horses had—and how fortunate we were to spend time with them.

➤ **[Is] there a standout in your book, one of the horses that really touched you?** — Cedar Rapids, Iowa

Wow, what a great question, and the first answer, of course, is that they were each a standout in some way. But, of course, some were incredible shining stars who literally changed my life. Three come to mind: Tall Glass O'Water is an old Vanderbilt mare, and I was a tremendous fan of Mr. Vanderbilt (who wasn't?). I included two Vanderbilt mares in the first *Old Friends* and it just made me feel good, so I sought out Tall Glass O'Water for *More Old Friends*. I loved her when she was racing—after all, she had a great name, she'd won at Saratoga, and her son Ewer All Wet was a very successful stakes winner. I found Tall Glass O'Water through an Internet search as she was sold at the Vanderbilt dispersal years ago. Her owner told me he'd bred her for a few years but was unable to get her in foal, and that he wasn't sure what to do with her. I contacted buddy Jeanne Mirabito, who contacted ReRun's Shon Wylie. Soon thereafter, Tall Glass O'Water, or Tally, became a ReRun gal. She's a happy, healthy (albeit somewhat rotund!) pensioner at Lori Neagle's farm, where she's spoiled with oatmeal cookies,

BARBARA LIVINGSTON

fortune cookies, and similar treats. She seems the picture of contentment, and I can't express how grateful I am that Mr. Vanderbilt's "old friend" is so beloved.

Sugar and Spice is another mare who, unbelievably, I helped out (which shows everyone can make a difference!). Sugar, an old grade I winner for Calumet and a half sister to Our Mims and Alydar, was living in a field of pensioners but wasn't doing well. They lived outside and, when I met her, she could barely walk. As such, she couldn't fight for her supper, and she was slim with a dull coat, skin rash, and sad eyes. One knee was permanently bent, a foot was wrapped in weathered duct tape, and her hooves were severely split. Despite that, she was unbelievably kind when I approached her, and as I petted her a long time that day, she seemed to melt under the touch. When I finally left, she tried to follow me the best she could, limping after me. As I drove away, I could still see her watching after me. It was heartbreaking. My friend Jeanne Mirabito—who'd tended to the aged Our Mims—was considering creating a haven for older, unwanted mares. I contacted her: Might she be interested in Sugar and Spice? She readily agreed and, days later, she became Sugar's owner for $1. Sugar didn't last long, but before she died she put on weight (under a carefully regimented diet which included her favorite treat, apples), her coat blossomed, her eyes brightened, and she began holding her head high. As Jeanne said, Sugar said "thank you" for every kindness extended to her. When Sugar died, Calumet Farm kindly allowed her to go home, and she was laid to rest near Alydar, Our Mims, and other relatives on a beautiful autumn day. We were fortunate to attend her burial. A bucket of apples was buried with her.

And then there is Highland Bud, two-time Breeders' Cup Steeplechase winner, and his Betsy Wells. Betsy, Jonathan Sheppard's foreman and exercise rider, tended to Bud through much of his career. She adored him, and everyone adored Betsy for her generous and happy spirit. Bud and Betsy eventually parted ways, but she never forgot him and kept tabs on where he was. Over the years Betsy was diagnosed with various cancers and she underwent treatment after treatment. Racetrackers held fundraisers for her, and friends helped her out whenever they could. She maintained her positive attitude throughout. In early 2005, however, she received a discouraging diagnosis and was told she should have a goal, something she could attain. She chose to ride Bud again. Friends transported Bud back into her life, and she spent happy days riding him. Bud, always "hot," seemed quite content to be loved again. It was a beautiful arrangement. Betsy, I'm afraid, did not last long enough to see *More Old Friends* published. I so wish she had. She was such an important part of it—such a beautiful woman—and I'm so grateful to her.

➤ **Who was the easiest horse to work with and who is your favorite to photograph (past or present)?** — Woodstock, Georgia

I'm not sure who was the easiest, but I don't remember any easier to work with than Affirmed or Cigar. Cigar was more difficult to show in a "beautiful" light, as he had a white-rimmed eye that is a bit odd, but he sure knows how to pose! I was fortunate to photograph seventeen of his last twenty races. And Affirmed, well, he was just a lovely individual inside and out. Sugar and Spice was very easy to photograph due to her kind nature; she'd basically look wherever you wanted, for long periods of time. But she just comes to mind now as I just wrote about her in an earlier response. Among my favorites, ever, have been horses most people might not often see photos of (which is perhaps why they'd be favorites). Puchilingui, a paint-colored Thoroughbred foundation sire who stands in Michigan, is a stunning model (he's in *More Old Friends*), and I absolutely loved photographing California's Bargain Day at age thirty-six (the first, and still only, thirty-six-plus-year-old Thoroughbred I've ever seen). Sip Sip Sip, an old claimer, is my all-time favorite racehorse, but I never got any great shots of him as I was only a teen when he was racing. And every few years I come up with new favorites, like Sightseek, Saratoga Dew, Gander, Lite the Fuse, Turnback the Alarm, Cigar, Bernardini, Invasor—oh my ... talk about a long list!

➤ **How are the trainers to deal with? Do most allow you free access?** — Istanbul, Turkey

Trainers are very accommodating, for the most part, although there've been a few over the years who made it clear we (the media) weren't welcome. Most trainers allow us to walk around their barns and photograph their horses as they are walked, bathed, and so forth. I stop short of stepping into shed rows without asking, however, as I realize security is a serious issue. I know that, if I owned a horse, I wouldn't want people I didn't know wandering about. So I'm careful to be respectful of people—trainers, owners, hotwalkers—and with our long lenses, we can usually get fine photos without getting too close.

That being said, there have been occasions we've had to work a bit harder, and push trainers a bit more, than I'm comfortable with. When Cigar arrived at Arlington for his date with destiny in the 1996 Breeders' Cup, photographers ran thick everywhere! I worried they'd spook Cigar, as everyone clicked, and some popped flashes, as Bill Mott walked his champion in the shed row. Photographers soon entered the shed row, too, standing at the ends and shooting Cigar as he walked. Cigar, amazingly, took it all in stride. Bill even let the horse walk right into a photographer who was kneeling on the ground (in a playful way, that is), providing us all a laugh. Bill laughed, too. He was always a great sport about our intrusions.

➤ **Your photo of [Halo] in your first *Old Friends* is one of my favorites— those eyes! Tell me more about him.** — Hampton, Connecticut

Halo ... ahhhh. Sometimes I still can't believe death finally got him. If ever a horse reflected "do not go gentle into that dark night." I was absolutely smitten with Halo, who would watch the world in a most unusual way: without moving his head. I might have mentioned this in the book, but he had this terribly unsettling habit of watching you like a cat—seemingly unblinking and with the most calculated look. His head would not move, but his gaze would follow you everywhere; it still thrills me to think of it! What a grand, grand, grand creature he was—like something out of a fantasy. He was "The Black Stallion" in the ship scene, tearing everything apart and bowing down to no one. I've never found a stallion so fascinating, and how nice that you are intrigued by him, as well.

➤ **The photo you took [of] Precisionist the day before he was put down goes beyond words. Were you alerted that his time was running out, prompting your visit to Old Friends?** — Vermont

I wasn't contacted by Old Friends before Precisionist's death. In one of those moments of serendipity, I visited Lexington for a one-day whirlwind trip and had a few spare hours before heading back to Louisville's airport. I called Old Friends to see if a friend and I could come see Precisionist. They kindly allowed my visit while warning us that Precisionist was in grave shape. When I got there, Michael Blowen was in a paddock with Precisionist, and it was clear the old horse was ailing terribly. They'd done all they could, but Precisionist wasn't able to rally, and he was euthanized the next day. I can't express how much I cherish the fact that they allowed me that last visit to say goodbye.

➤ **How difficult is it to get the perfect, unique shot when there are other photographers vying for the same result?** — Ottawa, Ontario, Canada

For racing imagery, which is where I sometimes meet up with hundreds of photographers, most magazines aren't necessarily seeking a particularly unique shot. They're generally seeking "bread-and-butter" shots—simple race win photos with four feet off the ground, and standard winner's circle pictures that clearly show the owner, trainer, and jockey. I just keep the faith that publications will occasionally have an interest in the other shots I take: unique portraits of our sport's athletes, scenic shots that reflect a track's spirit, and so forth. That is where I try to stand out, and I'd guess it's a matter of patience, passion, and dedication that keeps me "in the game."

➤ **What was the best picture you ever took?** — Louisville, Kentucky

Each time I'm fortunate enough to take a special photo it becomes my short-term favorite. But I do have one shot that stands out as a "classic" Saratoga image, which shows a horse galloping around the first turn just before dawn. It just had all the right elements—muted but lovely color, Saratoga's historic building as backdrop, and a galloping horse in just the right stride. If you feel inspired, just visit my gallery at www.barbaralivingston.com/gallery/ and put "before dawn" in the search engine.

➤ ***More Old Friends* is one of the most beautiful books I've seen. Do you [write] from notes, or did you just sit down with the photos of each subject and write from memory?** — Xenia, Ohio

Thanks for your very kind words. When I photograph a horse for a future book or story, I either jot down notes from the day or tape record my thoughts after a shoot. I also ask the horse's caregivers about [the horse]: temperament, special moments, special needs. Some events are really burned into my mind, however, such as Sugar and Spice's funeral. That will always be part of me.

Before writing horses' stories, I find old articles, photos, and so forth, from their racing and/or breeding days as it helps me get a fuller picture. I then look at the photos I took, remembering the day, and then the writing usually comes surprisingly easily.

TALKIN' HORSES
WITH
RANDY MOSS

Randy Moss, the lead horse racing analyst for the ESPN network since 1999, also covers horse racing for ABC Sports. Before his move to television, Moss was a reporter, columnist, and handicapper for the Fort Worth Star-Telegram, Dallas Morning News, Arkansas Democrat, *and* Arkansas Gazette. *Moss, who grew up in Hot Springs, Arkansas, home of Oaklawn Park, began co-authoring a daily newspaper column at age fourteen. He eventually left pharmacy school for a full-time newspaper job. Moss also developed the Moss Pace Figures that are calculated in conjunction with the Beyer Speed Figures.*

➤ **I am fourteen years old, and after I get out of college, I want to cover horse racing on TVG, HRTV, or maybe even ESPN. Do you have any advice about covering horse racing?** — Louisville, Kentucky

I was in the newspaper business for twenty years, covering horse racing and occasionally other sports before I started in TV. But there were more racing-specific media then. I'll give you the same advice I gave my twenty-three-year-old son, who is graduating next month with a degree in broadcast journalism: Focus on other sports and even hard news, get plenty of experience, and then if you still want to slide over into horse racing and a position becomes available, go for it.

➤ **When handicapping, do you consider any trainer more dangerous in stakes races on the turf or dirt? Do you believe that trainers have specialties and are better on certain surfaces?** — Elmont, New York

Horsemen like Bill Mott are great trainers for any surface and distance. Mott seems to be typecast as a turf specialist in recent years, but I remember his early years as a trainer, when he had a barn full of standout dirt horses and hardly a grass runner in the bunch. Some trainers do better with first-time starters than others. Some are better with [horses off] long layoffs, and so forth, but I'm a believer that success on grass or dirt is primarily a function of the types of horses trainers are provided.

➤ **Ragozin and Thorograph sheets, as well as Beyer and other speed figures, have greatly changed the way people handicap races. You've introduced the Moss Pace figures; what's the feedback?**
— East Saticoy, California

The feedback has been good thus far, but I must admit that I've been so busy trying to keep my head above water that I haven't had much time to survey the landscape, if you know what I mean.

➤ **What do you think of the Trakus system at Keeneland and its potential for the sport?** — Louisville, Kentucky

I love the data generated by Trakus. I thought some data [at first] was a little suspect, but the kinks seem to have been ironed out. I especially like the distance-traveled statistic used in tandem with the horses' individual times to get a feet-per-second figure. The "sheets" and Thorograph guys have got to be loving that stuff.

➤ **How would you change racing for the better?** — Ozone Park, New York

I wouldn't be a very popular racing czar. I'd immediately slash the number of racing days at most tracks. Racing is obviously my favorite sport, and I think it's wonderful, but you can get too much of a good thing. In my opinion, no race meeting should be longer than five or six weeks.

➤ **Of all the racetracks you have visited, which one is your favorite, and why?** — Elizabethtown, Kentucky

My favorite is Del Mar because of the laid-back beach vibe. I'd love to live there someday, if I can afford it. Others high on my list, in no particular order, are: Keeneland (young and enthusiastic crowd), Arlington (best facility in the U.S.), Saratoga (you can still hear Man o' War running), and Oaklawn (my hometown track). I also enjoyed Emerald Downs during a trip there a couple of years back.

TALKIN' HORSES

RANDY MOSS

➤ **The horse racing community is such a close-knit group. Has it been difficult not showing any bias in your announcing? Now that so many of the really great jockeys have retired, tell us who were some of your personal favorites and why?** — Atlanta, Georgia

The racing community is close-knit, but I'm not really a part of that. I'm on the periphery, if that makes sense. For example, I very seldom have dinner or socialize with owners, trainers, or jockeys. So showing bias isn't really a problem. The bigger issue is knowing when to criticize and when to keep your mouth shut because racing is much more complex than most sports. In the NFL, if a receiver drops a pass, he drops a pass. But if a jockey gets shut off, he may have made a lousy decision or the trouble could have been caused by factors beyond his control. If a jockey gets involved in a speed duel, he may have used bad judgment, or he may have had specific instructions from the owner or trainer to get the lead. I make an effort to praise or criticize only when appropriate, but we make mistakes, too. More frequently, I hear from owners and trainers who are upset because I disrespected one of their horses. But anyone who gives opinions is bound to rub some people the wrong way. I will say this—in the newspaper biz, I occasionally covered the NFL, NBA, major-league baseball, and college sports, and that gave me an increased appreciation for the many quality people in Thoroughbred racing. We're lucky. As for recently retired jockeys, other than my colleague Jerry Bailey, the ones at the very top are hard to separate. Laffit Pincay, Pat Day, Chris McCarron, Eddie Delahoussaye, Gary Stevens ... they were all so good that, in my opinion, the differences between them were minute. If you gave them the best horse, they all got the job done.

➤ **With all due respect to your employer, do you think televised racing coverage in general needs to be more objective?** — Crawdad, Kentucky

You'll never see an NFL broadcast between two 2-10 teams begin with a dissertation about how pathetic and unimportant the game is. The name of the game in television is ratings, and the objective is to try to give people a reason to watch, not encourage them to change the channel. If you have a lemon, you try to at least mention the positives, if they exist. We do have a journalistic responsibility to be objective, and if we have a weak race, we don't ignore that fact. But it probably won't be the first thing we talk about at the beginning of a show. In racing, this is a little easier than in other sports. For example, it's an impossibility for that game between 2-10 teams to have an impact on the post-season. But although a particular Hollywood Gold Cup might have a weaker-than-usual field, the possibility exists that a horse could deliver a breakthrough performance and go on to win the Breeders' Cup Classic. It happens all the time in major stakes. And we don't do claiming races.

➤ **My question has to do with the Bud longshot. Why haven't the sponsors put up some real money and given fans watching the telecast an opportunity to win big?** — Estero, Florida

I'll give Howie Mandel a ring. Actually, I once met Vanna White at LAX airport. She was sweet and tiny. Seriously, I'll pass along your idea to the department that tries to get sponsors to spend more money. It would add pizazz to the show, but the funds have to come from somewhere.

➤ **Who do you think is the greatest racehorse you have ever seen and why?** — Holland, Michigan

The best horse I've seen was Spectacular Bid as a four-year-old. As Buddy Delp said, he was the greatest horse ever to look through a bridle. I actually think he could have beaten the three-year-old Secretariat, who I would place at number two.

➤ **How important do you think it is for a Kentucky Derby horse to be "battle tested" before the race, specifically, racing in big fields or overcoming an unforeseen obstacle during a race?** — Louisville, Kentucky

To me, it's an advantage for a horse to have seen large fields prior to the Kentucky Derby. But this is one of those vague preferences. It's hard to quantify exactly how important this is.

➤ **With all the talk of "invaluable experience" horses need to win the Kentucky Derby, why are there no races carded at 1¼ mile prior to the Derby?**
— Henderson, Nevada

If racing secretaries carded a 1¼-mile prep race, few horses would enter. Trainers consider it enough of a challenge to get a three-year-old to run that far on the first Saturday in May, much less a month earlier. Sheikh Mohammed tried this. A few years ago he changed the distance of the UAE Derby from 1⅛ to 1¼ miles, but after a couple of runnings he realized his mistake and switched it back.

➤ **What do you make of the outside posts on Derby Day? Does a stalker/pacer have a chance past the 12th hole?** — West Islip, New York

Outside post positions—even on the extreme outside—are actually an advantage in those Derby runnings in which the pace is out of control. That's because the front-runners move over to the inside positions and then go into reverse on the second turn, clogging up the inside paths. But if the pace is only moderate, the far outside posts are at a big disadvantage because the field is more bunched into the first turn and there are fewer gaps that permit a rider to angle over and save some ground.

➤ **Why don't the powers in racing do more to promote jockeys?** — Indian Orchard, Massachusetts

We've been talking about this for years, and it just never seems to happen. Horses come and go, but top jockeys remain good stories for a much longer period of time.

➤ **Who is your all-time favorite racehorse that you have ever seen run? Who is your favorite racehorse from the old days whom you haven't ever seen run, [but] only read about?** — Glen Gardner, New Jersey

I mentioned the best horse earlier [Spectacular Bid]. I think I mentioned my recent sentimental favorite [With Anticipation]. My all-time favorite horse is one that few have even heard of—Barbizon Streak. It was an adolescent thing. My favorite from the old days would probably be Swaps. He might be the most underrated horse in history.

➤ **Do you feel that the Derby post position should be based on graded earnings or "quality wins" rather than luck of the draw?** — Minnetonka, Minnesota

The graded-earnings rule has exhausted its usefulness and needs to be changed. I wrote a column specifying how I would change the Derby eligibility, and it has to do with qualifying performance similar to the Masters in golf. The top three finishers from the Blue Grass, Wood Memorial, Florida Derby, and

Santa Anita Derby automatically get Derby berths, as do the top two from eight or ten other races, and the winner of a dozen more races. It works.

➤ **With top-class horses running less each year than they have in the past (example, recent Horses of the Year run four to six times), is it time to put greater than two starts before the Derby to rest as a factor?** — Pittsford, New York

The way racehorses are being trained at the top levels is in the middle of a seismic shift, so all the old Derby "rules" won't be long for this world. In the old days, horses ran so frequently that midseason layoffs were always a sign of a serious physical problem. Back then, the horses that had only two three-year-old preps before the Derby were walking wounded. That isn't the case any more. By design, trainers are choosing prep schedules of fewer starts. So most of the old rules no longer apply.

➤ **I love the commentary you and the team provide; it brings a lighthearted and often humorous approach to handicapping. What was your favorite Derby of the nineteen you have covered?** — New York, New York

We try not to take ourselves too seriously. Before every show Jack Whitaker used to remind himself, "This isn't brain surgery." We aren't covering Iraq. This is life's toy department. My favorite Derby was my first, Genuine Risk in 1980. Back then press box seating was according to tenure, and through an odd quirk of fate, I wound up watching the race from spot number two between Red Smith and Dick Young. Imagine that shaggy-haired, twenty-one-year-old punk watching his first Derby beside Red Smith. He seemed to take it in stride, though.

➤ **Do you use the Ragozin Sheets? If not, why and what's your major handicapping tool?** — Toronto, Ontario, Canada

For about twenty years now I've been part of the team that assists Andy Beyer in producing the Beyer Speed Figures. So I'm a strong believer in the Beyers and in the value of an accurate set of figures. But the Ragozin Sheets and Thorograph are also top-quality products. The numerical scales are different, but the methodology behind the making of the three sets of figures is essentially the same. The primary difference is that Ragozin and Jerry Brown factor in ground loss and weight carried, and the Beyer numbers don't. I also have a distinct fondness for pace figures, by the way.

> **How hard is it for you, as an expert handicapper, to translate artificial track performances into potential dirt performances, and how will the synthetic Derby preps play into your handicapping come Derby day?** — Louisville, Kentucky

I'm not sure anyone can effectively translate it, other than the process of looking at a horse's prior experience on synthetic tracks and conventional dirt.

> **What do you believe will attract more people to this great sport/ entertainment?** — Cranford, New Jersey

Racing can be improved in many areas, but an important one is a simple supply-and-demand equation. Look at what Keeneland has become—large crowds of enthusiastic college-age kids mixed with veteran gamblers. Keeneland has become the "place to be" for the college crowd, and as a result lifelong racing fans are being formed. And what causes this? Three weeks of racing in the spring and three in the fall. Racing should be an event to be eagerly anticipated, not something that drags on and on every month of the year. There is no longer a racing "season" in many areas, and when there is a glut in supply, demand decreases. This is something that American racing could learn from the European model. If the NFL played every day of the year, it would lose popularity as well. The problem is, try telling racetracks and states that they need to make less profit in the short term for a healthier long-term product. Horsemen's groups typically fight any proposed reduction in racing dates as well.

> **How much time do you devote to learning names, facts, and figures prior to a major broadcast?** — Mt. Gretna, Pennsylvania

I'm usually at the telecast site at midday Thursday, and Jeannine [Edwards], Jerry [Bailey] and I are going full-bore up until the time the light goes on Saturday afternoon. Lots of computer research, phone calls, and visits to the barn area and paddock. Overpreparation is my comfort level. If we have some kind of oddball delay, I know I'll always have something to throw out there.

TALKIN' HORSES
WITH

BILL NACK

Retired Sports Illustrated *writer Bill Nack participated in two of the most widely read "Talkin' Horses" online chats, in 2006 and in 2007. An authority on the great racehorse Secretariat, Nack wrote* Secretariat: The Making of a Champion *and* Ruffian: A Racetrack Romance. *A former writer and columnist for* Newsday, *Nack spent twenty-three years as an investigative reporter and general feature writer at* Sports Illustrated. *During his tenure with the sports weekly, Nack covered all sports but focused primarily on boxing and horse racing. In 2003 he compiled an anthology of his magazine writing in the book* My Turf: Horses, Boxers, Blood Money and the Sporting Life. *Born in Chicago and raised in Skokie, Illinois, Nack graduated from the University of Illinois before serving a two-year period in the Army, the second in Vietnam. After leaving the service, he was a political and environmental writer at* Newsday *for four years, a Turf writer for three years, and then served as a* Newsday *sports columnist for four years before joining* Sports Illustrated. *He has three daughters and a son and lives in Washington, D.C. Nack was also a consultant on the ESPN-made movie* Ruffian, *based on his book about the filly.*

➤ **I read your book on Secretariat and loved it. What was he like, both on the track and at Claiborne?** — Hanover Park, Illinois

Secretariat was a chivalrous prince of a colt who was playful and mischievous—he once grabbed my notebook out of my hand with his teeth, when I was talking to his groom, Ed Sweat—and stayed the same as a stallion at Claiborne. A kid could have ridden him. The older he got, it seemed, the more of a ham he became, and throughout his life he used to stop and pose whenever he heard the click of a camera.

TALKIN' HORSES

BILL NACK

➤ **Do you believe Pat Day lost [the 1989 Preakness] for Easy Goer [against Sunday Silence]?** — Atlanta, Georgia

When Easy Goer lost that stretch drive to Sunday Silence in the Preakness, many people blamed Pat Day because Easy Goer's head was cocked to one side, and that certainly did nothing for the colt's chances. I don't think he'd have won if they had gone around again. That Preakness was one of the epic struggles in the history of the turf, a ding-dong stretch battle that left thousands breathless.

➤ **How did you find those bits of information, which aren't common knowledge, to weave into the book [on Secretariat]?** — Nauvoo, Alabama

I collected many facts for the Secretariat book by studying old newspapers, books, and magazine clips. I also talked to many people who were around in the days of yore. For instance, I got the story about Nasrullah's death in the paddock from Claiborne's legendary old groom, Snow Fields.

➤ **Are you still carrying a certain feather around? Readers of your book on Secretariat will know to what feather I refer.** — La Mesa, California

The pigeon feather remained in my wallet—along with an old laminated picture of Swaps—until the wallet was lifted at a prizefight (Roberto Duran vs. Davey Moore) in Madison Square Garden in New York in the mid-1980s. Too bad the crook wasn't considerate enough—as many pickpockets are—to take the credit cards and money and toss the wallet into a mailbox so that the U.S. Postal Service could have returned it to me.

➤ **What are your top five horse racing moments?** — Springfield, Missouri

1. Secretariat's Belmont victory.
2. Ruffian's Spinaway victory.
3. Forego's nose victory over Honest Pleasure in the 1976 Marlboro Cup.
4. Cigar's triumph over Soul of the Matter in the 1996 Dubai World Cup.
5. Seattle Slew's magnificence in defeat in the 1978 Jockey Club Gold Cup, when he lost the lead to Exceller at the top of the stretch but battled back to nearly win it all.

(Bonus I): The last seven-eighths of a mile of the 1978 Belmont Stakes between Affirmed and Alydar, with Affirmed winning the Triple Crown in a squeaker.

(Bonus II): Sunday Silence winning Horse of the Year in 1989 by holding off a final desperate charge by Easy Goer in the Breeders' Cup Classic.

➤ **Which accomplishments do you consider most important in predicting success in the Kentucky Derby?** — Las Vegas, Nevada

I look for a solid two-year-old record and sure signs that a horse is "on the up-tick" in his form cycle. I also look at the trainer because a handful of them win most Derbys. Pedigree is also important: Speed and routing blood make for happy endings.

➤ **Can you tell us your favorite personal moment with "Big Red"?**
— Tustin, California

The early morning of the Belmont Stakes, when he burst from his stall and commenced walking around a cinder ring behind the barn like a stud horse going to the breeding shed, his eyes bulging as he walked on his hind legs, his forelegs pawing at the sky. That day, he was fitter than any horse since Pegasus took off above the treetops. And, at Pimlico, catching that pigeon feather.

➤ **As a [fellow] writer, I am interested in your approach to writing the chapter on Secretariat's Belmont. I go back and reread those passages when I need a horse racing fix.** — Houston, Texas

By the time I got to writing [about] Secretariat's Belmont, I was nearly finished with the book and I got so pumped that I think my nervous energy infused my prose. I loved writing that section of the book. I watched the Belmont about twenty times, talked at length to Ron Turcotte about it, then quizzed all those syndicate members about their reaction to it. And put it all together. It was a blast.

➤ **Apart from Secretariat, of course, which Triple Crown winner do you consider the best?** — Mt. Morris, Michigan

I think Seattle Slew was one of the greatest racehorses of all time, and I suspect that he would have given Secretariat his greatest competition. The other Triple Crown winner I love, though never saw, was Count Fleet—a true freak of nature. But Slew was a monster. I've always said that one of the greatest races of all time would feature three horses at Belmont Park going a flat mile:

TALKIN' HORSES

BILL NACK

Seattle Slew, Dr. Fager, and Swaps. Three true milers going at it with the sun shining and flags flying. What a horse race. By the way, one horse who rarely gets mentioned in conversation as a deserving member of the upper pantheon of modern horses is Kelso. He was a magnificent racehorse. Jockey Eddie Arcaro once told me that Kelso was the greatest racehorse he ever rode. "What about Citation?" I asked him. What Arcaro replied, word for word, was this: "Kelso would have beaten the s**t out of Citation!"

➤ **I know some people who have seen the Ruffian movie are very upset or distressed about the breakdown scene. They say it's extremely graphic. In light of Barbaro, why get so graphic?** — New York, New York

It was the hardest part of the movie for me to watch, but this is what happened to her: Ruffian shattered the two sesamoids in her right front ankle, and I think it's ill-advised and a cheat to make such a catastrophic breakdown less graphic than it was. I've thought about this, but I just don't think that Barbaro's accident and fate should have any bearing on how the Ruffian tragedy was handled on film. The Ruffian movie project was started long before Barbaro came on the scene, and I just don't see how and why one should influence the other. While the breakdown was graphic, it was very brief, and I thought the scenes following the accident were handled with abundant sensitivity. In fact, there was nothing of that horrible scene at the barn that I witnessed and described in my book, with Barbara Janney wailing; with an uninvited vet, Dr. William Reed, giving her a shot he should not have given her; and with Ruffian going into shock, trying to lie down as she bled continuously from the ankle.

These were scenes I witnessed at the barn and none of them is in the movie. When Ruffian awoke from surgery and started thrashing around, according to witness Frank Tours, she threw people around like rag dolls. None of this violence is in the movie. In fact, from her breakdown to her destruction, the scenes are very quiet and subdued. Some would say it's too quiet and subdued—too far from what really happened after she broke down. You be the judge.

➤ **Is it true that you ran across the track after Ruffian broke down and almost got run over by Foolish Pleasure?** — Glen Burnie, Maryland

This is true. It was a damn fool thing to do, but I was caught in the hot whips of the moment, and my sole thought was to get across that racetrack to find out what had happened to that filly. A guard had prevented me from crossing the track when I got there, and I would have had clear sailing if he had let me go. By the time he walked away, diverted by a bunch of photographers, Foolish Pleasure was racing through midstretch and I was ducking under the gate and on my way. Jockey Braulio Baeza saw me and yelled. I heard him scream and I heard the thunder of Foolish Pleasure's hoofbeats as they approached. I froze on the crown of the track. He swept past me. I could feel his wind. The hairs stood up on the back of my neck. All of this is told in my Ruffian book.

➤ **Much has been written about illegal drugs and medications in the sport. The babying of horses also seems to be prevalent today with supplements, massages, and a host of other high-tech treatments. Did [Secretariat] receive any of these so-called advances in the sport or was he just allowed to be a horse?** — Kissimmee, Florida

So far as I know, he was always encouraged and allowed to be a horse, and he retired in 1973 as sound as he was on January 20, 1972, the day he left The Meadow, in Doswell, Virginia, and was vanned to Hialeah to learn how to be a racehorse. I don't know if racetrack speeds have changed much, but I doubt if they've gotten any slower (dirt tracks, that is). The horses were certainly better in the 1970s—the greatest in history, in fact, a period in time when America was at its absolute height in producing the finest racehorses in the world. The gene drain to Europe and Japan had only begun. Our Thoroughbred gene pool was at its fullest and most active, like a pond stocked with thousands of trout, filled with the fastest and stoutest lines from Europe and America. Sorry. The 1970s were the golden age. Not a few horses ran some monster Beyer Speed figures in the 1990s—Formal Gold, Gentlemen and Will's Way each ran a126 Beyer in 1997—but that decade did not have the abundant talent of the 1970s.

➤ **Who would you pick as the best five fillies ever?** — New York, New York

American fillies:
1) Ruffian
2) Twilight Tear
3) Busher
4) Lady's Secret
5) Personal Ensign

TALKIN' HORSES

BILL NACK

➤ **Why haven't we had a Triple Crown winner in many years?**

— Hudsonville, Michigan

If a horse is good enough to win the Triple Crown, the chances are he will win the Triple Crown. If he's not good enough, the racing gods will thwart him and he will lose one of the three. Even if he wins the first two [à la Silver Charm, Real Quiet, and Smarty Jones], he will stub his toe at Belmont Park if he is not worthy of wearing the title. It is amazing how the racing gods have protected the Triple Crown. You have to be really a superior horse to win it—fast, durable, and blessed with stamina—and we are not breeding that caliber of horse these days, not like we used to. Yes, I do believe it will be done again. Someday a monster will come along, and he will dazzle us through all three races. I'll never give up that hope.

➤ **How has racing journalism changed since you first started? Are you concerned there is too much focus on speed figures and other rating systems and less subjective journalistic analysis? Which is easier, writing extended biographies of the greats or filing stories on everyday events?** — Sydney, Australia

The last, first: Writing shorter pieces on weekly or daily deadlines is much easier because they are easier to shape. I wrote a 900-word column four times a week for nearly five years for *Newsday* newspaper and it got easier and easier as time went on and as I got comfortable with the distance, a kind of journalistic sprint. Much more difficult were the 6,000- to 7,000-word stories I later did for *Sports Illustrated*. They took vastly more reporting, of course, and were far more unwieldy and difficult to organize. They were the middle distances, journalistically. But nothing was more daunting than doing a 70,000- to 100,000-word book. When I first sat down to write the Secretariat biography, I felt like a man toeing the line for a marathon. There were days very early on when I didn't know if I could get there or not. But I started it with Secretariat's birth, flashed back through the Chenery/Hancock/Vanderbilt family sagas leading up to the birth, then continued chronologically through his racing career as it culminated in the Triple Crown. Has racing journalism changed? So much coverage has shifted to the Internet that I no longer have to call anybody to find out the names of Steve Haskin's latest Derby Dozen, nor do I have to wait for the next day's papers to find out who won the Florida Derby or the

Lexington Stakes or the Santa Anita Derby.

No, I do not think there is too much focus on the speed figs. I have always been a "beader of horses," as the species is known—a guy who likes to take a bead on horses and values visual impressions as much as numbers on paper, but I've known Andrew Beyer for nearly thirty-five years, since the days when he was inventing the figs and refining them in his Washington, D.C., aerie, and I long ago came to appreciate what a breakthrough he made in the craft of handicapping. Very quickly, hanging around Andy, I came to understand what a useful tool speed figures can be in determining just how fast a horse really ran in any given race, and how solid a performance it was. Or wasn't. I don't think consulting speed figures in any way obviates beading or makes beading for visual impressions any less relevant, and, in fact, I've come to the conclusion that they complement one another as I form my own subjective judgments on Triple Crown or Breeders' Cup candidates.

➤ **Who do you think were a couple of the most underrated horses in racing? Who was the most difficult horse to handle that you covered?**
— Portland, Oregon

John Henry was one of the most ornery horses I've known, a cranky old bastard who insisted on doing things his own way, but oh, how he could run! Underrated? I've always thought title belonged to Old Rosebud, the 1914 Kentucky Derby winner. The late, great Turf writer Charles Hatton once told me: "There was nothing like watching Old Rosebud cut up a field of horses. It was like watching an artist at work." He won the Kentucky Derby in a common gallop and set a new Derby record, 2:03⅖. Rosie held the mark until Twenty Grand raced the mile and a quarter in 2:01⅕ in 1931. Almost totally forgotten, Old Rosebud remains lost in history. Mom's Command has certainly been underrated. Swoon's Son was absolutely one of the best horses to race in America in the mid-1950s, and was underrated and largely forgotten because he did not run in New York. Heck, he won close to a million dollars more than fifty years ago, and he did it in the toughest venue for summer racing in the land—the Middle West, old Arlington, and Washington parks. For four straight years, he was very near the top of the Experimental Free Handicap. He beat Round Table. He beat Bardstown. And he beat Needles, his peer in age, the only time they met, the 1956 American Derby, a grade I race if they'd been grading them in those days.

TALKIN' HORSES

BILL NACK

➤ **How did you develop your eloquence in writing about horses?**
— Saint Paul, Minnesota

I developed affection for horses very early, around the age of eleven or twelve, when our parents bought my sister and me a parade horse to hack around with (he was all white with a black head and we called him Bandit). I also worked two summers at Arlington/Washington parks outside Chicago, first as a failed track photographer who kept forgetting to remove the lens cap and then as a hotwalker/groom. So I had hands-on experience with animals since I was a kid and out of this flowed a lifelong fondness for these magnificent herbivores, particularly the hard-charging, nose-thrusting, uncomplaining Thoroughbreds. That is the horse end of the answer.

Years later, in another incarnation, I developed a great respect and affection for a variety of writers: i.e., F. Scott Fitzgerald, Emily Bronte, H.L. Mencken, William Faulkner, and Vladimir Nabokov. I also became a kind of student of two Irish poets who won the Nobel Prize for literature, W.B. Yeats and Seamus Heaney. I ended up memorizing a lot of Fitzgerald, Mencken, Nabokov, and the two Irish poets. And so I mixed a lot of very diverse writers into my own literary pot. I am very conscious of pace and meter when I write, and rarely compose a serious sentence in which I do not count the syllabic beats, at first consciously, now unconsciously: Stuff reads smoother and often sweeter when you count the beats. This impulse certainly derives from an early and sustained admiration of the work of William Shakespeare, the greatest of all the great masters of English literature. Old Willie counted the beats, as did every other writer I liked and studied from Keats to Yeats to Eliot to Thomas Wolfe, and so I started doing it myself, too—to less poetic effect, of course, but nonetheless …

➤ **I would love to hear your thoughts regarding the latest book on Secretariat [by Lawrence Scanlan] and his relationship with his groom Eddie Sweat. I'm curious why, according to the book, the "racetrack" seemed to ignore his passing.** — Chicago, Illinois

I thought it was wonderful that writer Scanlan took the time to pay such an eloquent tribute to Ed Sweat, the great groom of Secretariat, Riva Ridge, and Chief's Crown. I once wrote a long piece for *Sports Illustrated* on the life of racetrack grooms, and I asked to write it because I was a groom once myself and wanted to tell people what kind of long, arduous hours went into that work and how the racetrack swipes are the unsung heroes of the backstretch, the men and women who toil daily with the horses. It was called "Nobody Knows Their Name." The piece caused an unpleasant stir because I pointed out that, while their horses lived in the very lap of luxury, the grooms often lived in dirty, roach-infested hovels not fit for mice or men. I noted in the story how the groom of Sunday Silence came to Belmont Park, with his horse being trained for a Triple Crown sweep, bedded down the colt in a clean stall with mounds of golden straw and then went to unpack his things in his assigned racetrack room at Belmont. The place was a disgrace. It had to be bombed with a pesticide to kill the army of roaches he encountered there and he had to call rodent-control to get rid of the varmints.

On the great racetrack pecking order, grooms are near the lowest rung. They come and they go like the horses that they care for. Sweat's death was very sad. He was a tremendous man, always upbeat, very talkative and expressive, even eloquent when you got him on the subject of Secretariat, and he was doing with his life precisely what he wanted to do. "What I was born to do," he once told me. I do not know why racing people did not show up at his funeral, but it certainly wasn't for lack of admirers and friends, of which there were legions.

➤ **As you watched "Big Red" in the paddock that day before the race [Belmont Stakes], did you ever think another horse would come along to equal what you were witnessing?** — Sarasota, Florida

Here's what led up to that paddock scene on Belmont Day: After Secretariat's record-breaking Kentucky Derby, when he went from last to first through the first one and one-sixteenth miles of the race, when he ran each successive quarter mile faster than the preceding one, when he went the last half mile in :46⅖, I began to believe what I had only hoped was true before: That this was the best horse I ever saw and maybe the best horse that ever lived. His stunning charge around the tight first turn in the Preakness only fortified that notion, and I can still hear longtime Maryland handicapper Clem Florio striding through the press box saying: "Preakness horses don't do what Secretariat just did! They just don't do that! No, I've never seen one take that first turn like that … and win! Never." And on and on Clem went like that.

Even though the colt had just set two track records (Florio, as well as *DRF*'s Frenchy Schwartz, among others, clocked him in a record 1:53⅖ in that

Preakness Stakes), even though he had worked three times at Belmont Park before the June 9 Belmont Stakes— [three quarters] in 1:12⅕ on May 27; a mile in 1:34⅘, up nine furlongs in 1:48⅗, on June 1; and a half in :46⅗ on the Wednesday before the race—I was still surprised to see him walking on his hind legs around the paddock outside Barn 5 at 6:03 a.m. on the morning of the race, floating around it like a dressage horse as poor Charlie Davis begged him to come down. He moved as if on springs. I was surprised at this because, in spite of the fact that he was the fittest racehorse I had ever seen, he had never done anything remotely like that in all the mornings I had spent around him. But that little girl kept rattling her water bucket in the nearby pony barn and he kept rising up, looking like a great blue marlin breaking water, pawing at the sky as he walked on his back legs, until finally an alarmed Henny Hoefner told Charlie to take him in before he hurt himself. No, I never saw anything like that, and don't suspect I'll ever see it again.

➤ **What do you think the industry as a whole should be doing to attract young racing fans?** — Louisville, Kentucky

I am not a marketer, so this is a little out of my realm, but I was drawn to the racetrack as a kid because I enjoyed watching good horses perform consistently and well and because I was able to form attachments to a host of horses who ran in the Chicago area over several years: i.e., Round Table, Swoon's Son, Bardstown, Sir Tribal. I also grew fond of some of the low-rung claiming horses who kept coming back, year after year, for more: i.e., Fleet Argo, Abby Sting, Sanders Road, et al. Do you know what would happen to a Round Table or Swoon's Son today if they were in the hands of Coolmore or Godolphin? They'd be retired at the end of their three-year-old year, as Bernardini was last year, and we certainly would not have enjoyed Round Table or Swoon's Son through their five-year-old years, as I did. I saw each of them race dozens of times in the 1950s. No sport eats its young as voraciously as horse racing, and because of this the young fan of today is unable to make attachments to any of its stars—I mean "emotional" attachments—because most of the good horses quickly disappear into that great money-pit known as the breeding shed. I thought the retirement of Secretariat, following his three-year-old year, was one of the most fan-destructive things that any major sport had ever done to itself. The breeders in the syndicate simply couldn't wait to get him to the breeding shed so they could earn big dollars selling his foals or seasons to the horse. At the end of his three-year-old year, naïve as I was, I remember hoping that the greatest sportsman on the syndicate, Paul Mellon, would call a meeting of the group and urge them to let this extraordinary horse race through his four-year-old year, with the members divvying up what money he earned along the way. I mentioned this to one syndicate member and he looked at me like I was some kind of loony.

It was the first time I realized how badly the game missed all those old families of the 1920s and 1930s and 1940s, families who bred horses to race, who bred them not for sales rings but rather for winner's circles. These were the days when sportsmen ruled the sport, and those days were clearly no more. Just think about it. There is no good analogy in other sports, but imagine, for whatever reason, the New York Giants sending Willie Mays into retirement after his second or third year in centerfield. Too bad that Secretariat's breeder, Christopher Chenery, did not live to see his finest creation. The man's death forced the sale to the syndicate. Had the horse stayed sound, Chris Chenery might have raced him through his five-year-old year, into full maturity as a racehorse. Anyway … Here racing had its biggest star in history—a true iconic figure, in living flesh, as fit as ten fiddles—and suddenly he was whisked off television screens forever so a bunch of fat cats could get fatter. In terms of the overall health of the sport, was there anything more insane than that? Can you imagine what Secretariat would have done as a mature racehorse? He'd have carried the proverbial refrigerator, as short-coupled as he was, and probably broken records that would have stood for years: 1:44 for a mile and an eighth? How 'bout 1:56⅕ for a mile and a quarter?

After conquering this American world, the syndicate and Penny Tweedy might have taken him to Paris for the Arc de Triomphe. The great Allez France won the Arc in 1974. What a race that would have been! Who knows? Too bad we will never know. What a shame. Anyway, when he left the scene, a lot of young fans surely threw up their arms and left with him.

➤ **I was wondering if you could pass on a good recollection [of the Belmont].** — Chicago, Illinois

The 1978 Belmont, when Affirmed was striving to win the Triple Crown, and his foil in the Derby and Preakness, Alydar, moved to him at the seven-eighths pole at Belmont Park, driving to Affirmed's side in a bold bid to make a race of

TALKIN' HORSES
BILL NACK

it early and deny Affirmed the ultimate crown. Belmont Park became instantly electrified as Alydar drove to Affirmed's flanks. For the rest of that epochal event, no more than a head separated them, and deep in the stretch a roar went up when it seemed as though Alydar had thrust his nose in front. But Affirmed dug in and battled back. At the finish, his right eye looking rearward—he reminded me of Moby Dick staring back at Ahab lashed to the spearing ropes—he seemed to say to Alydar, "Come get me if you can!" What a finish! What a Belmont!

➤ **Is there anything writers like yourself have gained or learned from the whole experience [of Barbaro]?** — Newmarket, England

Barbaro's breakdown and ultimate demise constituted the first time in my experience that racing, as a sport, was not badly wounded by such an incident—by a catastrophic injury leading to a horse's death. I thought that Ruffian's breakdown during the great match race with Foolish Pleasure—and her death following surgery some eight hours later—hurt the sport grievously. I met many people over the years who told me that they never went to another horse race after that. It was simply devastating, and much of the ensuing anger and disillusionment grew out of the fact that it all happened so suddenly, on national television, and the very next day the headlines seemed strung like black crepe across the length and breadth of the sport. I had seen Black Hills break down on national television in the 1959 Belmont Stakes, but Ruffian's catastrophic breakdown was really the first time that a horse of giant stature—a genuine superstar who had already achieved iconic status, who had a huge following among nonracing as well as racing fans—had broken down before our very eyes and then died. It caused as much confusion as it did shock: "Did they shoot her?" one tearful woman asked me the next day.

"No, they don't shoot horses," I told her. "They put her to sleep."

And: "Why couldn't they save her?" and: "Does this happen a lot?"

The death of Go for Wand was equally wrenching. Here was another champion breaking down in a nationally televised race, only this time she went sprawling in the middle of the homestretch at Belmont Park, her jock looking like a rag doll as he smashed to the ground. The lovely little Wand was euthanized right where the outrider had pulled her over on her side. My mother, a long-time racing fan and avid race-watcher on television, called that night and said, "That's it; I'm not watching this on television anymore. What's happened to our sport?" Her reaction was very typical. The sport was wounded once again.

Barbaro's breakdown and long struggle to survive did not have the same negative effect. Why? I think it actually became a positive because the sporting public in America—many not racing fans to start with—got involved in his struggle to live and ultimately saw how devotedly hard so many people worked to save him. Because he lived as long as he did, people came to understand how difficult it is to keep laminitis at bay in a horse with only three good legs. They came to understand, through the education provided by television features and newspaper and magazine stories, that convalescing horses are not like convalescing people, that they simply cannot lie down for weeks on end as their bones heal, that healing a horse with broken bones is vastly more daunting and complicated. So, in the end, there was a great sense of sadness when Barbaro died—he had become America's favorite pet—but there was no confusion and there was no anger, at least none that I heard. If anything, there was a renewed interest in the sport from people who had followed Barbaro's ordeal to the end. There was an emotional carryover into this year's Triple Crown, a genuine interest from people that Barbaro had introduced to racing, and I believe this was behind the 12 percent spike in TV ratings for the Derby.

So the Barbaro experience, from the standpoint of the sport as it is viewed by the public, was more of a positive than a negative. The other major positive, of course, is the medical strides made by Dean Richardson and his staff at New Bolton in the treatment of catastrophically injured horses. They know a lot more now about saving these injured animals than they did a year ago.

➤ **I recall in the week prior to [Secretariat's] loss to Onion that he broke the track record at Saratoga for a mile and a sixteenth while doing a morning workout; did your research verify that?** — Lexington, Kentucky

On July 27, 1973, Secretariat worked a mile at Saratoga in 1:34 flat. Jockey Ron Turcotte, who was on him that morning, later told stableman Frank Tours that he didn't like the work. Heavy rains had washed out the track, and the inside of it, down by the rail, was hard sand with no cushion, like the part of a beach where the waves pound ashore. The track was blazingly fast. Turcotte told Tours, "Don't believe that work. The horse doesn't feel right to me."

In fact, he was incubating a virus, and eight days later, running a temperature, he lost the Whitney Stakes to Onion, a decent horse that did not belong on the same track with him. Yes, it was a brilliant mile workout, but probably the last thing he needed as a horse who was getting sick.

➤ **After "Big Red," which horses do you consider have come the closest to his greatness as a racehorse?** — Caracas, Venezuela

I am citing only horses that I've seen, and they are: Swaps and Nashua, Kelso, Damascus and Dr. Fager, Ruffian, Forego, Seattle Slew, Affirmed and Alydar, Spectacular Bid, and Cigar.

➤ **In a world of what ifs, who wins the Ruffian/Foolish Pleasure match, and a Dr. Fager/Secretariat at a flat mile?** — Versailles, Kentucky

I think she was a faster and better racehorse, but his busy career—against the best and toughest colts of his generation—gave him the edge in the match race. I talked to a lot of trainers about this before the event, and while they thought Ruffian was the greater of the two as a racehorse, most of them thought that he was the one who was going to take the most beating.

I think Secretariat beats Dr. Fager doing anything. Most people don't realize how truly fast Secretariat was because he became a legend winning at classic distances, but Turcotte always said that Secretariat was the fastest, pure running machine he'd ever been on, regardless of distances and that, in a match race against Dr. Fager, he would run head and head with him until the turn for home. Then, with that giant heart pumping Secretariat home, would draw away to win it. The really great match race is Dr. Fager and Seattle Slew at a flat mile, Belmont Park, 126 pounds each. How do you see that one?

➤ **Mr. Nack, excluding your own, what top racing books [should] every fan read?** — Taos, New Mexico

1). *The Sound of Horses*, by David Alexander

2). Anything written by Jay Hovdey, especially on Whittingham and Cigar

3). *Racing in America*, by Walter Spence Vosburgh

4). *Bull*, the biography, by Howard Wright

5). *Seabiscuit*, by Laura Hillenbrand

6). *McIlvanney on Horse Racing*, by Hugh McIlvanney

7). *Picking Winners*, by Andrew Beyer

➤ **Is there one racetrack that whenever you get there that fond memories just overwhelm you?** — Scottsburg, Indiana

I love Arlington Park, even though the old one burned down, and can still walk through the new place, smell the cigar smoke of the gamblers, and instantly think of my cigar-puffing dad. I also love Saratoga, with its ancient traditions dating back to Gettysburg and that wonderful stable area stretched along the backside.

➤ **Congratulations on your latest masterwork, *Ruffian: A Racetrack Romance*. It is a very emotional, as well as poetic, book. Was it as emotionally exhausting to write as it has been to read?** — Wayne, Illinois

There were days, in the writing of *Ruffian*, that I had to walk away from it. One thing really surprised me in working on it, after more than thirty years, the emotions are as raw as they were when it all went down at Belmont Park that July afternoon. I guess I'd just buried them. It was not easy going back to that barn after the race, not all these years later, but I needed to go.

Today I feel more pride in writing this story than I've felt in anything I've ever written about the Turf, with the possible exception of "Pure Heart." The Ruffian book is much longer than "Pure Heart" and says precisely what I wanted to say when I launched into it. The story had been percolating inside me for many years—I was always going to include it as a major chapter in a memoir I'd been planning—and it was a wonderfully cathartic experience to sit down and let it flow. As I mentioned in the acknowledgements, thank goodness I had followed her so closely through my work at *Newsday*, as a Turf writer, and also through my weekly work as the New York correspondent of *The Thoroughbred Record*. Between those two publications, I had a kind of Ruffian diary from which I could draw in writing the book. Plus, reading those old stories reminded me of things unwritten that I had long ago forgotten.

TALKIN' HORSES
WITH
ALAN PORTER

Pedigree adviser Alan Porter has been professionally involved with Thoroughbreds for almost thirty years, has written about racing and breeding for more than twenty-five years, and has planned Thoroughbred matings for eighteen years. Porter has been involved in the matings for more than one hundred stakes winners, including champions or classic winners in at least ten countries. He has written columns for the Daily Racing Form, Thoroughbred Daily News, Pacemaker, The Australian Bloodhorse Review, *and* Owner and Breeder International, *as well as contributed to numerous other publications in Europe, Japan, and North America. Porter has also authored three books, appeared as a speaker at numerous seminars and conferences around the world, and provided pedigree television commentary for several networks.*

➤ **On stallion potential alone, if you had to take a well-performed horse with a modest pedigree or a moderately performed horse with a good pedigree, which would you choose as a stallion?**
— Lexington, Kentucky

There are always exceptions, but I think, historically speaking, if you look at achievement relative to expectation and opportunity, it has been [the] moderately performed horses with good pedigrees that have outperformed initial opportunity/expectations. [It's the] high-class horses with modest pedigrees that tend to be among those who are more disappointing. Strawberry Road is an interesting one; he was a very good horse whose pedigree wasn't fashionable, and he was by a well-bred modest runner (Whiskey Road) who turned out to be a pretty good stallion in Australia. Not to take anything from Strawberry Road, who was a good sire (and looks a promising broodmare sire), but he was also helped by the fact that his owner had a good broodmare band

and was happy to have later developers and turf horses, which Strawberry Road frequently got.

➤ **At what point do you ignore a conformational flaw because the pedigree is very good, or when do you ignore a poor pedigree because the conformation is stellar?** — Sacramento, California

I don't think I would ignore a poor pedigree for stellar conformation if I was breeding to race. That kind of horse is probably better for producing for the sales ring. For a runner, we are primarily looking for athleticism. From the point of view of using a stallion who has conformation flaws—which most do, including some of the very best—I would first be concerned whether he was athletic enough to run through them. I would then be concerned to send a mare who did not herself duplicate or throw those faults. Other than that, I wouldn't lose sleep about conformation flaws in a well-bred, well-performed horse; he would certainly have a better shot than a beautiful individual who couldn't run or had a poor pedigree.

➤ **You suggest in your writings that the breed has reached a new pinnacle, [and] that there is now far less genetic diversity. As I recall your conclusion was based on the following: 1) [There has been] no final time improvement in [the] Triple Crown and similar distance races. 2) [There is an] inability of the present and recent past stallion population to establish a relatively consistent upper hierarchy. What other evidence—empirical evidence, if any—have you to support such conclusions?** — Wynnewood, Pennsylvania

Actually, this is not quite my hypothesis. My opinion would be not that the breed has reached a new pinnacle but that the standard of the best horses (in the U.S. and leading European countries) ceased improving significantly around thirty to fifty years ago. There's nothing particularly odd about this; it's happened in human athletics in some events. For example, in the 800m [race] only one person has bettered the time set by Sebastian Coe about twenty years ago. I don't recall suggesting that there is less genetic diversity; in the U.S., however, there is more of a specialization of type focused on horses who are most effective between seven to nine furlongs and who can gut it out to a mile and a quarter on occasion.

TALKIN' HORSES

ALAN PORTER

I have never actually conducted the study you note in [your first point]. What is clear is that final times of races are not dramatically improving. Dr. Fager's world record for one mile on dirt, for example, has not been beaten on that surface (it was tied by Najran). However, a low 1:33 mile (a record when set by Buckpasser) is not particularly rare, and an awfully lot of ordinary horses can run 1:09 and change, 1:22 and change, and so on—times which would have been exceptional fifty years ago. What I would suggest is that the standard of the very best horses is not significantly improving, but the standard of the average horse has, so there is less of a gap between the best and the rest. This means that competition at the highest level is more intense, and one of the results is that the best horses can't compete as often as in the past.

It's fairly clear that, if you look at the best stallions of say twenty years ago, there was a dominant group—Seattle Slew, Mr. Prospector, Nijinsky II, Alydar, Fappiano, Nureyev, Danzig—and I don't think anyone would suggest that there is such a well-defined hierarchy now. Another indicator is that (from memory) ten of the last thirteen Kentucky Derby winners have been sired by stallions who were standing at $15,000 or less when they sired the Derby winner. The best stallions aren't able to dominate the greatest race.

➤ **So many big name stallions are [breeding] 100 to 150 mares a season. How many mares do you think a stallion can responsibly be bred to, provided the demand is there?** — Baltimore, Maryland

In terms of the [stallions' ability] to handle bigger books, there is the potential because the number of covers per mare has come down with improved veterinary techniques.

In terms of the effect on the commercial market and the breed as a whole, I think the real question is, unless there is some outside regulation imposed (highly unlikely) or self regulation (also somewhat unlikely), large books for the most popular stallions are a reality for the immediate future, so how do we best deal with the situation? For a breeder, I think it is very important not to overbreed a mare as a buyer is going to have so many other weanlings or yearlings to choose from. The bigger books also mean that stallions [whose performance is disappointing] get found out in a shorter period of time. For good or bad, however, it's something we're going to have to live with for the moment.

➤ **Are many breeders taking into account [veterinary procedures such as] airway surgeries, bleeding, and procedures on foal legs in selecting matings?** — Sunnellon, Florida

It's pretty difficult—if not impossible—at the moment to know which stallions and mares had some procedures when they were foals. I've known of correct mares who consistently threw very crooked foals to a variety of stallions, suggesting [the mares] might have had corrective surgery. I don't know about the airway surgery, although I know one major claiming owner said he did a myectomy on every horse he claimed. I think we have to accept that virtually all horses are going to race on Salix/Lasix as long as it is perceived [as] being generally performance enhancing.

➤ **Who will win the Kentucky Derby first: a) German-bred runner b) Japanese-bred runner?** — Bethesda, Maryland

I don't see either happening in the near future, but I'd go for Japan, as they have more U.S. bloodlines and some dirt racing whereas German horses are exclusively turf.

➤ **Do you think Alysheba is underrated as a broodmare sire?**
— Cave Creek, Arizona

I think he's more of a wise guy horse than underrated. That is, those who are into pedigrees recognize him as a very nice broodmare sire, albeit more for turf than dirt. The problem with trying to find a younger one is that he didn't get such good mares as he got older, so the younger daughters tend not to have such good pedigrees.

➤ **It seems like we're getting more of a trickle of Sunday Silence progeny in this country than we've had in the past. How would you have expected him to perform as an American sire all these years had he stayed, and will the influence of his offspring be significant in the United States? Was his influence overrated in Japan for any reason like race restrictions or purse inflation?** — Raleigh, North Carolina

Given that the best Japanese horses are clearly very good, we'd have to acknowledge Sunday Silence as an outstanding stallion. He probably received better opportunities in Japan in relative terms than he would have received

ALAN PORTER

here, but it's hard to believe that he wouldn't have sired some very good horses in the U.S. as well. He's probably not going to have a huge influence in the U.S. as it's unlikely that we are going to get one of his top sons to be commercial here; so, unless there is a top-class U.S.-sired horse out of a Sunday Silence mare which goes on to be a stallion, his influence will probably be limited. [He is] a very good stallion by any standards, but best regarded as a seminal influence in his time and place like Star Kingdom in Australia and Sir Tristram in New Zealand.

➤ **Is your expertise sought in the Southern Hemisphere?**
— Auckland, New Zealand

I'm fortunate enough to have been able to work with many clients in the Southern Hemisphere and have been lucky enough to be involved with the matings for a Melbourne Cup and a Golden Slipper winner, as well as the winner of this year's Victoria Derby.

➤ **Pardon my ignorance on the subject, but why can't a horse go to stud and also remain in training to race?** — Columbus, Ohio

Actually, some horses have done just that, one notable example being Seabiscuit. In general, however, a horse is frequently injured, or [is] at or passing his peak when the decision to retire him is made, so there would be no upside in bringing him back to race. It would also be hard to get a horse back to fitness for major fall contests after a full stud season (and that assumes he isn't shuttling to the Southern Hemisphere). Of course, there is also the question of how focused on racing a horse would be after discovering the delights of breeding!

➤ **What tests are done on a horse to determine if he will be a good breeding prospect? Is this done by the owner before [the decision is made] to retire this horse to stud?** — Newark, Delaware

The only formal test which usually happens is, if there is going to be a financial transaction, there is an inspection of the horse to determine that he is insurable as a stallion prospect (testicles of normal size and consistency and so on). Apart from that, it is a question of whether a horse's performances and pedigree will lead to a buyer purchasing him for duty as a stallion, or whether the owner considers it worth the expense of standing him.

➤ **Why [are] so many horses gelded [castrated] at such an early age? Wouldn't that diminish their eventual value as there will be no stud careers for them?** — San Francisco, California

Funny Cide was cut because a testicle interfered with his action, so if he hadn't been gelded, we'd probably never have heard of him. Forego was gelded because of his extreme size and difficult temperament. Actually, relatively few horses are cut here early in their career, as opposed to say, England. Usually, if a horse is cut, the decision is taken because of physical (too heavy fronted, testicles interfering with action) or temperamental concerns. Owners do not generally lightly do away with the potential stud careers of promising and well-bred youngsters!

➤ **Please comment on Roberto's influence on the breed and explain why breeders were historically reluctant to embrace his bloodlines.**
— Locust Valley, New York

Roberto has generally been traveling in the direction of being a turf influence. I think that was the biggest problem with him commercially. Of his best active sons, Dynaformer has established himself as a high-level force and will stand at $100,000 while Red Ransom, who started in the U.S., has been exported to Europe, where he is highly regarded. It will be interesting to see if either Dynaformer gets a stallion son or Rock Hard Ten (a grandson) can establish a male line. As a grade I winner from seven to ten furlongs, and out of a Mr. Prospector mare, he is probably the last, best hope. Unless that happens, I think the Roberto influence will become more marginalized as far as U.S. dirt racing is concerned. Afleet Alex is an extended reverse cross to Rock Hard Ten—Mr. Prospector/Roberto (the dams of these two are by Nashua and are related). However, Roberto is going to be back in the fourth generation of his pedigree, and probably less of an influence.

➤ **I believe I understand breeding "type to type" and nick ratings. Are they equally important? If not, which should be given more weight when selecting a stallion for your mare?** — West Friendship, Maryland

All of these things are a general guideline. Nick ratings are just a generalized measure of affinity between the stallion (or sire line of the stallion) and the broodmare sire (or his sire line). In the most generally popular commercial application, this is a nick rating based on hypothetical opportunity. It is, however, a broad guide to general trends. In terms of breeding type to type, it's generally acknowledged that breeding radically different individuals doesn't [seem] to work well. If I was finalizing a mating, I would want to be happy with both the "nick" (or whatever other pedigree criteria I was using) and with the physical match.

➤ **Can the great sire Danehill have the same worldwide effect on the breed as his grandsire Northern Dancer?** — Jersey City, New Jersey

It's unlikely, as with dirt and turf bloodlines growing more disparate, he's unlikely to have the same impact on U.S. dirt racing as he has had on turf in Australia and Europe.

➤ **Do you feel that certain turf sires are better suited to producing runners for racing in California where the surfaces are harder? If so, which sires?** — Davis, California

That's a good question. I originally come from England, and there we do note that some sires get turf horses that are better on firm ground and some, with give in the ground. In fact, in the spring you would always get a lot of winners by horses who liked soft ground. The soft-ground sires were well known just like horses whose runners do well on wet or muddy tracks here. I would think that firm ground sires would be better for California, but I must admit I haven't done a study on U.S. horses which would tell me which do better on firm turf. It is a very good point, however.

TALKIN' HORSES
WITH
DR. DEAN RICHARDSON

Dr. Dean Richardson, the head of surgery at the George D. Widener Hospital for Large Animals at the University of Pennsylvania's New Bolton Center, was thrust into the public eye when he began treating 2006 Kentucky Derby winner Barbaro for a catastrophic injury sustained during that year's Preakness Stakes. Beginning with the injury and ending with the decision in January 2007 to euthanize Barbaro, Richardson handled all the pressure associated with treating such a high-profile animal responsibly and with professional calmness. An avid golfer who resides in Landenberg, Pennsylvania, Richardson is married to a veterinarian, Laura Richardson. Born in Honolulu, Richardson is the son of a Navy captain who was a physician specializing in internal medicine. Richardson enrolled at Dartmouth University at age sixteen with plans for a career in acting. His plans changed after he became hooked on horses while horseback riding as part of a physical education course. A 1974 Dartmouth graduate, Richardson earned his doctorate of veterinary medicine at Ohio State and has been at New Bolton since 1979. Prior to Barbaro, one of Richardson's highest-profile equine clients was steeplechaser McDynamo, who earned a second Eclipse Award in 2005 after undergoing surgery performed by Richardson.

Richardson received an unprecedented number of questions during his two online chats—one while Barbaro was under his care at New Bolton and the second a year after Barbaro's Derby victory and four months after his death. These excerpts are organized by date, to avoid any confusion.

➤ **Were you watching the Preakness when Barbaro's accident occurred and what were your thoughts?** — Poplar Grove, Illinois

Yes, I was watching it and I felt very sick to my stomach when is saw it. I knew immediately it was a very, very severe injury. I pretty much thought exclusively in medical terms, about the nature of the fracture [and] whether the skin was broken. Considering where he was, I figured right away he would come to me.

➤ **My daughter wants to become an equine veterinarian. Can you offer any advice on how to best prepare for veterinary school studies?**
— Monkton, Maryland

[She should] do as well as she can do in high school so that she gets into a good university and then do well there. Get appropriate guidance from counselors to take the required courses. Learn about the profession; spend time with veterinarians before she commits to this path. Most important, she should understand that being a [good] veterinarian is not just about loving animals; it requires critical thinking and a genuine sense of scientific curiosity.

➤ **Since [Barbaro's laminitis] was caused by uneven weight distribution, is he still going to be able to eat grain and alfalfa?** — Conroe, Texas

This is a common misconception. Alfalfa and grain do not cause laminitis in a case such as this. Overeating can cause laminitis, but the mechanisms are quite different. A horse in Barbaro's condition needs to eat a lot of high-quality feed in order to maintain his weight and optimize healing.

➤ **Is the fact that Barbaro is still a relatively young horse a benefit to the healing process, particularly with respect to the laminitis?**
— Lake Orion, Michigan

There is no question about it. A younger horse heals more rapidly. Both his fractures and his left hind hoof would be far more difficult to manage in an older horse.

➤ **How hard is it to separate your emotions from a patient you have dedicated so much of your time, energy, and expertise to? Has [Barbaro] captured your heart, too?** — Brookfield, Illinois

I have been very attached to a lot of my patients. The type of work I do (unfortunately) does not always result in a quick fix, so some of my successes and many of my failures stay in the hospital for a long time. I became a veterinarian because I loved horses, so it isn't too hard to get attached to those that you work on for a long time. I am certainly not alone; we have had patients that are so popular that the nursing staff will show up to see them when they come back to the hospital for a follow-up visit.

➤ **What are the chances of Barbaro developing [laminitis] in one of his front legs, and are horses more prone to developing it again after they've been through it once or no more so than a horse who hasn't had it?** — New York, New York

Right now his chances of developing it in his front feet are fairly low because he is healthy and bearing good weight on both hind limbs. If he has any serious setback in terms of his hind limb comfort, his front feet will definitely be at more risk. He absolutely will always be at higher risk of having laminitis and other foot problems in the left hind foot. A horse that has had it once definitely is at higher risk of having it again. [The decision to euthanize Barbaro was due to laminitis in his left hind foot and not the initial injury he sustained in his right rear leg.]

➤ **Were you surprised at the intense media interest following the surgery (all those network morning TV shows) and the fact that it continues?** — West Palm Beach, Florida

The level of interest and its persistence is surprising.

➤ **Why are you so passionate about horses? Was there a particular part in your life that made you very interested in working with them?**
— Elmont, New York

Briefly, I decided to become a veterinarian after falling in love with horses as a rider/horseman.

➤ **Can you please describe a day with Barbaro in regards to his schedule (including the grazing outings)? What occurs in regard to his treatments and caretaking and at what times?** — Pittsburgh, Pennsylvania

He gets ICU checks by the nurses four times daily (vital signs, checking how much he is eating, drinking, manure/urine production, and so forth). He is fed grain mixes four times daily. He receives free choice alfalfa and timothy mix hay. I change his LH [left hind] foot bandage around 6 a.m. and walk him about thirty minutes in the late afternoon. He is no longer being put in a sling. Previously,

DR. DEAN RICHARDSON

we were letting him out of the sling from about 7 p.m. until 9 a.m. The Jacksons [owners Roy and Gretchen Jackson] and Mr. Matz [trainer Michael Matz] visit at various times, and Mrs. Jackson always brings some Lael Farm grass handpicked for him. He gets groomed and bathed at various times. Medications are given at various intervals. Previously, he was on a number of constant intravenous infusions and epidural pain medication. His management is much simpler right now because he is doing so well.

➤ **Do you enjoy informing the public about [Barbaro], or do you view the media as an intrusion upon your time?** — Philadelphia, Pennsylvania

I view it as a duty to the public that cares so much about this horse. I personally care a lot about the equine industry, and I want people to understand that there are people like the Jacksons who truly care about their horses.

➤ **When you did the surgery on Barbaro, were the bones still "in place" or did you have to piece the bones back together? Was some of the bone removed? How much grafting was needed?** — Bloomington, Illinois

They were markedly displaced. The long pastern bone was essentially exploded. Only a few free fragments of cortical (dense) bone were removed. These were pieces that were unattached to any shred of soft tissue. We used about 40 cc of cancellous bone graft taken from his right tuber coxae ("point of the hip").

➤ **What has been your favorite part of taking care of Barbaro? Is he very affectionate?** — Weston, Connecticut

My favorite part initially was the challenge of the procedure and the aftercare. My favorite part now is simply trying to save his life. He is a very personable young colt, truly charismatic.

➤ **What are you using to treat the hoof for laminitis?** — Seattle, Washington

I have been reluctant to and will not say what brand names we are using, but it is a very simple treatment. He basically gets his foot cleaned daily and a very generic antibiotic; the only thing we are putting on it is a silver sulfur diozine that is nonirritating. We put a padded bandage on his foot and put the foot in a boot that has several pieces of foam in the bottom.

➤ **Given a perfect world and an optimum recovery for Barbaro, what is the best we can expect for him?** — Mount Laurel, New Jersey

I still believe there is a chance to save him to be a breeding stallion, capable of naturally [and comfortably] covering mares.

➤ **Has the experience of having Barbaro as a patient changed your life in any way, and, if so, how?** — Madison, Mississippi

Certainly, right now, it's very odd to go to the racetrack at Saratoga and have people ask for your autograph. That just does not happen to vets. But really, no, it has not changed my life. I am still busy here in the hospital with other cases and my regular clients. It's just that Barbaro takes up more time. I have always been a pretty busy surgeon. I have not played as much golf lately.

➤ **Why did you decide to take on Barbaro's case with its high profile when other veterinarians have said they probably wouldn't have touched it?** — Versailles, Kentucky

That's what I do. This is why I get up in the morning. This is the type of cases I have worked my whole career to get better at. I certainly can't imagine not wanting to try this. I am sure some would not have wanted it because it is so high profile. I certainly don't think I am the only person who could have helped him.

➤ **What percentage of euthanized racehorses would have a shot at survival if their owners were as committed to their horses' well-being as the Jacksons are with Barbaro? Is there anything you'd like to see racing do about it?** — Los Angeles, California

It is important for people to understand it is quite expensive. If money was no object and there was a commitment by the owners, there are a fair number of euthanized horses who could be saved. Certainly, many horses are put down because the expense of saving them is more than their value and that is certainly an understandable decision on the part of many people. It is also important to keep in mind that Barbaro has not been saved yet. It is not like anyone can say it has been proven. I certainly can't emphasize that enough, and, unfortunately, it is the truth. Until he is doing what a normal horse can do, I am not going to consider it a success.

TALKIN' HORSES

Dr. Dean Richardson

➤ **How far along is the pastern bone fusion in the right rear leg [original injury]? How long will it be before the bone is fused completely?**
— Bensalem, Pennsylvania

It looked excellent during the last cast change. We only assess it carefully when we have the cast off because the X-ray doesn't go clearly through the cast. It looked like it was really progressing well. We did that procedure in early July, and the soonest I would expect it to be solid enough to take out of the cast would be early September. But it could be later. It is all depending upon what it looks like.

➤ **What is the most important thing you learned from this experience and do you feel it will be helpful in the future for treatment of other horses facing similar injuries?** — Boyce, Virginia

I've tried to emphasize throughout the last few months that I don't want people to think that there were too many really straightforward lessons in the Barbaro case. As with any complicated case, you figure out that you might have done some things different, but you really don't know if doing them differently would necessarily have resulted in a different outcome. Learning is often very gradual in clinical practice, and I definitely believe that we could manage the next case slightly better just for having learned minor lessons from Barbaro. I truly hope that the support coming in for equine research will be what makes a significant difference in the long run for other injured horses and those with laminitis.

➤ **How [did] Barbaro's status change so quickly, from talk of discharging him in early January to his death on January 29? What was the turning point (or was there a single turning point)?** — Pasadena, California

The biggest problem is that he began to get more sore on his laminitic left hind foot. That occurred even though he had been fairly stable on it for several months. This is not unusual, however. All of us who work on this type of case have seen one be comfortable for months to years and then suddenly have a crisis. In Barbaro's case, when he became lame on the left hind, he badly overloaded the right hind limb. The latter, as you know, was healed but not perfect. The result of the overload on the right hind leg was that he developed a severe subsolar abscess on that foot. We tried to protect the RH foot by placing him in transfixation pins. This allowed him to bear full weight again on the RH, but it wasn't enough to offset the development of laminitis in both front feet. I have described it as a deck of cards falling and still find that to be an apt analogy.

➤ **Is there any particular group, kind, or class of horse that is more likely than another to suffer laminitis? Do you think the tragic disease has anything to do with diet?** — Philadelphia, Pennsylvania

This is too complicated a question to answer other than to say that there are many different causes of laminitis, and it is very difficult for us right now to even relate a case like Barbaro to the laminitis that we see in an obese pony on spring grass, a mare with a retained placenta (afterbirth), an old horse with Cushing's disease, or a very ill horse with diarrhea. There may be some definable genetic markers for horses predisposed to laminitis, but this will need a lot more research. Diet certainly plays a role in the onset of some forms of laminitis but probably not at all in others. It is also very important to keep in mind that laminitis includes an enormous spectrum of severity. Some horses can be treated and return to work and others cannot be saved despite heroic efforts.

➤ **[Published] articles suggest that you would have done the surgery on Barbaro's broken leg differently; is this true, and in hindsight, what would you have done differently?** — Columbus, North Carolina

I honestly don't know if I had a similar case come in tomorrow if I would do it much differently other than some subtle changes in the way that the pastern joint was fused as part of the original repair. This is a fairly subtle detail in terms of the overall management of the case. I hope people understand exactly how difficult it is to always know exactly what is right and what is wrong if you are doing a relatively uncommon procedure. You don't always know what will work, but you try to apply solid principles into practice and you try to adapt to changing circumstances.

➤ **Considering the advancements made in veterinary medicine and technology, do you feel that the injury suffered by Ruffian in 1975 would still be considered catastrophic today?** — Plantsville, Connecticut

It would still be considered a very serious injury, but the chances of Ruffian surviving today would be much, much better. "Simple" fetlock fusions are done

Dr. Dean Richardson

today with considerable success. There are some injuries, especially those in which the blood supply is badly damaged or the skin is broken so badly that major infection is inevitable, where we still have a very poor chance of saving the horse. We need to keep pushing the envelope about what is repairable and that requires more research, dedicated owners, and more experience.

➤ **It's obvious that you and your colleagues learned a great deal about treatment of musculoskeletal injuries following Barbaro's accident. How will you be sharing [this information] with your fellow surgeons and veterinary medicine students from an academic perspective?**
— Miami, Florida

I think it is a major misconception that we did something all that unusual on Barbaro. We tackle difficult cases regularly that just don't get much press. The veterinary profession has extremely active continuing education programs throughout the world, and some of them specialize exclusively in training veterinarians in the newest techniques for managing the most difficult types of cases. These continuing education programs also allow the experts teaching the courses to learn from one another. In addition, publications in scientific journals allow others in the profession to learn from others' experience. Barbaro's case is already in press as simply one of thirty-one horses treated with similar technology.

➤ **Given the intricacies of equine physiology in the hoof, do you feel that one cure for laminitis is attainable or will laminitis need to be addressed in the same way as cancer (such as multiple approaches depending on horse, degree of involvement, and so forth)?**
— Pittsburgh, Pennsylvania

The answer here is a categorical yes. Especially in terms of prevention, it is likely that enormously varied approaches will be required. Treatment of the laminitis after it has occurred will probably be more similar than prevention.

➤ **What is your fondest memory of Barbaro?** — Falls Church, Virginia

Walking with him outside in the sunshine and hearing him munch grass when there was no one else around except the cattle and horses in adjoining fields.

➤ **What did you learn about yourself from your experiences with Barbaro?** — Houston, Texas

That I am capable of being somewhat patient with the media.

➤ **What changes would you personally like to see Thoroughbred racing institute that might make racing safer for the horses?**

— Nicholasville, Kentucky

I think that good epidemiological data about injuries in Thoroughbred racing should be supported by the industry in an effort to define what sorts of things can be done to minimize breakdowns. There is currently a surge in interest in the newly available racing surfaces and noninvasive methods of recognizing damage to the musculoskeletal system. To really evaluate both will require serious investment in time and resources over the next several years.

➤ **Have you ever treated any injury to a horse that was that severe? In light of the huge focus on curing laminitis, [will] we find some sort of viable, successful treatment for this tragic disease?** — Seattle, Washington

We have treated other horses with what I would consider to be more difficult problems. Some have made it and some have not. I honestly believe that we can save at least 50 percent of horses with injuries like Barbaro's if we have the financial resources. It is important for everyone to recognize that treatment of severe injuries is expensive and not everyone has the financial resources to do what is required. That is a fact of life in veterinary medicine. I absolutely believe that major improvements in preventing and treating laminitis can be realized within the next five to ten years. I fervently hope that one of Barbaro's legacies will be that increased awareness of this disease resulted in more research.

➤ **Aside from complications due to injury, what is the most common cause of laminitis that you see, and what one thing would you advise horsemen to do to help prevent laminitis?** — Nottingham, New Hampshire

This is an interesting question that again brings out the important point that most laminitis is associated with some precipitating cause such as colitis, retained placenta, other types of colic, Potomac Horse Fever, and so forth. The only prevention is to try to avoid those types of illnesses, a tough task. The major preventable form of laminitis is probably that caused by obesity and older horses with uncontrolled Cushing's disease (pituitary dysfunction). Both of those can be prevented or managed.

➤ **When, if ever, is amputation a viable option for horses with severe lower leg injuries?** — Dallas, Texas

There are a few success stories of horses with amputations, but the great majority of horses the size of Barbaro will develop laminitis in the opposite foot.

➤ **Why can't a horse stay off its legs for any extended period of time (as a human could with a broken leg)?** — Marco Island, Florida

It is remarkable how different one horse is to the next in terms of how they deal with being in recumbency for extended periods, but the majority of large horses (like Barbaro) develop serious decubital sores, lose their appetite, waste away, and often develop lung and gastrointestinal problems when they lie down too many hours per day. I have seen horses that survive for a long time in recumbency, but it is definitely the minority. The nursing care required is also phenomenally taxing in a large horse. Most horses simply give up if they are in enough pain that they are lying down most of the day.

TALKIN' HORSES
WITH
STEVE ROMAN

Steven A. Roman is a New York City native who earned a B.S. in chemistry from City University of New York in 1963. He also earned a master's degree in organic chemistry from Columbia University in 1964 and his Ph.D. in physical-organic chemistry from Columbia in 1967. Roman has been involved in the horse industry for more than thirty years as an owner, breeder, and early stage trainer of performance and conformation show horses; more than twenty of those years have been in the Thoroughbred racing business as an owner, consultant, writer, and educator. As the creator of the "Dosage Index," a technique for classifying Thoroughbred pedigrees according to aptitudinal type, he is an internationally recognized authority on the relationship between Thoroughbred pedigree and racing performance. His book, Dosage: Pedigree and Performance, *was published in 2003. The* Daily Racing Form *has also named him as one of the ten most influential people in twentieth century Thoroughbred handicapping.*

➤ **The modern Dosage formula is a version of an old formula that included important broodmares. How can a formula be effective if it excludes the influences of half of the gene pool?** — Lexington, Kentucky

The original introduction of Dosage theory by Col. J.J. Vuilier in the early twentieth century identified only eight historically significant prepotent sources among early nineteenth-century Thoroughbreds, including just one mare. He was able to identify a total of only fifteen such sources, or chefs-de-race, in the entire nineteenth century, none of the additional chefs-de-race being mares. In any case, neither Vuillier's work, nor Dr. Franco Varola's [work], nor ours exclude any part of the gene pool. Every chef-de-race is the result of all the genetic influences behind him, both male and female. Since our work is based on population statistics, the focus on sires has little impact on the statistical results because of the huge difference in the number of foals descended from individual sires and dams.

➤ **Do Arkansas and other small states have the sire power for a classic Dosage?** — Fayetteville, Arkansas

Dosage is an expression of aptitudinal type and is only marginally related to what we usually refer to as class. A horse bred to stay a classic distance can be bred anywhere if the sire and dam contribute the appropriate balance of speed and stamina. Whether or not that horse can be competitive at a classic distance at the grade I level is a separate issue. That said, a horse bred in Arkansas with a classic pedigree should have a better opportunity in a classic distance race than a horse from Kentucky bred to stay five furlongs.

➤ **The stamina numbers [for Derby contenders] have considerably decreased over the past ten years. [Why]?** — Jacksonville, Florida

One of the motivations for developing contemporary Dosage methodology was to have at hand a tool that would help identify trends in the aptitudinal evolution of the Thoroughbred. For that purpose it has functioned very well.

The shift toward speed, especially among winners of American classic races, is dramatic and extends well beyond the last ten years. The average DI of Derby winners in the 1940s, 1970s, and 2000s are 1.02, 2.67, and 3.22, respectively. If you plot the DI of Derby winners versus year since 1940, the trend suggests that within ten or fifteen years, half of all Derby winners will have a DI over 4.00. My only comment is this is the path owners, breeders, and fans have taken. It is what the market demands despite the protests of traditionalists. You can change the direction by mandating more races at longer distances or on grass, but that will never happen. It also can change if the continuing trend results in a loss of interest in the sport. Nevertheless, racing can still be exciting and some horse still has to win the Derby even if the field is comprised of twenty sprinters. I must say, however, the depth of quality today is inferior to what it was. Despite the occasional Cigar or Ghostzapper, I do miss the likes of Secretariat, Spectacular Bid, Seattle Slew, Affirmed, Dr. Fager, Damascus, and so many of the other truly great horses who populated racing in an earlier time.

➤ **Will American breeders continue to shun European-based stamina lines in their ongoing quest for the commercial product? Will the Kentucky Derby have to be shortened to a one-turn mile before they realize the folly of their ways?** — Chicago, Illinois

American breeders will continue to respond to the commercial market as they see it. Stamina-oriented European sire lines generally have less appeal because of the emphasis on distance and grass. Obviously, there are exceptions, like Sadler's Wells and Danehill, but for the most part it is difficult for European sires to break through unless they have extraordinary stud credentials. The trend toward increasing speed at the expense of stamina is real and it is ongoing. It will change only as market conditions change. Nevertheless, it is not all doom and gloom. There are still many horses out there bred for classic distances and which perform well in the American classics. At the same time, the evolution toward speed presents an opportunity for those breeding to race rather than sell. I believe you still want your classic prospects to display the kind of early maturity required to withstand the rigors of the Triple Crown trail, but you don't want to sacrifice stamina for precociousness. As in many things, the proper balance of attributes is often best. You should maintain a balance between speed and endurance. And you should maintain a balance between early maturity and continuing development. Those things will give you at least an edge. Let's hope, however, that it never comes to the point where, as a notable trainer once suggested, the Derby be dropped back to nine furlongs.

➤ **I rigorously evaluate the Dosage Profile in each category of each [Kentucky Derby] contender. [However] the Dosage itself and Center of Distribution do not seem to have as strong of an indicator of predictive performance.** — Pittsburgh, Pennsylvania

The Dosage Index (DI) and Center of Distribution (CD) provide a quick summary of a horse's aptitudinal type. But as you suggest, the Dosage Profile (DP) is the key. The DI and CD are the result of how the elements of inherited prepotent speed and stamina are arranged within the DP. You can learn much more about a horse's likely performance type from the DP than from the DI or CD, although all three are helpful. To better understand the significance and importance of the DP, I refer you to an article at my Web site that deals with this very issue. The article is entitled "The Relationship Between the DI and CD:

STEVE ROMAN

DP Patterns." The significance of the DP becomes apparent when you realize that, for example, a horse with a DI of 3.00 can have a CD anywhere between 0.25 and 1.25 depending on how the points in the DP are distributed. The aptitudinal type of a horse with DI 3.00, CD 0.25 is quite different from that of a horse with DI 3.00, CD 1.25.

➤ **Would you please tell us why Nearctic hasn't been assigned as chef-de-race?** — Lexington, Kentucky

For a sire to be recognized as a chef-de-race, he must exhibit an undeniable prepotence for aptitudinal type. That is the main criterion for consideration and is something quite distinct from a sire's success at stud. Not surprisingly, this distinction is often a source of great confusion. The chef-de-race list was never meant to be the equivalent of an honor roll of great stallions. Many great sires are aptitudinally prepotent. Many are not, despite their achievements. And since a primary objective of Dosage is to facilitate the most accurate aptitudinal interpretation of a pedigree, nothing is gained by including stallions among the chefs-de-race that are not demonstrating aptitudinal prepotence. There are several ways to evaluate aptitudinal prepotence. One way, for example, is to compare the Dosage figures of a population of Thoroughbreds having a common ancestor to the figures for the general Thoroughbred population displaying similar performance characteristics. If those figures are close to one another, it is unlikely the common ancestor is contributing a significant prepotent influence. If the figures are very different, the opposite may be true. One example is Storm Cat, arguably the most successful North American sire currently standing. When you compare the average CD of runners with Storm Cat in their pedigree to the average CD of the general population of runners having the same average winning distance (AWD), you'll find the figures are essentially identical. Accordingly, there is no aptitudinal type we can ascribe to Storm Cat that adds anything useful to the aptitudinal interpretation of the pedigrees in which he appears. Contrast that situation with an earlier example, Apalachee, a premier sire of sprinters. In his case the difference between the average CD of his descendants and that of the general population with a similar AWD was enormous, mainly due to the very strong stamina influences contributed by his sire, solid chef-de-race Round Table. When you define Apalachee as a source of brilliance (certainly derived from his dam) and recalculate the figures, the two populations begin to mesh, confirming Apalachee's prepotence for speed.

Storm Cat and Apalachee are excellent examples of a great sire with no observable prepotence for type beyond what his own ancestors bring forward, and a good-but-not-great sire with easily identified prepotence for type. Since the evolution of Thoroughbred type is dynamic, not static, it is possible a prepotent influence may appear more clearly after a couple or three generations. That could be the case with Storm Cat who, in the long term, appears also to represent speed. In other words, the book on Storm Cat is not closed.

As for Nearctic, he fits the Storm Cat mode rather than the Apalachee mode. Nevertheless, whatever influence for type he may transmit is now captured through his sons, chefs-de-race Northern Dancer and Icecapade.

➤ **Do you see any trends in inbreeding or the "Rasmussen Factor" of inbreeding to dams of different sires?** — Dayton, Ohio

The obvious trend in inbreeding over time is toward a lower coefficient of inbreeding (a fraction which, when multiplied by 100, affords the amount of inbreeding as a percentage). Clearly, the intensity of inbreeding is diminishing with successive generations. I will leave the significance of this trend to the inbreeding experts. My experience with the Rasmussen Factor (RF) is limited; however, I do know that pedigree authority Roger Lyons published an article questioning the significance of the original RF study based on the fact that inbreeding is not distributed evenly across the Thoroughbred population. I did publish my own research article several years ago about the influence of the RF on the racing and breeding career of stallions. That study of over 800 stallions, available at http://www.chef-de-race.com/articles/rasmussen_factor. htm, indicated that the presence of the RF in their pedigree had no effect on either their racing performance or their breeding performance.

➤ **What criteria are used to name a chef-de-race? [Will] the dual category chefs ever be determined/revised to be of a single influence? [Can you explain Conquistador Cielo?]** — West Palm Beach, Florida

To address your first point, I'll provide the introduction from the announcement of Pleasant Colony and Buckaroo as chefs-de-race in 2004:

"Contrary to a misconception held by many critics of Dosage, the selection of a chef-de-race is not necessarily an affirmation of a superior record at stud.

TALKIN' HORSES

STEVE ROMAN

That chefs-de-race usually emerge from among prominent sires is generally true because prominent sires are more likely to generate sufficient data for an accurate analysis of their aptitudinal influence through one or two generations, directly and through sons and daughters. Nevertheless, the overriding criterion for chef-de-race selection remains the identification of a prepotent influence for type that has a direct bearing on the correct aptitudinal interpretation of the pedigrees in which the sire appears."

The original chef-de-race list was entirely that of Franco Varola as later modified by Abe Hewitt in the 1970s to better reflect trends in American racing. Split aptitudes were a direct consequence of Varola and Hewitt disagreeing as to the proper aptitudinal assignment. Since then, split assignments are based solely on statistical analysis and are useful because they create a more realistic continuum of aptitudinal influences, particularly along the linear CD scale. I seriously doubt there is a relationship between split aptitude chefs-de-race and the performance of individual horses in a given race. Conquistador Cielo doesn't necessarily contradict Dosage theory. He could be considered a statistical outlier common to any statistical distribution. On the other hand, his high Dosage figures actually may be an accurate reflection of his true type. Speed was his dominant trait as he won almost every race on the lead with a few exceptions where he was no more than a length or two behind. He won the Belmont Stakes from the front end, unchallenged and on a sloppy track, not an unusual scenario. He later did not quite stay the mile and a quarter in the Travers Stakes when challenged early and by far his best performance was his record-setting effort in the Metropolitan Handicap at a flat mile. I'm not suggesting his Dosage figures are perfect; however, you can describe him as a speed horse capable of getting beyond a mile on class, the factor often overlooked by critics who focus only on the figures. One shouldn't evaluate the figures out of context.

➤ **Is there really an ideal number for a Kentucky Derby contender?**
— French Camp, California

There are no ideal Dosage figures. There are guidelines suggesting that too much speed in a pedigree is a disadvantage in the classics. However, within the Dosage guidelines there are many types capable of winning. Derby winners have been early maturing speed horses and they have been late-developing come-from-behind horses. These are distinct types, most likely with significantly different figures.

➤ **It seems since [Lasix became legal], the Dosage system has become more flawed. Is it the Dosage system or [drugs]?** — New Orleans, Louisiana

I expect that performance-enhancing drugs, or as some might prefer to call them, performance-enabling drugs, could affect a whole range of things, including the type of horses winning races and especially their speed and pace figures. Drugs do more to make the playing field uneven than anything else I can think of.

➤ **Have you ever considered reclassifying a chef-de-race based upon further race result data?** — Louisville, Kentucky

There was some reclassifying of chefs-de-race in the early days following the initial publication of our work in the early 1980s. Since then the assignments have a much stronger statistical basis, so there is less incentive to make changes. That said, from time to time there are individual sires that I reevaluate, but it doesn't happen very often. Should the data warrant it, I would have no hesitation making a change, although I suppose the commercial databases selling Dosage data might be a little annoyed.

➤ **With speed so dominant, is there any advice you can give in modifying the way the Dosage can be used?** — Bethpage, New York

I don't think much has really changed even with the evolution toward more speed in pedigrees. In a competitive environment everything is relative. Other things being equal, if a field is filled with speed horses, those with any stamina edge should have an advantage at a classic distance. [Use] a horse's Dosage figures as a baseline and make mental adjustments to them by adding an appropriate speed or stamina influence from non-chef-de-race sires in the pedigree. I recommend this approach, and to facilitate the process I publish an annual list of such sires with notional aptitudinal assignments. Keep in mind that such modifications should be made conservatively because these sires have not been confirmed as truly prepotent for type. Nevertheless, if you see a Derby contender by Grand Slam, for example, you can be reasonably sure there is more speed in the pedigree than the raw figures indicate.

TALKIN' HORSES

STEVE ROMAN

➤ **With the changes [literally] in the landscape in racing, is there any way to include artificial racing surfaces in regards to the Dosage formulas?** — St. Louis, Missouri

Absolutely, although it will be a while before there is enough data obtained from races on synthetic surfaces to have a meaningful impact. My initial studies have shown that the general Dosage model correlating Dosage figures with winning distance holds up equally well on both surfaces. Preliminary data indicate that at the same distance, the figures on synthetic surfaces are marginally higher than they are on dirt although it is far too early to draw a definitive conclusion. If that pattern continues, it will suggest that speed in a pedigree can carry further on the synthetic surface.

➤ **What is your opinion on the weights that horses are assigned? Do you think [a few] pounds make a difference?** — Springfield, Pennsylvania

My experience is that the correlation between weight and performance is nonlinear, although weight can and does matter. Unlike the historical scale of weights, where a pound at a specific distance is essentially equivalent to some number of lengths, I have found that many horses are affected only marginally by additional weight up to a certain point, after which the effects can be very great. It is more like a breaking point than a continuum. Horses seem to have their individual limit of weight-carrying ability where, for example, one may begin to suffer when asked to carry more than 110 pounds while another may not show any obvious distress until asked to carry 125 pounds. I believe trainers tend to be oversensitive to the weight issue and put far too much emphasis on whether their horse will be assigned 112 or 114 pounds. Weight-carrying ability is related to the individual horse's physical characteristics and strength.

➤ **If the male line of a pedigree determines distance and perhaps the surface where a runner will be most successful and the female line determines the runner's racing class, [isn't it] important to get an overall appraisal of a runner's aptitude by incorporating this female line into the Dosage Index?** — Columbia, Maryland

Dams, because they produce so few foals compared to sires, have a minimal impact on the statistical basis of Dosage. Nevertheless, they are at least as important as the sires in the development of Dosage theory. Usually, aptitudinal prepotence in a mare will be adequately captured by the influence assigned to her chef-de-race descendants. A good example is Rough Shod II who shows up in the pedigree of chefs-de-race Nureyev, Sadler's Wells, and Apalachee. Of course, whatever influence she may be transmitting has been modified by the other prepotent influences in the pedigree of each chef-de-race descendant. I know some people who find it useful in their analysis to separate the Dosage contribution into a sire component and a dam component. In this way they can see if a pedigree represents speed over speed, speed over stamina, and so on. As far as I'm concerned, Dosage information can be used, abused, and manipulated as one pleases if it increases a person's understanding of how pedigree affects performance.

➤ **How many horses are under consideration to become professional chefs-de-race?** — San Pedro, California

I am continually monitoring aptitudinal developments within the breed as the database grows. New chef-de-race prospects emerge periodically awaiting more data to confirm or deny aptitudinal prepotence. Right now the most likely candidate is Unbridled. I won't discuss in which aptitudinal group or groups I think he may wind up, but just think of this sequence: Unbridled to Unbridled's Song to Songandaprayer.

➤ **Could you please explain the pace parameter requirements as succinctly and plainly as possible.** — San Dimas, California

Pace parameters are a series of performance-related numbers that capture the pace characteristics of a horse in classic prep races at a mile or longer. They include expressions for fatigue rate, early speed, and energy utilization efficiency. In addition they include calculations of the horse's velocity at various points within the race as well as projections of final time, turn time, and last quarter-mile time in a hypothetical ten-furlong event. We can compare these numbers to those generated by previous classic winners in their prep races to determine which contenders best fit the classic winner profile. I generally limit my selections to the top five contenders in several key pace categories and then narrow the selection even further by focusing only on those which have achieved a guideline minimum Performance Figure (PF) in at least one of their route prep races.

STEVE ROMAN

Since 1998, the Derby winner has been among the top five contenders eight times in fastest velocity from the second call to the finish, five times in lowest percent of total energy utilized through the second call, six times in fastest projected ten-furlong final time, seven times each in fastest projected turn time and last quarter-mile time, and eight times in best PF. Details are available at my Web site, including current data for this year's Derby.

➤ **I respect the theories of Dosage [but] unfortunately, Dosage figures cannot even be referenced in racing literature anymore lest the author be labeled a fool by the masses.** — Seattle, Washington

I'm not convinced the picture is as bleak as you describe. Commercial databases such as Bloodstock Research among others continue to offer Dosage figures more than twenty-five years after their introduction. Dosage figures still are provided prior to the Derby by numerous online and print outlets. My book continues to sell well five years after its initial publication. My Web site gets a thousand page views a day and multiples of that leading up to major racing events. Frankly, I don't spend much time fretting over the critics. I understand the subject matter is technical and not easily understood by people, especially those without any training in statistics and scientific method. I have no control over that. As for the timing of chef-de-race assignments, it should be noted that the body of work surrounding contemporary Dosage methodology is largely academic in nature. Accordingly, I'm not nearly as concerned about the timing of publications as I am about the accuracy of the data and its interpretation.

➤ **I have read about this system many times and still don't get it—is there an easy way to understand this and learn it?** — Palm Beach, California

Everything you need to know is available [on my Web site], including a basic review of Dosage and a tutorial. I can also recommend a brief article by Kathleen Jones called "Dosage in a Nutshell" available at http://www. thoroughbredchampions.com/dosage/. Of course, you can always e-mail me.

TALKIN' HORSES
WITH

GEOFFREY RUSSELL

A native of Dublin, Ireland, Geoffrey Russell was named director of sales at Keeneland in 2001 after serving five years as assistant to Rogers Beasley, who became director of racing. Russell had previously served as director of sales administration for the Fasig-Tipton Company from 1987 to 1996. Russell became acclimated to the auction scene when he attended sales in Ireland with family friends. After working in insurance and a short stint as a bid spotter for Ireland's Goff's auction company, he decided to travel to the United States in 1982 for a three-month visit, which turned into a permanent relocation. Starting on the muck crew at Fasig-Tipton, Russell became involved with a sales management training program that resulted in his eventual career within public auction sales. After serving as administrator at Jack Kent Cooke's Elmendorf Farm, Russell returned to Fasig-Tipton in 1987 before joining Keeneland in 1996.

➤ **What are the rights of a potential buyer in utilizing the newest technology in analyzing traits of a consigned horse such as heart score, gait analysis, or other biometrics?** — Jersey City, New Jersey

Although we see more of these services at the two-year-olds in training sales than we see at yearlings sales, there are many different companies that provide these services and you should contact them directly. Many buyers use these services while many prefer to do it the old-fashioned way.

➤ **How do you determine hip number order [at an auction]?**
— Hockessin, Delaware

We use an in-house computer system that ranks all the horses that are entered into the sale. We also receive information from the consignors where they feel their horses should be placed—their "wish lists." We take all this

GEOFFREY RUSSELL

information, as well as conformation notes with regard to the yearlings, and assign each horse a session. Once the sessions have been assigned, we then randomly select a letter from the alphabet that we have not used in three years; for example, this year's September sale starts with "J."

➤ **Is [there] a difference in the style and pace of the major Thoroughbred auctions in the United States compared to those in the United Kingdom or Ireland? Also, do you perceive any peculiarities that set apart the American from the European buyers?** — Miami, Florida

Yes, the European auctions are run at a slower, more sedate pace than here in the United States. In England, the bid spotter is only [a] pointer, and all bids must be recognized by the auctioneer, while here the bid spotter is allowed to accept bids. This adds to the excitement of the auction. Personally having attended auctions both in Europe and here, I prefer the U.S. auction system.

➤ **I have been an owner [of claimers] for many years but do not know a thing about buying a yearling at auction. What is the best way to learn about yearling conformation, and what do you look for?** — Westerton, Pennsylvania

Great question, but a difficult one to answer in this type of forum. I think that the first step would be to attend one of the many new owners seminars that are conducted by the Thoroughbred Owners and Breeders Association and other organizations. At these seminars you will find professionals who will discuss conformation in great detail. Attend as many Thoroughbred auctions as you can and look at the horses in the back walking ring. Depending on what you are looking for—a sprinter or a distance horse—there are different things you will be looking for in a horse's conformation. In general terms, you are looking for a horse that has balance and athleticism, [with] a strong shoulder, deep girth, and a good hip, and with no serious angular deviations or deformities.

➤ **[Will you] share your comments or anecdotes on the appearances of different yearlings [such as whites or heavily spotted] each year through the sales ring?** — San Juan, Puerto Rico

Good racehorses come in all shapes, sizes, and colors, but there is no mistake that people have biases against certain colors and markings. There is an old horseman's saying: "One white foot, ride him for your life; two white feet, give him to your wife; three white feet, give him to your man; and four white feet, sell him … if you can." Then along comes The Minstrel and he had four white legs and was an outstanding racehorse. Some people do not like peroxide manes and tails, but both Grundy and Generous had peroxide manes and tails and were genuine and great racehorses. One of the greatest racehorses and influences on the Thoroughbred industry was Hyperion, and he had four white feet.

➤ **Please tell me why you think Keeneland should charge a 4½ percent commission on horses that fail to meet their reserves?** — Chicago, Illinois

Keeneland charges the lowest sales commission in the entire Thoroughbred industry. Some Thoroughbred auction houses charge as much as 10 percent commission and the art auction houses even charge more. We charge 4½ percent on all horses that use our facilities. The entry fee for the September and November sales covers the commission up to $22,000, and above that you are charged 4½ percent. We market each sale, distribute sale catalogs worldwide, and have the most extensive mailing list worldwide. We recruit buyers from all over North America and the world to come and purchase at our sales. The consignor—not Keeneland—is the one who establishes the reserve and, in some cases, may overestimate the value of their horse.

➤ **Do you think it is fair that the entry fee for the [top-selling horse] is the same as the last horse sold in the September sale?** — Lexington, Kentucky

The entry fee to the Keeneland September sale is $1,000 for all horses. This entry fee covers the commission up to $22,000. Our fixed costs are the same for every horse in every sale. The sale topper will pay 4½ percent commission above $22,000, while the last horse may not have to [pay a commission fee].

➤ **What factors determine if you have a successful sale?**
— Frankfort, Kentucky

We all love high-priced horses and world-record prices. I want buyers to be able to buy what they want at a price they believe is fair, and I want sellers to sell all of their horses. So what I like [is for] the clearance rate to be high and that the median price improves over the previous year.

TALKIN' HORSES

GEOFFREY RUSSELL

➤ **How has the market [been changed by] so many yearlings by certain sires?** — Wilmington, North Carolina

The size of the stallion books, and thus the number of yearlings by those stallions offered at public auction, has had a huge effect on the market. With the majority of these stallions representative of the middle market, it has expanded the middle market to be now books 3, 4, and 5.

➤ **We read stories about [the purported] shady dealings at horse sales. Why don't the sales companies try to help straighten things out?**
— Lincoln, Nebraska

Sales companies strive to create a fair marketplace for all. Keeneland is very involved in the sales integrity program.

➤ **A TOBA survey showed many buyers don't want horses that have had corrective surgeries. Why should [breeders] continue [to allow corrective surgeries]?** — Memphis, Tennessee

The decision to do these surgeries is up to the breeders. Some buyers do not consider these important in making their buying decisions.

➤ **What are your thoughts about Polytrack and the effect it will have on the April two-year-olds in training sale?** — Lexington, Kentucky

I personally, as well as Keeneland, believe strongly in the Polytrack surface. We believe that what is good for the horses is good for us and the industry, and we believe that Polytrack is good for the horses. A safer racetrack is vital to the success both of our racing and North American racing, as well as [to] our sales program. Will the times at the April sale be slower? I don't know. Our sale topper this year did not work overly fast but still brought over $1 million. I believe that buyers will look at the motion of the horses more than the time.

➤ **I love the fact that you have the auctions live online. Are there any plans to further the use of online bidding?** — Midlothian, Texas

The most important part of an auction is the excitement of the moment and live bidding. There is nothing like the drama created by bidders intent on owning the horse in the ring. Online bidding does not deliver that aspect.

TALKIN' HORSES
WITH
RIC WALDMAN

Ric Waldman, bloodstock adviser and consultant, has been actively involved in the Thoroughbred industry for more than thirty-five years and is president of Lexington-based R. Eric Waldman Consulting Services. In addition, Waldman's company is syndicate manager for Overbrook Farm and Windfields Farm. In that capacity, REWCS has managed the successful careers of such prominent stallions as Storm Cat and Deputy Minister, who collectively were leading general sires for four consecutive years. Previously, Waldman was founding president of, and partner in, Stallion Access Inc., a stallion seasons and shares trading company; served as business manager of Airdrie Stud; and was assistant general manager of Fasig-Tipton Company in Elmont, New York.

➤ **I'm really into the breeding of horses, and would like one day to get involved. For someone who has little experience, what would be the best way to enter the business?** — Toronto, Ontario, Canada

I am going to assume that you are young with your career ahead of you. First, find a way to work with horses, at [a racetrack] or at a local farm, or if you are really adventurous, find your way to a larger racing center or breeding center. That way you will find out quickly whether you like horses or are just attracted to the seemingly fashionable part of the industry. Once you decide that it is for you, your next direction should fall into place. Also, read, read, read as many publications about racing and breeding as you can.

➤ **Do you think horse breeders should be held accountable for the unsoundness in the breed today?** — Toronto, Ontario, Canada

I have contended that we should be held accountable, that the "buck stops" with us, although many of us who are commercial breeders are influenced to produce a horse which buyers want, and that is one with speed, speed, speed, regardless of soundness. If you look at many of the successful stallions in the past thirty-plus years, you will find that their careers were relatively short, e.g., Raise a Native (four starts), Danzig (three starts), and so forth. Would our breed be better off without their influences? Of course not. So, there is no right answer, nor immediate solution, but we must be careful not to move entirely in the direction of breeding slow, sound horses.

➤ **Do you think we'll see more stallions bred to books [number of mares to be bred] of two hundred or more or do you think we'll see no more than a handful bred at this level? What is your position on limiting book sizes?**
— Lexington, Kentucky

I am a believer in allowing the market system to dictate what our practices are. In this case, I believe that we are seeing a backlash against large books, and 200-plus is definitely large; in fact, I think 150 is large. If a breeder is not bothered by a stallion breeding a large book, then he/she will continue to support a particular stallion, with price likely being the factor which attracts that breeder. Thus, the farm which stands that stallion will have to price that stallion so that it is attractive to enough breeders in order to have a book size acceptable to the stud farm. The downside to large books is the furthering of an already shrinking gene pool.

➤ **What do you look for the most in the mares that are approved to breed to horses like Storm Cat and Deputy Minister? Do you lean more to pedigree or race record?** — Edmonton, Alberta, Canada

With Storm Cat, at his stud fee and age, we are basically looking for young mares with clean reproductive histories, owned by breeders who are known to us (for credit worthiness). At the beginning of Storm Cat's career, we were trying to get numbers, pure and simple, because he was not particularly popular. As he became more successful, we were able to be choosier with respect to pedigree and race record. Having to choose between the two, I prefer pedigree over race record, as I believe that most good horses come from good families.

Since it is not practical to inspect mares which apply to stallions, a stallion manager is left to rely on mares' sales prices, progeny sales history, and pedigrees as indicators of their conformation or rely on the breeder to wisely select a mare when risking so much money on an expensive stud fee. Regarding the influx of Storm Cat's sons at stud, we are seeing successful sons and grandsons at stud. The extent of Storm Cat's impact on the breed has not yet been fully realized. Another trait of his that he seems to pass on to his sons is his virility. That should help carry the Storm Cat line further into the future.

➤ **It must be such a thrill to see Storm Cat every day and be the person that has helped shape his career. What type of mare fits him best?**
— Savannah, Georgia

Generally, I believe in trying to breed out faults in either a stallion or a mare. In Storm Cat's case, that would mean that a breeder would be looking at a mare with good knees and perhaps no less than medium size. However, my guess is that, if we lined up all of the dams of his group/graded winners, you would likely see all sizes and shapes. As for pedigree of his mares, I prefer to avoid close inbreeding and like to see mares which possess classic pedigrees; most breeders are taking care of these preferences on their own, without any input from me. His success has been so broad that mating a mare to Storm Cat should not be that complicated.

➤ **What makes Storm Cat such a special stallion?** — Durham, North Carolina

I can give you 500,000 reasons. [Storm Cat's stud fee was $500,000 per mare].

➤ **What goes into choosing the stallions with which Overbrook's mares will be mated? How much is commercial and how much of it is finding the best match possible for the mare (regardless of price)?** — Pittsburgh, Pennsylvania

Our intent is usually with the idea of producing a racehorse. Our decisions of which yearlings to sell are usually not contemplated until late winter/early spring. In many cases, the yearlings we decide to sell are those which we like, but feel we can sell well. I still have trouble with the ideology that breeding commercially is mutually exclusive from breeding to produce a racehorse. That does not speak very highly of yearling buyers. I think that, if a breeder is trying to breed a very good-looking yearling and he/she succeeds in doing so, then shouldn't that yearling have a good chance of being a racehorse?

TALKIN' HORSES

RIC WALDMAN

➤ **Obviously, there will be life after Storm Cat. How do you prepare the farm for that?** — San Antonio, Texas

We have been trying to develop new stallions, regardless of the age and status of Storm Cat. A successful stud farm cannot have too many high-powered stallions, but realistically, it is a longshot that any farm will be fortunate enough to have a Storm Cat.

➤ **What was it like working for W. T. Young? What lessons did you learn from him?** — Lexington, Kentucky

I learned so much about life from him. He was generous with his time and wisdom, and I am a better person with a more wholesome and well-rounded perspective from having known him. He was the first to admit that he was not a horseman, but he was a businessman who understood the business of running a stud farm. He was also a builder with an uncanny sense of design and layout. He had a hand in every structure and in the planting or moving of most trees. He loved Overbrook and derived a great deal of pleasure coming by and making his presence known.

➤ **How important is nicking in determining which stallions you should breed your mares to?** — New York, New York

It is hard to ignore a successful nick, and when that nick works a second time, look out. Every breeder will try to replicate it. So, many of these successes are self-fulfilling because they encourage a plethora of the same or similar crosses, which naturally, will result in more successes with that nick.

➤ **When you consult with people about their breeding decisions, do they then hold you responsible if they get disappointed in the final outcome of what you suggest?** — Atlanta, Georgia

Most people with whom I work have been in the business before we connected, and they have understood the risk well before I was hired. Come to think of it, I am not sure if I have ever been hired by a client who was freshly coming into the business. If that were to happen, the first thing I would explain would be the risks and that their operation needs to be well funded. If an investor is not able to make a considerable investment before expecting a return, then they better rethink their decision to invest in the first place. Bear in mind, I make recommendations, rarely decisions. Investors/owners derive pleasure out of making the final decision, but many of mine—because most of my larger clients have been longstanding—trust my recommendations and go along with me. All recommendations carry some degree of risk, and experienced clients know that. Inexperienced clients will soon find out.

➤ **In your experience, which combination of sire/dam would create the ultimate classic horse?** — Elmont, New York

It is easy to breed stamina into a horse, but the trick is to breed enough speed so that it can win. The Kentucky Derby trail is full of many plodders and even more speed horses which cannot get the trip. The right combination is an inexact fine-tuning of both speed and stamina. My gut thought, as unscientific as it is, is that the female family has to possess enough stamina in order for her offspring to get the trip. Occasionally, a Derby winner will be by a sire which appears not to possess enough stamina to ensure a Derby winner but ends up surprising us. Only after the race can we reevaluate that sire as to his siring capabilities.

➤ **Overproduction appears to be a major worry for many in the business. Should there be a maximum number of mares bred to any one stallion in each season?** — Yorkshire, England

I am a big believer in allowing the market system to take care of itself, as far as dealing with only price/demand/supply. However, this proposal addresses a bigger issue, and that is dealing with the shrinking gene pool. In my opinion, breeding limitless numbers of mares to stallions has weakened the breed, and likely will continue this weakening. Limiting book sizes should reverse this. Whether this violates antitrust laws is for a higher authority than I to decide.

➤ **When you're starting out, what is the best way to network and gain clients?** — Atlanta, Georgia

My involvement with horses began with being interested in the business aspect of this industry. I next had a limited experience working with horses, and how could anyone not enjoy that? I wish I had grown up with horses and had more hands-on experience with them, but I am where I am because I was hooked on the business. The horse industry is unique in that so many socio-economic levels interact on a daily basis. Once someone gains entry in the business, whether rubbing horses, working in racetrack administration, or—as I did—performing various odd jobs with a sales company, that person will have the opportunity to be exposed to interesting and successful people in and outside the horse industry. Gaining entry is the tough part, but perseverance and willingness to do anything should allow one to accomplish that.

➤ **I was told that some mare owners breeding to stallions with high stud fees, especially those in their first year, don't always pay the amount published. Do stud farms make allowances [if one promises] to breed the mare back?**
— Miami, Florida

I think to what you are referring is the discount offered to breeders who commit to breeding to a new stallion for three to four years. It makes a lot of sense. Given that market breeders jump from first-year horse to first-year horse, seeking safety, discounting a three-to-four-year package of services 25 percent, provides an incentive to breeders to stay with a stallion for most or all of the entire unproven years (years one to four). From the perspective of the stud farm, selling a number of the packages eases the pressure of having to sell out an entire book of mares each of those unproven years. It is reasonable to expect a breeder who is breeding to one of the discounted stallions to pay the full, nondiscounted price for a one-year breeding. Fees are also adjusted on stallions who stand for lower fees, mainly due to the general lack of demand. I do think a farm has to be careful with the inconsistency of pricing the same stallion at different price levels to different breeders without any improvement in progeny performance being the catalyst.

➤ **How do you think the artificial-style surfaces will affect your matings plans going forward in the next few years?** — Lexington, Kentucky

I think you will see an annual increase in artificial surfaces, especially if the early returns continue. As you see a proliferation of artificial surfaces, then we will have a larger sample of sire line successes to judge. The easy answer is that some sires' progeny will take to it, and some won't. There will likely be some, but not all, turf sires to be included in that group. Some breeders are already changing their matings plans to consider the "artificial track effect." After a few years, breeding for artificial tracks will be as predictable as it is now—that is to say, an indicator, but not absolute. As it stands now, some horses bred for dirt racing can handle the turf, but very few horses bred just for turf racing handle all dirt tracks. It will be interesting to see how this plays out in the next few years. This reminds me of a comment about "turf foot" (big, small, flat, and so forth) attributed to Hall of Fame trainer LeRoy Jolley, who said, "A turf foot is a foot which is attached to the horse which handles the turf." The same may be able to be said about sire lines and artificial surfaces.

➤ **What is the criteria you use for determining the potential value of a young stallion? I've heard as a ballpark figure four hundred times whatever stud fee [people] believe a stallion can command.**
— Louisville, Kentucky

Much depends on the demand for the stallion prospect from competing farms. If the prospect is a "farm maker," one that has a realistic, limitless potential for a farm, then the farm is more apt to stretch out the multiple to four hundred, or thereabouts. If a stud farm stretches itself to a four hundred multiple for a stallion, then it may try to make up for its exposure by taking additional breeding rights. Unfortunately, the breeder, if he/she wants to play, will have to pay an excessive stud fee just because the farm paid such a large multiple. Most farms are far more comfortable with a three hundred-plus multiple and won't play at the four hundred level.

➤ **What kind of racing resume, breeding requirements, and special talents would you expect to find on the next non-Northern Dancer/ non-Mr. Prospector future trendsetting chef-de-race?**
— San Juan, Puerto Rico

A race record reminiscent of Seattle Slew's and the soundness nonexistent in today's American stallions, combined with the human conviction to support him for four years with ample books because such a stallion will likely have to be imported.

➤ **What advice do you give mare owners with respect to stud fee range? For instance, in mating a $20,000 mare, what fee range would you suggest and why?** — Bloomington, Indiana

It used to be that a breeder should pay at one-third or one-quarter of mare value for stud fee. That is no longer the case, and it is not uncommon

Ric Waldman

for a breeder to pay stud fee at par to mare value. That may work out fine as long as the market continues to go up, but look out if it turns down and the breeder has overbred his mare. On your $20,000 mare—I assume that is her value "empty" [not in foal]—I would spend $10,000 on stud fee. Keep in mind that there are good "10s" and bad "10s," so do your homework thoroughly; after all, we are talking real money.

➤ **What are some things you look for in a stallion that give you an indication of what they will be like at stud?** — Louisville, Kentucky

First, I would like to think that a stallion can be a success, but a real close second is whether I think he can be marketed. These two considerations are not necessarily mutually inclusive. In order to be able to be marketed, he has to have pedigree, race record, and conformation—the same ingredients which are so common whether a breeder is selecting a stallion for his/her mare, or a stallion farm is selecting to sell to that breeder. Of those three ingredients, there is give and take, but a stallion prospect from an obscure sire line [or which has] unacceptable conformation has an uphill battle.

➤ **With many good sons of Storm Cat now standing at stud, who is the most likely to carry on the great influence of Storm Cat?** — Boston, Massachusetts

From what we have seen thus far, Giant's Causeway, Forestry, and maybe Johannesburg, and look out for Discreet Cat when his time comes. There are quite a few lesser-known sons of Storm Cat who possessed a world of speed, like Yankee Gentleman, and then there are many affordable, successful sons like Cat Thief, who might be the best value at stud.

Meet
RON MITCHELL

Ron Mitchell is the online managing editor for bloodhorse.com, consistently voted the industry's top Web site, and was the longtime moderator and host of the online series "Talkin' Horses." Mitchell's experience includes serving as a writer with *The Thoroughbred Record* and *Thoroughbred Times* and as a researcher with the Dick Lossen Bloodstock Agency before joining Blood-Horse Publications in 1992. Since then, Mitchell has been an editor at *The Blood-Horse*, and he also is a contributing writer to many Eclipse Press titles, including the very popular *Top 100 Racehorses of the 20th Century* and *Horse Racing's Top 100 Moments*. Mitchell lives in Lexington, Kentucky.